PROKOPIOS

The Secret History

with Related Texts

PROKOPIOS

The Secret History

with Related Texts

Edited and Translated, with an Introduction, by
Anthony Kaldellis

Hackett Publishing Company, Inc.
Indianapolis/Cambridge

14 13 12 11 2 3 4 5 6 7

For further information, please address
Hackett Publishing Company, Inc.
P.O. Box 44937
Indianapolis, Indiana 46244-0937

www.hackettpublishing.com

Cover design by Anthony Kaldellis and Abigail Coyle
Interior design by Elizabeth L. Wilson and Erica Finkel
Composition by Professional Book Compositors, Inc.
Printed at Versa Press, Inc.

Library of Congress Cataloging-in-Publication Data
Prokopios.
[Secret history. English]
The secret history : with related texts / Prokopios ; edited and translated, with an introduction, by Anthony Kaldellis.
p. cm.
Includes bibliographical references and index.
ISBN 978-1-60384-180-1 (paper)—ISBN 978-1-60384-181-8 (cloth)
1. Byzantine Empire—History—Justinian I, 527–565—Early works to 1800. I. Kaldellis, Anthony. II. Title.
DF572.P813 2010
949.5'013—dc22 2009032270

CONTENTS

Introduction

By 550, Prokopios felt that he had been living in a nightmare for most of his adult life. His view of government was that it should guard the borders of the state against barbarian aggression, promote the welfare and respect the rights of its subjects, appoint competent and honest people to high office, and enforce just laws. During the course of the past few decades, however, a regime of men and women, most of whom were unqualified for office, had set out to destroy both the stability of international order and the very foundations of lawful society. They had initiated two horrific wars on flimsy pretexts. Though they preached liberation, they had brought only ruin upon the lands they had sought to liberate as well as upon their own armed forces, which they ground down through protracted service, often incompetent leadership, and penny-pinching fiscal policies. The liberated peoples were exposed to constant attack by local insurgents and to the rampant corruption and arbitrary rule of the imperial officials in charge of pacification and reconstruction. Moreover, while promoting such "glory" abroad, the regime had actually exposed the homeland to sudden and devastating attacks by enemies both old and new. Major cities, centers of commerce and culture, were destroyed by foreign attacks that could have been prevented. Few felt safe. And a new plague swept through the world, carrying off millions.

At home, the regime inaugurated an era of bigotry, repression, corruption, and injustice. Those viewed as sexual and religious deviants were targeted and persecuted, while funds, often illegally obtained, were funneled to the priests of the only approved faith. Religion was made an instrument of government to a hitherto unprecedented degree. Its rhetoric shaped imperial ideology, but often it seemed only a cover for the regime's corruption and greed. Laws were canceled, enacted, or modified to suit the interests of the moment. Rights of property and persons were trampled on when they stood in the way of personal whims or ideological imperatives. Properties were seized without cause, citizens made to disappear or held and tortured without trial. Officials squeezed money from their subjects by inventing new fees and indirect taxes. Deficits soared while living standards declined. Power was given to lawless elements to terrorize the population and act outside the law. Critics were silenced, the cultured and intellectual classes scorned by a government that plotted all in secret behind a screen of religion.

These are the charges that *The Secret History* levels against the rulers of the most powerful state in the world at that time, the Roman emperor Justinian and his wife Theodora. Prokopios set out to expose the mechanisms and personalities behind this type of regime. It is no wonder that it also recounts so many actual nightmares, frightful demonic visitations, and dream-visions of devastation.

The Secret History is a unique historical document. No previous author had yet exposed the crimes of a regime by combining institutional, legal, and military analysis with personal attacks and salacious rumor quite as Prokopios does here. In this dense, behind-the-scenes pamphlet, he artfully combines the roles that today are divided among tabloid reporters, investigative journalists, public intellectuals, and "disgruntled" administration insiders. Its effect on Justinian's reputation has been devastating. It is worth considering what that reputation might have been had the works of Prokopios not survived, or not been written. Justinian would surely be remembered and even celebrated as one of history's great rulers: a builder of magnificent churches on an unparalleled scale, especially the cathedral of Hagia Sophia in Constantinople; a codifier of Roman law and major legislator in his own right; an emperor who reconquered provinces that had been lost to the barbarians, chiefly North Africa and Italy, temporarily reversing the empire's "decline"; and an ascetic Christian monarch who worked tirelessly to restore the Church to unity, contributing personally to the theological debates.[1] In the absence of Prokopios' dissident voice, historians would have placed their trust in the emperor's many pronouncements, which were designed to project precisely such an image of greatness, as well as in the favorable testimonies of the chroniclers who sought his favor and echoed the official version of events. The many other voices of criticism that were raised against Justinian during his reign would have been too scattered, obscure, and insufficiently prestigious to prevail against his pervasive and cunningly designed

The footnotes to the Introduction cite English scholarship with only a few exceptions. For full citations to the primary sources, see A Guide to the Main Sources; for scholarly studies of various aspects of the reign, see A Guide to Scholarship in English.

1. These aspects of the reign are covered in more detail later in this Introduction.

propaganda.[2] It was only by providing detailed and abundant inside information and by deploying the literary techniques and conceptual resources of classical historiography and political thought that Prokopios succeeded in undermining the emperor's reputation.

In fact, *The Secret History* played a decisive role in the transformation of Justinian's image in European thought. Before the document's discovery in 1623, Justinian was more a cultural icon than a historical figure. His name was associated with the codification of Roman law that formed the basis of legal science in the West (beginning in the eleventh century). His legacy was entrusted more to jurists than to historians. Until the seventeenth century, moreover, the controversies that surrounded his name concerned the legitimacy of his interventions in the Church and his heavy-handed treatment of the popes (in a word, the problem of "Caesaropapism"). But these legal and theological concerns emerged from the controversies of medieval and early modern Europe. They did not reflect the concerns of Justinian's own time or provoke efforts by historians to evaluate the reign as a whole. That began to change in 1623, when Vatican archivist Nicolò Alemanni discovered the text of *The Secret History* and published it under the double title *Anekdota* and *Historia arcana*. The former word is where English gets *anecdote*, but in Greek it means "unpublished material." *Anekdota* is what the work is called in its first definite attestation, in the tenth-century Byzantine encyclopedia *Souda*.[3] Like *Historia arcana (The Secret History* in Latin), *Anekdota* is less a title than an editorial description of contents. We don't know what Prokopios would have called the work. Interestingly, Alemanni did some editing of his own to the text, specifically omitting Chapter 9, the pornographic account of the early years of Justinian's empress Theodora. It was restored to the text in later editions.

The publication of *The Secret History* transformed Justinian from a legal abstraction to a human ruler with flaws, personal and political interests, and secrets. Prokopios' pamphlet has fundamentally shaped all subsequent efforts to come to terms with Justinian's momentous reign, as we see as early as Montesquieu's *Considérations sur les causes de la grandeur des Romains et de leur décadence* (1734), and culminating in Edward Gibbon's *History of the Decline and Fall of the*

2. For these other voices, see "The Contemporary Context of *The Secret History*" below.

3. *Souda* s.v. Prokopios Illoustrios, in A. Adler, ed., *Suidae Lexicon* (Leipzig: Teubner, 1971), 4:210–11.

Roman Empire (1776–1778), whose account of Justinian basically, even gleefully, followed *The Secret History*.[4] The problems posed by this single, brief, but indispensible text remain acute today. It is necessary, then, to situate it within its broader historical background and its more specific literary and political context, which is what the rest of the present introduction aims to do.

But before we turn to the Roman Empire in the sixth century, one more point is worth making about Prokopios' endeavor. He was the sole major historian of the Roman Empire to write about the reign of a living emperor. The rule among his predecessors and successors was to conclude their narrative at the point where the current regime took over, for one could not be both honest and safe when writing about reigning monarchs and their wives and servants. What they sometimes did was to treat past rulers as surrogates for the indirect discussion of present ones (so, e.g., Tacitus' Tiberius is a cover for Hadrian,[5] Ammianus' Julian is a partial foil for Theodosius I, etc.). Prokopios was unique and courageous not only in that he wrote a neutral and mostly critical history of the wars of Justinian, who was a dangerous man to offend, but also in that he dared to write *The Secret History* when Justinian, the great spider at the center of the vast imperial web, was still alive. This unique quality infuses his works with the suspense of secrets furtively told and outcomes not yet decided.

The Roman Empire in the Sixth Century

In 527, when Justinian ascended to the throne, the Roman Empire encompassed the Balkans (north to the Danube River), Asia Minor and northern Mesopotamia, Syria, Palestine, and Egypt. These regions were ruled by a single centralized state whose capital was at Constantinople, or New Rome. Since the fourth century, the empire had unofficially been called *Romanía*, namely the polity of the Roman people (their *res publica*, or *politeia* in Greek). The empire that modern historians call "Byzantium" was the direct continuation of this Roman polity, preserving for another thousand years the same name for its state and national identity. The Roman Empire of the sixth century, therefore, was a bridge between the classical

4. See A. Cameron, "Gibbon and Justinian," in R. McKitterick and R. Quinault, eds., *Edward Gibbon and Empire* (Cambridge: Cambridge University Press, 1997), 34–52.

5. R. Syme, *Tacitus* (Oxford: Clarendon Press, 1963).

empire of antiquity and Byzantium. It had a single, centralized set of military, administrative, fiscal, and judicial institutions; a single coinage and law; a predominant language (Greek); and increasingly one religion, though Justinian managed to split it irrevocably into two hostile churches. It was Roman identity that provided the primary basis of the empire's unity, not Christianity as is often stated. The faith actually created tensions and, by the reign's end, a permanent rupture. What stirred less controversy was what all agreed on, namely that they were Romans. The deepest and most stable ideologies are those that are most taken for granted.

The military and cultural resurgence of the sixth-century empire deviates from the conventional narrative in which the fall of the Roman Empire in late antiquity ushers in the Middle Ages. For one thing, it is by now understood that only half of the empire actually "fell," namely the western half, while the eastern half, "Byzantium," survived for more than a thousand years. Nor was the history of the eastern empire one of continuous decline. The reign of Justinian in particular (527–565) played an unexpected role in the historical transformation that led from the ancient world to the Middle Ages. It occupied that ambiguous pocket of time between the deposition of the last western Roman emperor in 476, when finally even Italy was openly governed by Germanic kings (albeit in a way that preserved many Roman traditions), and the mid-seventh century, when the Arabs began their conquest of the Near East and North Africa. After 700, only parts of the Balkans, Asia Minor, and Italy remained to the "rump" empire. Yet flanked as it was historically by the fall of the West and the rise of Islam, the sixth-century empire nevertheless asserted itself dynamically on the world stage, revealing unexpected sources of strength, resilience, and creativity. The groundwork had actually been laid down in the fifth century, when the political authorities at Constantinople managed to gain control over their barbarian allies and armies, the opposite of what happened in the West. Through diplomacy and bribery, they ensured a long period of relative peace that fostered economic and demographic growth. Military, civilian, and fiscal institutions were consolidated and placed on a sound footing, especially by the accountant-emperor Anastasios (r. 491–518), whom Prokopios and others whose careers were precisely within those institutions would uphold as a model of sober governance. Justinian was thereby enabled to launch a series of military ventures, seizing North Africa from the Vandals, Italy from the Ostrogoths (though only after a twenty-year war), and even parts of Spain from the Visigoths. The story of Roman "decline and fall" did not, just then, seem to be inevitable, and the emperor's daring general Belisarios was believed by many to rival the heroes of classical antiquity. In fact, Justinian repeatedly proclaimed his intention to restore the glory of the Roman Empire, and it was precisely Prokopios' intent to question and undermine that claim.

Drawing on a pool of new talent, Justinian pushed through internal reforms as well. Early in his reign, he appointed a team of jurists (ultimately headed by the scholar Tribonianos) to codify Roman law and bring it up to date. The fruit of their labor was a hugely influential compilation known in modern times as the *Corpus of Civil Law (Corpus iuris civilis)*, which is still the main source for Roman legal thought. The emperor continued to issue reform edicts, trying to improve administrative efficiency and, in particular, to constantly refine the law of property succession, creating considerable confusion among the propertied classes. He also sponsored extensive and innovative church building, which would be panegyrically described by Prokopios in the *Buildings* (after 554).[6] His crowning achievement was the cathedral of Hagia Sophia (Holy Wisdom) in the capital, completed in 537 by the architects Anthemios and Isidoros. Justinian also labored to solve the religious impasse of his age, namely the split between those who accepted and those who rejected the Council of Chalcedon (451). Here he vacillated between dialogue and persecution. The controversy generated a great deal of heated writing on both sides and the emperor's policies resulted in failure (and, many believed, heresy): the Church was split in two with few prospects of ever being unified again.

Toward other fields Justinian was either indifferent or hostile. That some flourished was often in spite of his efforts and due to the vitality of the culture at large. He cracked down on the non-Christian Platonist philosophers of Athens, closing their schools in 529–531 and leaving them no choice but to seek refuge in Persia, from where they returned under guarantee of protection in 532, and continued to write commentaries on ancient philosophy. Historiography attained classical levels of quality with Prokopios' *Wars*, whose narrative was continued around 580 by Agathias, a classically educated lawyer. The sixth century also witnessed the composition of annalistic chronicles in Latin and Greek that were favorable to Justinian; ecclesiastical histories and accounts of saints' lives in Syriac

6. For Prokopios' works and their relation to each other, see "The Works of Prokopios" below.

and Greek that were not; epigrams and erotic poetry; the compilation of medical encyclopedias as well of a massive gazetteer in sixty books by Stephanos of Byzantion; the *kontakia* of the great liturgical poet Romanos Melodos; antiquarian scholarship by Ioannes Lydos on Roman institutions and the Roman calendar (in Greek, but using Latin sources); the only history of the Goths to survive from antiquity, written in Latin and in Constantinople by Iordanes, who claimed to be of Gothic descent himself; a philosophical dialogue treating contemporary political issues; and the last Latin epic poet of antiquity, Corippus (who came of age in Vandal North Africa but sought patronage at the Byzantine court).[7] The literary scene, then, combined innovation, encyclopedism, and the continued development of classical genres. Little of this was sponsored by Justinian, though a fair deal of it was responding to the developments of his reign, in many cases negatively.

Greek was spoken by the majority of the population and in all parts of the empire. Other languages, except Latin, were mostly regional. Coptic was spoken by a large part of the population of Egypt as was Syriac (a form of late Aramaic) in some of the eastern provinces, but there was considerable bilingualism in both regions (with Greek). In contrast to Syriac, which produced a vast corpus of Christian writings in this period and afterward, the tongues of Anatolia (such as Phrygian) are sparsely attested and were soon to disappear. Many Armenians lived in the eastern provinces and had joined the Roman armies, especially after the formation of a field army for the northeastern frontier. Latin was spoken in some Balkan regions, at the top levels of the administration, and, after a fashion, in the army. The eastern Mediterranean had been governed in Greek by Roman officials ever since the time of the Republic. However, the universal extension of Roman citizenship in 212, the gradual concentration of the legions in the East, the creation of a New Rome in the East by Constantine in 330, and the expansion of the bureaucracy transformed the Greek-speaking East in accordance with Latin law and administration. Justinian's origins were in the central Balkans so, while he knew Greek, his native tongue was Latin. But two proponents of Latinity during the reign (Tribonianos and Ioannes Lydos) were speakers of Greek from Asia Minor. Use of Latin by the administration, however, was steadily receding, as

7. For a more detailed survey of sixth-century literature, see A Guide to the Main Sources; for its ideological diversity, see "The Contemporary Context of *The Secret History*," below.

Lydos complained.[8] In the early fifth century, all communication between subjects and the state had to be translated from Greek into Latin to reach the higher levels of the administration, whose responses then had to be translated into Greek to be understood by the original petitioners.[9] But since that time the requirement to use Latin was gradually dropped by bureau after bureau until even Justinian began to issue his edicts in Greek (with Latin translation). In the process, however, a great number of Latin terms entered the Greek vocabulary, as the reader of *The Secret History* can see.

Many chapters of *The Secret History* denounce Justinian's persecution of religious minorities. The population of the empire was by now overwhelmingly, but not monolithically, Christian. There were still pagans in the provinces while many intellectuals, especially in the capital and even high in the administration, subscribed to non-Christian philosophical systems. Pagan cults were still local and diverse in character, and they had no empirewide institutions. There was probably little in common between the pagans of Harran in Syria, of Athens, and of upper Egypt, and it would be mistaken to think of philosophers as "pagans." The Church, of course, lumped them all together and called them *Hellenes*, that is, Greeks (*paganus* was used in the Latin West). Jews could be found in many cities and regions of the empire, but they concerned the authorities less than did the Samaritans (a parallel branch of ancient Judaism), who repeatedly revolted in Palestine in the fifth and sixth centuries and had to be militarily suppressed. Christian heresies still survived from earlier phases of the Church, including Arianism and Montanism. A measure of religious diversity, then, characterized the empire in 527 when Justinian took the throne. Through persecution and coercion, he did leave the empire a more Christian realm by the end of his reign. Where Justinian failed, ironically, was in achieving Christian unity. In fact, his efforts to make all Christians accept the Council of Chalcedon, whether through dialogue, compromise, or persecution, resulted in open schism. In contrast to the persecution of the minority groups mentioned above, this was a development that Prokopios does not much discuss in *The Secret History*, in part because he found theological controversy distasteful and also because he promised to cover those events in a likewise scandalous *Ecclesiastical History*, a work that, in the end, he never wrote.[10]

8. Ioannes Lydos, *On the Magistracies of the Roman State* 3.68.

9. See F. Millar, *A Greek Roman Empire: Power and Belief under Theodosius II, 408–450* (Berkeley: University of California Press, 2006).

10. For this unwritten work, see p. xxvii below.

Another of Prokopios' main complaints in *The Secret History* concerned the cities. The Roman Empire in the sixth century was still a network of cities, each of which drew sustenance and revenue from its agricultural hinterland. But trade was a crucial part of the overall economy. The cities were less autonomous than they had been in the earlier Roman Empire. All law was now Roman law; local politics were subordinate to the imperial bureaucracy; and the cities' finances were often micromanaged by imperial officials. The tax rate was higher, so less money was available for local projects, maintenance, and new buildings. Cities had to petition the court for tax breaks and financial assistance, especially after natural disasters and barbarian raids. In many places the physical amenities of classical culture crumbled (e.g., gymnasia and baths), but there was extensive church building. The Church was now one of the greatest landowners and was continuously receiving gifts and bequests. Thus the topography, aesthetics, and power structures of most urban centers changed, though this did not sap their cultural vitality. The dynamic literary culture discussed above was produced by writers who originated in virtually every province of the empire. Talent flowed to the capital and administration, though these men did not lose pride in their native cities.

One of the goals of *The Secret History* was to expose how the corruption and fiscal oppression of Justinian's regime negatively impacted the cities and the economic prosperity of his subjects. Writers and intellectuals like Prokopios generally came from the more prosperous sectors of local society, but we lack precise demographic and economic data for the overall structure of imperial society. Small farms cultivated by free peasants probably formed the basis of both society and economy, but some have argued that large estates were on the rise (these are better documented in Egypt, where the papyri reveal the existence of fiscally complex, family-run agribusinesses).[11] A complicated system of contractually agreed rents, fees, and labor duties bound small farmers and large landowners in reciprocal, if asymmetrical, relationships. Slaves now constituted a smaller part of the workforce than in the earlier empire. In theory, the same law applied to all Romans. Power came from office, not birth or ethnicity, and career advancement was open to all. Some of the generals and civil administrators in *The Secret History* came from humble provincial backgrounds. The emperors of the late fifth and sixth centuries were former soldiers, peasants, or accountants, often of

11. See, e.g., P. Sarris, *Economy and Society in the Age of Justinian* (Cambridge: Cambridge University Press, 2006).

provincial origin. But in practice wealth conferred great advantage in terms of securing connections, credentials, and offices, whether local or imperial. Justin and Justinian, men of humble and even "rough" provincial origin, rose up through a system that deferred to families of wealth, illustrious descent, and entrenched power. Opportunity and conceit, then, as well as talent and privilege, made for a fluid and dynamic social scene.

By 500, therefore, what we call the Roman Empire was partly the nation-state of the Roman people (*Romanía*), an aspect that would emerge more fully in middle Byzantium, and partly a multiethnic empire, an aspect temporarily highlighted in the sixth century by Justinian's wars of conquest. The primary and unquestioned identity of the vast majority of the population was Roman, certainly of Latin and Greek speakers but also of Syriac speakers and in Egypt; likewise of pagans and Christians, Chalcedonians and Monophysites, rich and poor.[12] With a few exceptions (for example, among Samaritans, Jews, and possibly Isaurians), there were no ethnic or territorial groups that maintained a historical memory, ethnic identity, or social structure that differentiated them from mainstream Roman society. Regional diversity was mostly geographic or reflected only administrative realities. "Macedonians," for example, were merely Romans from Macedonia. We find throughout *The Secret History* references to Thracians, Paphlagonians, Bithynians, Kappadokians, Kilikians, Phoenicians, Palestinians, and others. These were not ethnicities but regional labels derived from the names of provinces or classical geography: almost all of these people were simply Romans. Yet negative stereotypes attached to certain regions. Under Justinian, the Kappadokians, who already had a reputation for being uncouth, were further reviled because of the harsh fiscal measures devised by Justinian's despised prefect Ioannes the Kappadokian, who appears often in the work.[13] That so many individuals in the

12. See A. Kaldellis, *Hellenism in Byzantium: The Transformations of Greek Identity and the Reception of the Classical Tradition* (Cambridge: Cambridge University Press, 2007), Chap. 2. For a Syriac narrative text that is just as Roman in outlook as any written in Greek and Latin, see F. R. Trombley and J. W. Watt, tr., *The Chronicle of Pseudo-Joshua the Stylite* (Liverpool: Liverpool University Press, 2000).

13. For Kappadokian stereotypes, see R. Van Dam, *Kingdom of Snow: Roman Rule and Greek Culture in Cappadocia* (Philadelphia: University of Pennsylvania Press, 2002). Justinian's *quaestor* Tribonianos invented rhetorical and mostly fictitious histories for each imperial province to accompany the reform legislation of 535; see M. Maas, "Roman History and Christian Ideology in Justinianic Reform Legislation," *Dumbarton Oaks Papers* 40 (1986): 17–31.

narrative bear these regional markers indicates, conversely, the widespread participation by provincials in what was by now a national and Roman political culture.

On the other hand, Justinian's conquests in the West, along with his incorporation of hitherto unconquered regions of the Caucasus into the empire, revitalized the sense that Romans exercised imperial hegemony over others.[14] Prokopios himself was not without Roman pride but he detested how Justinian linked this imperialism to his own aggrandizement and corrupt regime (to say nothing of the botched military planning). Moreover, the emperor seemed not to treat his Roman and barbarian subjects any differently. He extensively recruited soldiers from among the barbarians, both those within and outside the empire, and his imperial ventures in the West left the Balkans and the East exposed to barbarian attack. *The Secret History* reacts to these policies by demanding that the borders of the empire be defended against all enemies by armies recruited among, and loyal to, the population that they were charged to protect.[15] War should be waged only in the interests of *Romanía*, and not to feed a monarch's hunger for exaltation.

The Historical Background of *The Secret History*: An Overview of 518–551

Between 450 and 565, the imperial throne was occupied by provincials of humble origin who rose up through the ranks of the army or bureaucracy. Justin I (r. 518–527) was an illiterate Balkan peasant who, at an advanced age, was captain of the palace guard when Anastasios, himself almost 90, died in 518. Through intrigue with the guard, he had himself acclaimed emperor. The following overview will trace the history of the empire from that moment until 551, focusing on the events and people that Prokopios discusses in *The Secret History* (therefore excluding ecclesiastical history).[16] It will also follow the movements of Prokopios himself, to the extent that they can be reconstructed. Readers familiar with this historical background may

14. See M. Maas, "'Delivered from Their Ancient Customs': Christianity and the Question of Cultural Change in Early Byzantine Ethnography," in K. Mills and A. Grafton, eds., *Conversion in Late Antiquity and the Early Middle Ages: Seeing and Believing* (Rochester, NY: University of Rochester Press, 2003), 152–88.

15. See A. Kaldellis, "Classicism, Barbarism, and Warfare: Prokopios and the Conservative Reaction to Later Roman Military Policy," *American Journal of Ancient History* n.s. 3–4 (2004–2005 [2007]): 189–218.

16. See also the Timeline for the dates of important events.

skip this section. Studies of many of the events and topics mentioned here are cited in A Guide to Scholarship in English.

Politically, Justin's first concern was to secure peace with Vitalianos, a general who had been in rebellion against Anastasios for many years. In 518, Vitalianos was reconciled to the regime in exchange for offices, including the consulship in 520. But that year he was murdered in the palace, a deed that many blamed on Justin's nephew Justinian, who had risen to a position of great influence. Justinian would become consul in 521. A few years later, after the death of Justin's empress Euphemia, a law was passed allowing senators to marry former actresses; its purpose was to enable Justinian to marry Theodora.[17] In 526, the great metropolis of Antioch was destroyed by an earthquake that caused thousands of deaths. Justin undertook to rebuild it. Tensions had meanwhile been mounting with Persia during the 520s regarding the religious loyalties of subject peoples in the Caucasus, the Lazoi and Iberians. In 527, Justinian was made emperor just a few months before Justin's death.

Justinian immediately moved against pagans, Manicheans, and apostates, and soon (in 529 or 531) targeted the schools at Athens. At the same time, in 528, he appointed a commission to revise Roman law that concluded its work in 534 with the final version of the *Corpus iuris civilis* (mentioned earlier). By the end, the director of this project was the jurist and *quaestor* Tribonianos. In 529, there was a major Samaritan revolt in Palestine. The rebels captured Neapolis (Nablus) and set up an emperor of their own named Ioulianos, but the rebellion was crushed militarily. In 530, Moundos defeated a Slav raid in the Balkans (he was a Gepid who had served the Goths in Italy for decades and had recently taken up service under Justinian). In that year, a Persian offensive against Armenia was defeated by Sittas (married to Theodora's sister Komito); and the young general Belisarios defeated a large Persian army in a battle at Daras by the border. Prokopios of Kaisareia (the metropolis of Palestine) had been serving as Belisarios' *assessor* and private secretary in the East since at least 527 and would accompany the general for many more years.[18] The following year (531), Belisarios was defeated by

17. For the text of this law, see related text 1: "A Law for the Marriage of Justinian and Theodora."

18. For the rhetorical and legal training of most late Roman historians, see G. Greatrex, "Lawyers and Historians in Late Antiquity," in R. W. Mathisen, ed., *Law, Society, and Authority in Late Antiquity* (Oxford and New York: Oxford University Press, 2001), 148–61.

the Persians at Kallinikos and was recalled to Constantinople. Chosroes (Khusrow) meanwhile succeeded his father Kavades (Kavadh) on the Persian throne and began negotiations for peace with Rome. Before these could be concluded, a major riot, the so-called Nika riots, broke out in Constantinople in January 532 and escalated into an urban insurgency. The protesters, perhaps instigated by a senatorial faction eager to overthrow Justinian, demanded the dismissal of two hated officials, the praetorian prefect Ioannes the Kappadokian and the *quaestor* Tribonianos. This they obtained, but when they attempted to replace Justinian on the throne with Hypatios, a nephew of Emperor Anastasios, thirty thousand of them were massacred in the hippodrome by the soldiers of Moundos and Belisarios. A large part of the city burned down, including the church of Hagia Sophia, but reconstruction began immediately.[19] Later that year, a treaty was agreed upon with the Persians, the so-called Eternal Peace, according to which the empire would keep Lazike while Iberia would go to the Persians. Ioannes the Kappadokian was restored to the prefecture, where he implemented an ambitious policy of administrative and fiscal reform that was opposed by some (e.g., Prokopios and Ioannes Lydos). Tribonianos and his team continued to work on the *Corpus* despite his dismissal as *quaestor*.

With peace secure in the East, the following year (533) Justinian launched a major naval expedition under Belisarios against the Vandals in North Africa. The Vandals, who were Arians (a heresy according to which the Father and the Son were not of the same divine "substance"), were believed to be persecuting their Catholic subjects. In the fifth century, under the leadership of their king Gaiseric (r. 428–477), they had led a number of destructive naval raids against Roman lands from Carthage, even capturing Rome itself in 455. Attempts to reconquer the lost province had been spectacular failures. Yet Belisarios defeated their king Gelimer in two pitched battles in 533 and regained Carthage by the end of the year. In 534, Belisarios was slandered to the emperor (there was always fear that a successful general might set himself as a rival emperor in the provinces) and returned quickly to the capital, where a spectacular triumph was staged to celebrate the victory and honor Belisarios while highlighting his firm devotion and submission to Justinian. The general left Solomon in command of North Africa, but Justinian's civilian administrators were already implementing measures that were unpopular with the soldiers. Meanwhile, the Gothic

19. For Prokopios' account of the Nika riots, see related text 2.

regime in Italy was weakening. Amalasountha, the daughter of Theodoric the Great, was ruling in the name of her son Athalaric, but he died in 534. She made a tentative offer to surrender Italy to Justinian in exchange for a pension in the East, but changed her mind and associated her corrupt relative Theodahad with her in the kingship. In 535, he imprisoned and killed her (at the instigation of Theodora, according to *The Secret History*). Sensing weakness, Justinian sent Moundos to conquer Dalmatia (which he did, though he died in battle), while Belisarios, now sole consul, conquered Sicily in preparation for an assault on Italy. Prokopios had accompanied the African expedition from the beginning; presumably he had returned to Constantinople and then back to Sicily with Belisarios in 535. In 536, he was in Carthage when the army mutinied against the general Solomon. The rebels were defeated first by Belisarios, who arrived from Sicily, and then by Justinian's cousin Germanos.

Meanwhile, the Goths in Italy elected Vitigis as their king. Theodahad was arrested and killed. Vitigis then ceded southern France (Provence, ancient Transalpine Gaul) to secure the neutrality of the Franks and abandoned south Italy and Rome in the face of the Roman advance. When Belisarios captured Naples after a brief siege, some of his barbarian troops slaughtered many of its citizens, an atrocity that was widely noted and imperiled Italian loyalties. Belisarios occupied Rome at the very end of 536 and defended it against a Gothic siege for over a year. Prokopios was an eyewitness of this dramatic campaign. In March 538, the Gothic army retreated northward while the Romans pressed their advantage, taking cities and strategic locations in the north. The Franks sent an army across the Alps to aid the Goths, but it retreated in 539 after being struck by disease. The Goths slaughtered the population of Milan, but by 540 Vitigis had been confined to Ravenna. In May of that year, Belisarios pretended to accept a Gothic offer to become emperor of the West over both the Italians and the Goths, but when he was in possession of Ravenna he proclaimed himself loyal to Justinian and told the Goths to disperse. The king and his treasure were taken to Constantinople by Belisarios, who had again been slandered at the court, though this time there was no triumph. Prokopios, having served as an agent and military advisor in the Italian campaign, accompanied him back to the capital. Meanwhile, Sittas was killed in Armenia by rebels in 538 and was replaced by Bouzes, who imposed harsh measures. Solomon defended North Africa from Moorish raids and lay the groundwork for prosperity in the province (539–544). The new cathedral of Hagia Sophia was inaugurated in 537, after only five years of construction.

To this point, the initiatives of the regime could have been described as a stunning success. Peace in the East, a major legal codification, the construction of Hagia Sophia and many other churches, and the reconquest of North Africa and Italy testify to Justinian's vision and his ability to select talented men to implement his policies. But Prokopios would already have noted many disquieting signs. The massacre of the Nika rioters and the suppression of dissidents and "deviants" revealed the regime's ruthless authoritarian character. Too many of Justinian's officials were corrupt, which undermined justice at home and caused discontent among the non-Roman people brought under imperial authority. The emperor's stream of legislation created confusion and insecurity; some of his edicts seemed designed to serve particular interests, not the common good. More worrisome was the arbitrary and vindictive behavior of Theodora, who had to have her way and did not care whether the laws or the dignity of the state were trampled in the process. Belisarios also, for all his brilliance as a general, too often caved in to the demands of his soldiers, and he refused to stand up to his unfaithful wife, Antonina. This, at least, is the picture conveyed by *The Secret History*. The potential existed for a major miscalculation: Justinian's ambitious rhetoric thinly veiled an imperial edifice that was beginning to crack, both at home and abroad. The emperor had left the East and the Balkans dangerously exposed in order to pursue his adventures in the West, and he relied too heavily on bribing barbarians not to invade Roman territory, which soon turned into an extortion racket on their part. Even as Belisarios was returning to the capital in 540, with a second king and treasure in tow, all this potential for disaster suddenly exploded.

Before surrendering Ravenna, Vitigis had sent emissaries to King Chosroes of Persia, proposing an alliance against Justinian. Their plea was welcome: the Persian king knew how vulnerable the Roman East was and, moreover, he claimed that Justinian had violated the peace by trying to bribe some of Chosroes' own allies into a Roman alliance. In the summer of 540, Chosroes invaded Syria, besieging cities, sacking some and extorting payment from others, until he finally reached Antioch, which he captured and destroyed before carrying off tens of thousands of its citizens to southern Mesopotamia. The war was on. Meanwhile, a large Bulgar army raided northern Greece and Thrace, reaching the Long Walls near Constantinople.

In 541, Theodora and Antonina plotted and engineered the downfall of Ioannes the Kappadokian.[20] Belisarios was dispatched to the East but did not press deeply into Persia so as not, Prokopios claims in *The Secret History*, to be cut off from news of his wife, from whose affair with their adopted son Theodosios he could no longer avert his eyes. Lazike, meanwhile, rebelled against the oppressive imperial governors and invited the Persians in to expel the Romans. Chosroes marched to the Black Sea, captured the fortress at Petra, and accepted the vassalage of King Goubazes. The imposition of harsh taxes by corrupt officials was having the same effect in recently conquered Italy, straining the loyalties of the native population and allowing the Goths breathing space to recoup and elect a dynamic new king, Totila (Baduila), one of the noble heroes of Prokopios' *Wars*. It is not clear where Prokopios himself was during these years.

Totila rolled back many of the Roman gains in central Italy during 542. Some minor campaigning took place in the East as well, but much of it was put on hold because of the plague, which had spread out of Egypt in the previous year and reached Syria and Constantinople by late spring. For two hundred years this disease would ravage North Africa, Europe, and western Asia, and modern estimates of its death toll sometimes reach as high as one third of the population. Prokopios, who probably witnessed the outbreak in Constantinople, authored the most sober and reliable account of its symptoms, both the medical and the social.[21] It is possible that the Roman army faced recruitment problems after this point and that Justinian increasingly turned to barbarian mercenaries to wage his many wars. In 543, Totila continued to make gains in Italy. Bouzes and Belisarios were recalled to Constantinople under suspicion of plotting against the palace. Bouzes was imprisoned by Theodora for two years. Belisarios was disgraced, but later pardoned as a favor to his wife. It seems probable that Prokopios was no longer serving with Belisarios at this point; we know that he was already composing the *Wars* during the 540s. The following year (544), Belisarios was sent to Italy, but with few soldiers. He was to spend the next five years there playing a cat-and-mouse game with Totila and ultimately achieving nothing. Meanwhile, Solomon was killed in battle in North Africa. His nephew Sergios was given command of the province, which was to prove a disastrous decision. The province lapsed into anarchy and suffered from renewed Moorish raids. In the

20. For Prokopios' account of Ioannes' downfall, see related text 7.

21. For Prokopios' account of the plague, see related text 8.

East, Chosroes failed to capture the city of Edessa despite a determined siege. Perhaps it was after he had witnessed this string of disasters that Prokopios began to experiment with the idea that the world was governed by chance (*tyche*) and not the providence that Justinian so believed was on his side. This notion of random chance would feature prominently in the historian's works, including *The Secret History*.

In 545, Rome and Persia signed a five-year truce that excluded Lazike. The Goths captured more cities in Italy. In 546, the rebel commander Gontharis killed Areobindos, the governor sent to relieve Sergios in North Africa, and ruled the province from Carthage. He was soon killed by the Armenian officer Artabanes, who had once fought against the Romans in his native land but had now taken up service under Justinian. The command of the province passed to him, but he wished to be recalled to Constantinople to marry the emperor's niece, the widow of Areobindos.[22] The Goths took back Rome at the end of the year, but Belisarios retook it in a daring move the next spring (547). The general Ioannes Troglita was transferred from Mesopotamia to North Africa, where he found the province in a state of siege. In 548 he defeated the Moors in a major battle and began (again) to rebuild the shattered province. Theodora died of cancer that year, which altered the balance of power at the court. Antonina secured the recall of Belisarios in 549; he was sent to the East, though still under suspicion. Now the Lazoi again changed their allegiance, inviting the Romans to expel the Persians. The Roman general Dagistheus besieged the city of Petra but encountered fierce resistance. Meanwhile, Totila was besieging Rome, virtually abandoned by this time, and regained it in January 550. Dagistheus cleared Lazike of Persian forces except for the garrison at Petra, which was reinforced by the Persians. Justinian appointed his nephew Germanos to lead a new Italian expedition. Germanos married Matasountha, a daughter of Amalasountha and granddaughter of Theodoric, to legitimate himself in Gothic eyes, but he died of illness after fighting some Slavs near Serdica. The Slavs ravaged Thrace, reaching the Long Walls near Constantinople, while in the West Totila took the war to Sicily. This was probably the situation when Prokopios wrote *The Secret History*. In 551, the Romans took Petra in Lazike and Justinian appointed Narses to finish the Gothic War, which he did the following year at the battle of Busta Gallorum.

22. For the story of Artabanes, see related text 10: "A Plot to Kill Justinian."

At the time when the *Wars* and *The Secret History* were completed (in 550–551) everything was still unresolved. Three parts of the known world had been ravaged by nearly continuous warfare (Italy, North Africa, and parts of the East). The entire Roman world had been devastated by the most lethal plague in history and had endured Justinian's authoritarian rule. The wars of conquest had created more problems for the empire than they had solved. Armies had been deployed on too many fronts, leaving the core of *Romanía* unprotected. Possibly because of the plague, recruitment of native Roman soldiers declined and was offset by the hiring of increasingly more barbarian mercenaries. The latter, however, had no loyalty to the Roman people, least of all to the former Roman provinces they were now being paid to conquer, pillage, and occupy. Those territories, recently ravaged by war and political instability, were then squeezed financially to offset the cost of their own conquest and administration. It was difficult for imperial officials to come across as liberators under such circumstances (which is what Justinian's official rhetoric required them to be), and many turned out to be harsh and corrupt as well. As a result, Justinian constantly had to devise new ways to squeeze money from his former subjects in the eastern empire, and these are chronicled with indignation in *The Secret History*.

The Works of Prokopios

Prokopios has long been notorious for writing three different, even apparently contradictory, accounts of the reign of Justinian: the ostensibly neutral but occasionally critical *Wars*, the hostile *Secret History*, and the panegyrical *Buildings*. This ideological flexibility was taken as emblematic of the perfidy and subtlety of the "Byzantines" who were despised by the thinkers of the Enlightenment, while the corruption, deceit, and pornography on display in *The Secret History* were used to paint an equally negative picture of his society. It is only recently that scholars have come to terms with the fact that *The Secret History*, no less than Prokopios' *Wars* and *Buildings*, is a highly crafted literary representation of individuals and events with specific ideological and rhetorical goals. But how could one person let his words flow in such different channels? Which reflects the real Prokopios? To answer these questions, we must consider the circumstances under which the three works were composed and pay close attention to the ways in which they subtly allude and respond to each other.

It seems that Prokopios was already planning to write a major historical work in the late 530s, that is, after the conclusion of the Eternal Peace with Persia (532), and while that peace still held; after the conquest of North Africa (534); and while the prospects for a swift end to the war in Italy were still good.[23] In this early version, the narrative would move from the conclusion of the Eternal Peace to Africa and then to Italy. But the Persian invasion of 540 reignited war on the eastern front, and the war in Italy dragged on inconclusively during the 540s. Prokopios therefore decided to split his narrative into three theaters: the *Persian War* (Books 1–2), the *Vandal War* (Books 3–4), and the *Gothic War* (Books 5–7). This had definite advantages for the organization of material, but it also meant that some books were discontinuous (there was nothing to report from the eastern front between 532 and 540, for example), while events in the capital and Balkans (mostly raids by Slavs and "Huns") had to be placed awkwardly into narratives focusing on other theaters of war (mostly in the *Persian* and *Gothic War*). Prokopios wanted this to be a major work of classical historiography in the tradition of the ancient historians such as Thucydides, one of his models. But he could not, in a public work, reveal everything that he knew about Justinian. It seems, therefore, that he kept two separate files, one with material that would go into the *Wars* and another with all the dirt on the regime. The second he could never publish while Justinian and especially Theodora were still alive. But by the mid-540s, the emperor was in his sixties and had already ruled for a long time. It is likely that Prokopios was waiting for him to die in order to integrate much of the material in his *Secret History* file into what was slowly taking shape as the *Wars*. The death of Theodora in 548 must have relieved some of the pressure. It is possible that the account of the downfall of the prefect Ioannes the Kappadokian in the *Wars* came originally from the secret file, though Prokopios still could not tell the full truth because one of the protagonists, Belisarios' wife Antonina, was still alive.[24]

But by 550/551, Prokopios had, perhaps, run out of patience and decided to compose two separate works, the *Wars* and *The Secret History* as we have them (Justinian would in fact live on for another

23. The following account is based on the reconstruction by G. Greatrex, "The Composition of Procopius' *Persian Wars* and John the Cappadocian," *Prudentia* 27 (1995): 1–13; and "Procopius the Outsider?" in D. C. Smythe, ed., *Strangers to Themselves: The Byzantine Outsider* (Burlington, VT: Ashgate, 2000), 215–28.

24. Compare *Wars* 1.25 (translated in related text 7: "The Downfall of Ioannes the Kappadokian") with *Secret History* 2.16.

fifteen years). There is another reason why he may have delayed publication, namely that the 540s offered him no satisfying or convenient point at which to end his narration of the many ongoing wars. The war with Persia raged on in Lazike, with the Persians still holding out in the fortress at Petra; Totila seemed to have gained control over most of Italy; North Africa was more settled after the campaigns of Ioannes Troglita but ruined as a province; and Slav and Bulgar raids in the Balkans were intensifying. It did not seem as though things would improve anytime soon. That is why each of the *Wars* ends on such a negative note, and taken together, their conclusions are a massive indictment of Justinian's policy, fully in agreement with the accusations laid against the emperor on precisely this point in *The Secret History* (chiefly in Chapter 18): all these people killed, all these lands ruined, and for what? In fact, on closer inspection, the *Wars* is not all that neutral. Prokopios put serious attacks on imperial policy in the mouths of his speakers, including many spokesmen for Justinian's enemies and the peoples he conquered. He openly reveals the crimes committed by the officials whom Justinian appointed to govern those peoples as well as the fact that the emperor's western ambitions had left the East and Balkans dangerously exposed. The hero of his account of the 540s was the Gothic king Totila. Moreover, the historian laced his prose with subtle allusions to classical literature that imply damning comparisons between Justinian and ancient tyrants and barbarians, thereby revealing indirectly what he could not say openly. Each of the three *Wars*—the "wars that Justinian waged against the barbarians," as the preface programmatically announces (1.1.1)—ends badly.[25]

In short, the *Wars* quietly points to the thesis of *The Secret History*, while *The Secret History* bluntly corrects the omissions, misrepresentations, and even lies that had to be put in the *Wars* to ensure the author's safety. The two texts complement each other: they were not fused into one because of the constraints of Prokopios' circumstances. For example, in the preface to the *Wars* Prokopios promises that he will not hide the wretched deeds even of those who were close to him because history must be impartial (1.1.5). The same term ("wretched deeds") is used at the end of *The Secret History*'s Preface (1.10) to characterize all that is about to be divulged regarding Belisarios, Justinian, and Theodora. Not only

25. See A. Kaldellis, *Procopius of Caesarea: Tyranny, History, and Philosophy at the End of Antiquity* (Philadelphia: University of Pennsylvania Press, 2004), and

does this reveal the common purpose of the two works, it also indicates that the full purpose of the *Wars* will not be clear to one who does not also then read *The Secret History*. This is evident in the system of cross-references used in *The Secret History*: when Prokopios refers to the *Wars*, it is always *back* to what he calls "the earlier books." And at one point in *The Secret History* he summarizes his indictment of Justinian by calculating the destruction that he wreaked in North Africa, Italy, and the East (18.5–31), thus replicating his "signature" tripartition of the theaters of war. *The Secret History* is a kind of supplement to the *Wars*—and Prokopios's singular outlook is reflected in both texts.

The *forward* cross-references in *The Secret History* are also interesting, for they declare Prokopios' intention to write a separate *Ecclesiastical History* that would tell the history of the Church, or at any rate Justinian's policies toward it, in the critical and even scandalous manner of *The Secret History*.[26] That is why he leaves contemporary Christian controversies out of *The Secret History*, though he does cover Justinian's persecution of pagans, Samaritans, and the ancient heresies (such as Arianism). Prokopios never wrote his *Ecclesiastical History*, however, which is unfortunate because it would have cast an entirely different light on the history of the Church than do the other histories and hagiographies of this period. This was, as far as we can tell, the only other work that Prokopios was planning to write as of 551.

Two years later much had changed. The Romans had recaptured Petra in Lazike and Totila was defeated by Narses in a major battle, dooming the Gothic cause. In 553/554, Prokopios wrote an appendix to the *Wars*, which became Book 8, in which he covered events in each theater up to that date. While Book 8 contains many geographical and ethnographic digressions, it is, given the recent victories, surprisingly critical of imperial policy, even more so perhaps than the first seven books. The beginning of the preface to Book 8, moreover, copies the beginning of the preface of *The Secret History*, indicating the continuity of Prokopios' intention and providing an inside joke to those in his inner circle of friends who had read the

---

"Prokopios' *Persian War*: A Thematic and Literary Analysis," in R. Macrides, ed., *Byzantine History as Literature* (Aldershot, UK: Ashgate, 2009).

26. See *Secret History* 1.14, 11.33, 18.38, 26.18, 27.32; and the discussion by A. Kaldellis, "The Date and Structure of Prokopios' *Secret History* and His Projected Work on Church History," *Greek, Roman, and Byzantine Studies* 49 (2009): 585–616.

secret work.[27] In the preface to Book 8, Prokopios notes that the previous books had become famous in every corner of the Roman Empire. Readers of *The Secret History*, however, would know that this was not true of *all* that he had written. Yet Book 8 of the *Wars*, a public work, refers forward to the *Ecclesiastical History* (at 8.25.13), which was still unwritten. This was an odd announcement, as that work was likely to be critical of Justinian and the priesthood. Moreover, he had made it clear in the original version of the *Wars* that, in his view, theological disputes were stupid and a waste of time.[28] This public announcement of the *Ecclesiastical History* probably explains why the work was not written, despite the fact that Prokopios by that time had a large file of relevant material. The work was too inflammatory to publish while Justinian was still alive, and it is likely that the emperor outlived the historian. As of 554, there were still no signs that Prokopios planned to write any other work.

But then, sometime in the second part of the decade, Prokopios composed the *Buildings*, a panegyric glorifying Justinian's constructions, which were mostly religious but included military and civil engineering projects. It is not clear whether the work is complete, how it was delivered to its honoree, or what exactly it was meant to accomplish. Yet even though we cannot know exactly what induced Prokopios to reverse his stance in this way, we can still imagine the kinds of motives that may have led him to it. It has been proposed, for example, that Prokopios' repeated praise of the mercy that Justinian showed to conspirators, an odd theme to put at the beginning of a work such as this, may indicate that the historian had been implicated and had to clear himself.[29] Or, Justinian may have simply asked the famous historian of the *Wars* to write a panegyrical work, a request that he made of other learned men in his capital. One of them, Ioannes Lydos, who was also to write a critical study of the regime and may have been on close terms with Prokopios, claimed that Justinian had once asked him to write a panegyrical account of the victory over the Persians in 530, and noted later in the same work that "it was not safe to refuse the requests of an emperor such as

27. E.g., Ioannes Lydos: see A. Kaldellis, "Identifying Dissident Circles in Sixth-Century Byzantium: The Friendship of Prokopios and Ioannes Lydos," *Florilegium* 21 (2004): 1–17.

28. *Wars* 5.3.5–9. See below for a discussion.

29. This was suggested by M. Angold, "Procopius' Portrait of Theodora," in C. N. Constantinides et al., eds., *Philellen: Studies in Honour of Robert Browning* (Venice: Istituto ellenico di studi bizantini e postbizantini di Venezia, 1996), 21–34; here 24.

him."[30] Justinian, or one of his high officials, may have wanted the historian to position himself more favorably toward the reign than he had in the *Wars*. And the gifts of emperors were not lightly to be despised in any case.

Be that as it may, the *Buildings* should be read as an insincere work. Not only does it attribute to Justinian constructions that properly belong to Justin or Anastasios, but the first chapters are also laced with odd insinuations and many classical allusions that subvert the surface praise, in other words the same techniques that are used in the *Wars*.[31] While the *Buildings* reflects Justinian's own propaganda and is useful to have for that reason, we should be cautious in using it as a source for Prokopios' views. On many points it offers a completely opposing interpretation of events than we find *The Secret History*, for example regarding the Convent of Repentance founded by Theodora for former prostitutes (17.5–6).[32] Let us also remember how Saint Augustine described his own days as an imperial orator: "how unhappy I was . . . on that day when I was preparing to deliver a panegyric on the emperor! In the course of it I would tell numerous lies and for my mendacity would win the good opinion of people who knew it to be untrue."[33]

The Structure and Themes of *The Secret History*

For all that it consists of diverse material that Prokopios could not safely include in the *Wars*, *The Secret History* is not an unorganized dossier of notes. The historian did his duty by drawing it up into tight, thematically coherent, and interconnected narratives, which reveal few traces of their disparate origins. The text consists of three discrete sections. The first two are announced at the end of the Preface (at 1.10), in which Prokopios promises to reveal the wretched deeds of Belisarios (corresponding to Chapters 1–5 of the text) and then the wretched deeds of Justinian and Theodora (corresponding to Chapters 6–18). The third part (Chapters 19–30), a legal and administrative commentary on the regime, was added on

30. Ioannes Lydos, *On the Magistracies of the Roman State* 3.28 and 3.76.

31. Kaldellis, *Procopius* (see note 25), 51–61.

32. The *Buildings* passage is translated in related text 4: "The Convent of Repentance."

33. Augustine, *Confessions* 6.6.9; tr. H. Chadwick (Oxford: Oxford University Press, 1991), 97. Many Roman and Byzantine texts attest to the self-conscious mendacity of panegyrics.

afterward, possibly a few weeks or months later but in any case during the same year that the first two parts were composed.[34]

Part I (Chapters 1–5): *The Gynocracy*. This section is not, as promised, exactly about Belisarios but about his wife Antonina, or rather about how Antonina, in collaboration with Theodora and some eunuchs, managed to dominate and emasculate Belisarios. His displacement in the text by these two women reflects his lack of virtue and even dignity. In fact, the point of these chapters is to show what happens when masculine virtue is displaced by feminine vice, which draws its strength from the manipulation of sex and men's weaknesses. The dramatic low point for Belisarios comes when he is recalled to the capital under suspicion, disgraced, and made to think that his execution was imminent.

> In this state of terror he went up to his room and sat alone upon his bed, having no intention of doing anything brave, not even remembering that he had once been a man. His sweat ran in streams. He felt light-headed. He could not even think straight in his panic, worn out by servile fears and the worries of an impotent coward. (4.22)

The women make it seem that Antonina intervened to save her husband (again reversing the normal plotline in which the man saves the woman in distress).[35] The scene that ensues may allude to forms of sadomasochistic sex.

> He jumped up from the bed and fell on his face before his wife's feet. Placing a hand behind each of her calves, he began to lick the soles of his wife's feet with his tongue, one after the other, calling her the Cause of his Life and Salvation, promising that henceforth he would be her devoted slave and not her husband. (4.29–30)

Prokopios' point is always political, not merely to expose a personal weakness. For example, this episode foreshadows the humiliating new rite of prostration that Justinian and Theodora imposed on the court, forcing Romans to behave in a way that had always been associated

34. See Kaldellis, *Procopius*, 142–159; and "The Date and Structure" (see note 26).

35. See *Wars* 7.31.3, translated in related text 10: A Plot to Kill Justinian, and also Theodora's intervention during the Nika riots, which may have saved her husband's throne, translated in related text 2.

with "oriental" monarchies.[36] The personal emasculation of Belisarios in this episode had direct political consequences of its own. For one thing, it prevented the man from acting nobly as a tyrannicide, an accepted virtue in both the Greek and Roman traditions.

> Everyone was thinking that . . . Belisarios' plan was to stop wasting his time in Byzantion and that as soon as he found himself outside the city walls he would without delay take up arms and do something noble and befitting a man against his wife and against those who had violated him. But it was not to be. He . . . simply obeyed that woman. (4.40–41)

All this is intimately connected to the indictment of tyranny that runs through *The Secret History*, for one of the essential characteristics of tyranny in classical thought was the subversion of the public interest by the disordered private and family life of the tyrant and his associates. This is demonstrated strikingly in the episode of Chosroes in Lazike, which occupies the middle of the first part of the text. Facing a mutiny, the king read aloud a letter sent by Theodora to one of his officials, which proclaimed her absolute power in the Roman state. What kind of a state, he asked the mutineers, is governed by a woman (2.36)? The narrative then reveals how Theodora arbitrarily imprisoned officials and ruined imperial policy in pursuit of her private interests and vendettas. "Private comedy has turned into political tragedy."[37]

Prokopios wields narrative in a subtle way to highlight the subversion of family values as well. Belisarios adopted a young man named Theodosios, with whom Antonina, his mother by adoption, had an affair. Meanwhile, she turned against her biological son from a previous liaison, Photios, who sided with Belisarios to undermine his rival Theodosios. Lust and weakness triumph here over natural ties of affection. The low point in the narrative is when Belisarios begs his *stepson* Photios to help him against his wife Antonina (Photios' *natural* mother) and to kill his *adopted son* Theodosios (2.6–13), Antonina's lover. Belisarios claims that he raised Photios as both father *and* mother (2.7), but neither he nor Antonina would come to Photios' aid when he was later imprisoned by Theodora. The affair

36. See *Secret History* 15.15, 15.27, and especially 30.21–26; for discussion, see Kaldellis, *Procopius*, 128–42.

37. B. Rubin, *Das Zeitalter Iustinians* (Berlin and New York: W. de Gruyter, 1960), 1:199.

of Antonina and Theodosios reads in part like one of the ancient romance novels, in that the protagonists are constantly being driven apart by circumstances despite their great passion for each other, but in this case the virtuous and even pure premises of such novels have been turned on their head: the characters of *The Secret History* are always antiheroes, as we see in Belisarios' refusal to do anything heroic.

Part II (Chapters 6–18): *Justinian and Theodora*. This is the largest and central section of *The Secret History*, and it aims to capture the very different and complex personalities of the imperial couple. The origin of Justinian's family (6) and the chapter on his character and appearance (8) are separated by an account (7) of the violence of the hippodrome fan-clubs (basically sporting guilds that engaged in hooliganism and street crimes). The origin and character of Theodora (9.1–32) and the account of her appearance and marriage to Justinian (9.47–10.23) are also separated by a brief return to the topic of the fan-clubs (9.33–46). This establishes a coherent thematic counterpoint: the two main characters come together against a background of lawless violence and the disruption of social order. Most of the events in these chapters occur during the reign of Justin, but in Prokopios' view Justinian was the real power behind the throne starting as early as 518, which is the date from which, writing in 550–551, he counts the thirty-two years of Justinian's *power* rather than his *reign*, which technically began in 527.[38] The analysis of Justinian's reign begins in Chapter 11 with a discussion of his foreign policy and persecution of religious groups; Chapter 12 then introduces a major theme of the rest of the work—how the imperial treasury confiscated the properties of senators. This chapter introduces the suggestion that Justinian and Theodora were really demons (which is discussed in more detail later). The rest of this part of *The Secret History* alternates between the lifestyle and crimes of Justinian (Chapters 13–14) and the lifestyle and crimes of Theodora (Chapters 15–17), before reaching a crescendo of war, slaughter, and natural disaster in Chapter 18.

The goal of this central section of the text is not merely to document the specific crimes committed by Justinian and Theodora but to paint portraits of their characters. These portraits are subtle and quite unforgettable. Perhaps they are the most masterful literary images of rulers in the Greek tradition since the days of classi-

38. *Secret History* 18.33, 23.1, 24.29, and 24.33; see Kaldellis, "The Date and Structure."

cal tragedy. In Prokopios' mind, Justinian was a tyrant—there could be no question about that—but in decisive ways he did not fit the classical image of a tyrant. He is revealed in the text as a calm, accessible, apparently good-natured, hardworking ruler who hardly ate or slept. He did not abuse his power in order to indulge his bodily desires, as tyrants were supposed to do. Theodora, on the other hand, was his opposite. She raged furiously and nursed her grievances, slept and ate a lot, hardly worked at all, and was contemptuously inaccessible. Yet the narrative subtly reveals that these differences were superficial, or rather they reinforced each other. Prokopios claims that their apparent disagreements over matters of policy and personnel were an illusion, a theater devised to divide and conquer. More fundamentally, the two rulers were governed by their mutual love of money and their bloodthirsty eagerness to use violence in order to obtain it. Because of this, "even the good aspects of [Justinian's] nature were turned by him to the mistreatment of his subjects" (13.33). He was perfectly calm when he signed orders for the destruction of towns and the enslavement of populations (8.29, 13.2). He was malicious but also naïve and easily led around, a destructive combination (8.22–23). His *eros* was not for other men's wives, as with ancient tyrants, but for Theodora his wife on the one hand (9.30–32) and for murder and money on the other (e.g., 8.26, 11.3). Murder and theft are the major themes of *The Secret History* as a whole, namely how the private vices of two very different people ruined the Roman state.

The most sensational aspects of this part of the text have received the most attention in modern scholarship, namely the pornographic account of Theodora's past and the claim that Justinian was a demon. We will discuss them separately below. A more interesting aspect that has, however, been overlooked is the subtle structural analysis to which Prokopios subjects the regime, that is, his analysis of how Justinian's policies adversely affected the political, military, and economic balances of the empire. By bribing the Huns not to invade Roman territory, for example, Justinian unintentionally provided a supply that created its own demand. More and more tribes began to raid the empire in order to qualify for these payments, and some continued to plunder in violation of the agreement (11.5–10). In order to recruit them as mercenaries for his wars to liberate Roman lands abroad, he prohibited his generals in Illyricum from attacking them when they were raiding Roman lands that he already did control (21.26–29). When he persecuted heretics by confiscating their property, he caused many Orthodox Christians, whose livelihood depended on those properties, to lose their jobs and become destitute (11.16–19). He esteemed officials who brought him increased revenues even through illegal means and so, "[a]s a result, many would try hard to show him that they were in fact immoral, even though they were not, at least in their own private lives" (13.24–25). These counterintuitive results were perhaps not intended by Justinian, but Prokopios is astute in tracing the complex patterns of causality. Justinian apparently did not care what the results were so long as he got his way in the short term.

Part III (Chapters 19–30): *The Corruption of Laws, Administration, and Policy*. Prokopios presents this as an integral part of *The Secret History*, but it was evidently written later in the same year as a kind of appendix. It is a sustained critique of Justinian's administration, the men whom he chose for high office (especially his praetorian prefects, *quaestores*, and *magistri officiorum*), and the laws that he issued. In fact, Prokopios often alludes to the actual language of Justinian's edicts, which he must have had available to him as he was writing, making this section a kind of historical-legal commentary. This, along with its detailed analysis of fiscal and administrative policy, makes the final section of *The Secret History* a unique and unprecedented treatise by ancient conventions.[39] The major theme is to show how Justinian constantly changed or disregarded laws and manipulated the administration in order to consume the wealth of his subjects (Prokopios presents this image at the very beginning of the section as a nightmare seen by one of his informants; 19.1–3). Prokopios' outlook is not to be identified with that of any particular class, for he explains how the emperor victimized senators, landowners, merchants and craftsmen, sailors, the urban populace, soldiers and officers in the army, silk traders, residents of provincial cities, lawyers, artists, the poor, and those on public welfare. We should remember that "it is possible for a historian to complain of injustice without the complaints necessarily relating to his own experiences."[40] Besides, Prokopios was probably not a senator.

After Chapter 27, however, the exposition lapses into a series of scandals that are only loosely connected to each other by the theme of the emperor's avarice and stinginess. It seems that Prokopios dumped some leftover material into these final chapters. And whereas in the rest of the work the amount of repetition and overlap

39. See Kaldellis, *Procopius*, 150–59, 223–28.

40. G. Kelly, *Ammianus Marcellinus: The Allusive Historian* (Cambridge: Cambridge University Press, 2008), 124.

is insignificant, indicating the careful planning with which it was composed, in the third section he does repeat a handful of accusations that he had made in the second, such as paying off the barbarians and the wasteful constructions by the coast (19.6–16). Particularly strange is the way in which he "introduces" Justinian and Theodora at 22.23–32 as if all that he had written in the second part was not fresh in his mind. While the emphasis on witchcraft is a new feature here, he even repeats the charge that Justinian's will was "light as dust" that he had already made at 13.10, without referring us back to that passage as he normally does. Perhaps he was reworking his original notes anew.

Overall, the structure of *The Secret History* reveals considerable planning and tight consistency. There is, as just noted, little overlap. All of the many cross-references, both internal and external, and both forward- and backward-looking, pan out. Some material, as noted, has been inserted awkwardly, such as the final chapters; the material on Sergios and the younger Solomon at 5.28–38;[41] the story of Makedonia is not fully developed at 12.28; and the brief section on the *magister officiorum* awkwardly intrudes into the narrative of Petros Barsymes as praetorian prefect at 22.12–13. This digression was probably added later (the "he" with whom the text begins after the digression is Petros and not Justinian, with whom the digression ends). But these are minor flaws in a work that is otherwise artfully put together, considering that Prokopios did not employ a linear narrative sequence on which to hang his material and could have found little guidance for what he was attempting here in the literature of the classical tradition.

The Style and Images of *The Secret History*

Though Prokopios wrote in an elevated register of ancient Greek, the individual sentences that make up *The Secret History* are short and blunt and their syntax is usually uncomplicated. The same syntactical forms are repeated often and there are almost no rhetorical flourishes. Prokopios does not try to dazzle his readers with his eloquence or arcane style. That is done adequately by the nature of the material and his accusations. The intensity of the work stems from

41. This North African material may be intended to complement that from the East and Italy given earlier in the first part of *The Secret History*, showing how Theodora's political interference affected all three of Prokopios' "signature" theaters of war (see p. xxvii).

its contents, but these are related matter-of-factly. In fact, the vocabulary of the work as a whole can be called minimalist. The same terms are used to describe similar crimes, and the vocabulary deployed for motives and states of mind is likewise repetitive ("consistent" might be a more positive way of putting it). One comes across the same abstract verbs many times, while groups of people are typically designated via plural participles (which results in a high incidence of "those who . . ." in translation). In these senses, *The Secret History* can even be called a restrained work (certainly compared to the rhetorical pomposity of Justinian's own edicts). This stylistic uniformity, moreover, and the accuracy of its internal cross-references, reinforce the conclusion that the work is not an assembly of disparate notes but was carefully written in a relatively brief period of time in 550/551.

The language, however, is mostly faithful to Prokopios' classical models and laced with allusions to ancient literature, some of which are well chosen to enhance the argument of *The Secret History*. Consider, for example, the courtship of Justinian and Theodora:

> As it was impossible for anyone who had reached the rank of senator to marry a prostitute (this being prohibited from the earliest times by the most ancient of laws), he forced the emperor to annul those laws with another law, and so afterward he lived with Theodora as his lawful wife, effectively making it feasible for anyone else to marry a prostitute. (9.51)

The narrative here, in both structure and language, is modeled on Herodotos' *Histories* 3.31, which recounts the mad Persian king Kambyses' illicit desire to marry his sister. The king pressured his jurists to circumvent the ancient law that prohibited such marriages and discover an "other law," namely that "he who is king of Persia can do whatever he wishes." Prokopios thereby links Justinian to a mad oriental despot (and one of the subliminal themes of the *Wars* was how similar Justinian was to his Persian nemesis Chosroes). Moreover, there is a nice pun here: the "other law" (*heteros nomos*) that Justinian compelled Justin to pass so that he could marry Theodora alludes to the word for prostitute here, a high-class escort, or courtesan (*hetaira*), which is probably what Theodora was by this stage in her career. The story works on a symbolic level as well: Justinian's rise to sole power coincides with the overturning of the Roman laws of private life, a prominent theme of *The Secret History* and basic to ancient views of tyranny. Note that Justinian is then said to have "mounted" the imperial position (9.51—the pun works in Greek as well as in English).

The most frequently cited classical author in *The Secret History* is the comic playwright Aristophanes. At first glance this is surprising, for the contents of *The Secret History* are not really funny. But Aristophanes was not merely a comedian. His deeper themes were war, cultural decline, corruption, and demagoguery, and his plays have strong tragic dimensions (e.g., the ending of the *Clouds*, the most quoted play in *The Secret History*). The density of Aristophanic language and images is meant to mock Justinian and his minions, stripping them even further of respectability and legitimacy. This was Aristophanes' own goal in mocking the bellicose but vulgar Athenian politician Kleon, to whom some of the allusions in *The Secret History* point. For Prokopios, too, Justinian "acted like a barbarian in his manner of speech, dress, and thinking" (14.2) while "[t]he state resembled a kingdom of children at play" (14.14). The emperor may have been all-powerful but he was also gullible and easily led around by flatterers (13.10–12). This resonates powerfully with Aristophanes' caricature of "The People" (Demos) who ruled in the radical democracy of his times. The *Knights* is also referenced frequently in *The Secret History:* "O Demos, how splendid your rule! All men fear you like a Tyrant. But you're easy to sway, with flattery, fawning, and deceit" (1111–1117). Theodora, too, had not forgotten her theatrical instincts. "When it suited her interests, she converted even the most important matters into a farce, treating them like one of those stage skits they put on in the theater" (15.24). Both Prokopios and Aristophanes, then, exposed and mocked the rise and rule of vulgarity.[42] It is worth noting here that the first external mention of *The Secret History*, found in the tenth-century Byzantine encyclopedia of classical studies called the *Souda*, intriguingly refers to the text as "an invective and a comedy against the emperor Justinian and his wife Theodora."[43]

We must, then, be sensitive to the nuances and subtle allusions that may lie behind the language of Prokopios at any point. "The kingdom of children at play," for example, is an allusion to Herodotos' *Histories* 1.114, where Kyros, the future king of Persia, played the game of "king" with his friends. Beyond the surface mockery, the allusion is a way to compare Justinian to a Persian monarch. Other images serve similar aims. Prokopios concludes his

42. Compare the fourth-century historian Ammianus Marcellinus' "fondness for casting the officials of Constantius in the language of Plautine comedy"; Kelly, *Ammianus*, 172.

43. *Souda* s.v. Prokopios Illoustrios; A. Adler, ed., *Suidae Lexicon* (Leipzig: Teubner, 1971), 4:210–11.

description of Justinian's appearance by noting that he "retained a ruddy complexion even after two days of fasting" (8.12). He then conjectures that Justinian most resembled Emperor Domitian (r. 81–96), one of the most hated men in Roman history (also cited as an archetypical tyrant by Prokopios' contemporary Ioannes Lydos).[44] Prokopios tells a macabre (and unhistorical) story about how Domitian was hacked into pieces, which his wife had stitched together; then she set up a statue showing him in this grotesque form. Seeing this statue in Rome, Prokopios noted its similarity to Justinian. Beyond the image of a butchered Justinian that this comparison inevitably brings to mind (an image that Prokopios presumably wanted to become real), there is another, more subtle, parallel. Emperors became tyrants when they lost all shame, when they could no longer blush, and the word for it was the same as for a "ruddy" complexion. This is how Cassius Dio, an early third-century historian, described Nero's lapse into tyranny.[45] Regarding Domitian, it was said that his "ruddy face saved him from blushing with shame." By extension, this "ruddy expression, which fortified him against blushing at his acts, might be implicated in his tyranny."[46] Prokopios claims that Justinian did not blush (13.2), but how could he given his ruddy appearance? "As if the word 'shamelessness' were written prominently on his forehead, he casually and unscrupulously advances to the most abominable actions" (10.5). Theodora, by contrast, was "pale" (10.11); her utter shamelessness is so flaunted in the text (e.g., 9.14) that she presumably had no use for the cover of a ruddy complexion. She simply never felt any shame.

Remaining faithful to the language of their classical models, Prokopios and other authors in late antiquity avoided using Christian and Roman technical terminology or, if they had to use a word such as *monk* or *referendarius*, they explained it as though it were unfamiliar or attributed it to "the Christians" or "the Romans" (meaning Latin speakers). This practice was imposed by the autonomy of the conventions that governed classicizing literature and had no bearing on whether the author was himself a Christian or a Latin speaker. The linguistic mirage of a world that had not changed fundamentally since the age of Thucydides did not, however, affect

44. Ioannes Lydos, *On the Magistracies of the Roman State* 2.19.

45. Cassius Dio, *Roman History* 61.5.1; Nero is cited as an archetypical tyrant in *The Secret History*'s Preface (1.9).

46. Tacitus, *Agricola* 45; and J. E. Lendon, *Empire of Honour: The Art of Government in the Roman World* (Oxford: Oxford University Press, 1997), 107.

Prokopios' ability to discuss contemporary religious issues. The broader strategy of classicizing authors was to present their own times in terms of the classical models that had withstood the test of the ages. Writing in this way offered the best guarantee that one's own works would still be accessible in one or two thousand years. Those models, moreover, offered a range of transhistorical concepts of analysis that could be understood by educated readers regardless of their specific cultural context. So discussing the sixth century AD as if it were the fifth century BC avoided the parochialism that we encounter in less sophisticated writers of the time (for example, in the chronicler Ioannes Malalas). It did not preclude one from writing about contemporary religious issues. Prokopios was, after all, planning to write an ecclesiastical history, probably in the same stylistic register. He refers in *The Secret History* to baptism and Christian adoption (1.16), albeit with circumlocution, and often notes that his protagonists violated even "the most dreadful oaths that exist among Christians" (2.13). Justinian scandalously had himself proclaimed emperor "three days before the Easter celebration, at a time when it is not permitted to greet one's friends or even wish them peace" (9.53; because it was period of mourning). His condemnation of the servility with which the Senate, the priests, and the populace prostrated themselves before the whore Theodora—"as if she were a goddess" and with "upturned hands as though in prayer"—is infused with religious language, to highlight the pollution of their act (10.6–8).[47]

Furthermore, Prokopios was not above using Christian images and words to attack Justinian and Theodora. He has a monk call Justinian "the Lord of Demons," alluding to Scripture (12.26). The powerful climax of Chapter 18, which draws together the themes of death and destruction in every country, civil strife, war, foreign invasion, famine, plague, flood, and earthquake, replicates precisely the list of evils from which Christian congregations prayed to be spared in the Divine Liturgy: "Rescue, Lord, this flock, and every city and country, from famine, plague, earthquake, flood, fire, the sword, invasion by foreigners, and civil war."[48] The liturgy would, of course, have included ritual blessings for the emperor Justinian, which is why it is all the more ironic that Prokopios links his litany of evils to the notion that Justinian was the Lord of Demons. We must

47. See Kaldellis, *Procopius*, 138–40.

48. R. C. D. Jasper and G. J. Cuming, *Prayers of the Eucharist: Early and Reformed*, 3rd ed. (New York: Pueblo, 1987), 122 (the liturgy of St. Basileios).

remember, however, that this was all for the purposes of rhetorical invective and ideological polemic, and not necessarily an expression of Prokopios' own religious views.

There is probably subtle humor to be found in Prokopios' Christian forays as well. The youth Theodosios with whom Antonina has an affair in the first part of the text used to belong to the heretical Christian sect of the Eunomians; he was baptized and adopted by Belisarios, making Antonina legally his mother (1.15–16). Now, as it happens, the fourth-century heretic Eunomios had argued that God the Son was of a different nature and inferior to God the Father, whereas the Orthodox believed not only in the equality but the identicalness of their natures. Well, after his conversion and baptism, Theodosios "the son" definitely usurps the place of his "father," at least in Antonina's bed. He had truly embraced the Orthodox position.

Prokopios and Justinian: A Conflict of Ideologies

The Secret History is not merely a personal attack or indictment of one emperor's policies. What animates the text is an ideological conflict between two opposing views of government and religion.

The broad outlines of Justinian's religious and political ideology, that is, his beliefs regarding his powers and responsibilities as Roman emperor, can be reconstructed from his many legislative acts, those predating 535 in the *Codex*, the *Novellae* after that, and the edicts authorizing the *Digest* and *Institutes*. The image of imperial power projected by those texts was in some respects conventional, for they drew on a long tradition, and many of them were actually written by the emperor's *quaestores*. But they were written on his behalf, he authorized them personally, and, while they drew upon traditional concepts, the specific ideology that they project is distinctively Justinian's. In addition, the section devoted to the reign of Justinian in the *Chronicle* of Ioannes Malalas was based in part on the official announcements and notices that Justinian posted regarding important events. The entries in that text, then, reflect the emperor's propaganda.[49] *The Secret History* delivers an attack on precisely the ideology that emerges from Justinian's legal and other propagandistic texts, thus highlighting it through stark contrast. The third part of

49. R. Scott, "Malalas, *The Secret History*, and Justinian's Propaganda," *Dumbarton Oaks Papers* 39 (1985): 99–109.

the text engages directly, sometimes word-for-word, with the specific provisions of Justinian's legislation.

All Christian emperors up to this point had naturally believed that theirs was the sole "True Faith" and that all other faiths were erroneous and harmful. Yet even while they legislated in accordance with this belief, their policies were usually tempered by pragmatism and were passively reactive, at least compared to those of Justinian. For him deviance was a hateful pollution to be actively stamped out. From the time he took office he initiated full-spectrum campaigns of prohibition and persecution to wipe that stain clean and bring everyone into line with what he believed was the truth, thus taking religious exclusivity to a logical extreme. Justinian was "a genuine ideologue and a radical, a ruler determined to remake the world in accordance with his ideals."[50] His reign was marked by periodic and bloody purges in the capital. His persecutions targeted pagans and philosophers, Manicheans, Samaritans, Jews, heretics, homosexuals, and astrologers. Violence was an ideal method of correction. After all, God punished humanity collectively for tolerating deviance (homosexuality, for example, caused earthquakes). But God had also rewarded Justinian himself with military victories, because of his pious zeal.[51] In other words, both success and catastrophic failure could justify repression. In the *Chronicle* of Malalas, we catch echoes of the emperor's belief that "terror" and "public order" went together.[52]

In *The Secret History*, Prokopios criticizes this intolerant and oppressive approach to religious and social diversity. For him it was wrong to persecute others for their beliefs, even when those beliefs were idiotic and repugnant. While he does not set out the precise philosophical grounds of his position, we can infer them. For one, he was a pragmatist. The harmful consequences to Roman society of Justinian's persecutions were not worth the unity that they aimed to impose (and in vain, at that). He regularly criticizes Justinian for not foreseeing, and then disregarding, the political, military, and economic consequences of his policies. Legal discrimination against Arians in North Africa led to military revolts; the confiscation of the heretics' property caused many Orthodox Christians to lose their

50. C. Pazdernik, "Justinianic Ideology and the Power of the Past," in M. Maas, ed., *The Cambridge Companion to the Age of Justinian* (Cambridge: Cambridge University Press, 2005), 185–212, here 186.

51. Earthquakes: *Novella* 77; victories: *Constitutio Tanta*, Preface (confirmation of the *Digest*); *Institutes*, Preface.

52. Scott, "Malalas," 103–04.

jobs; the persecution of the Samaritans led to war and the devastation of Palestine; favoritism to priests meant that landowners were subject to the avarice of their clerical neighbors. In sum, the emperor's "firm faith as regards Christ . . . worked to the ruin of his subjects" (13.4). Better to tolerate diversity than incite war, injustice, and discontent. Put differently, Prokopios did not seem to like the new definition that Christianity had given to the word *heresy*, namely that it was an error to be wiped out. His outlook was closer to that of classical antiquity, when a heresy was a philosophical choice made freely. This corresponds to his emphasis throughout *The Secret History* on citizen rights over the emperor's alleged divine authority (see below). It is likely, moreover, that his *Ecclesiastical History* would have shown that Justinian's efforts to impose unity on the Church resulted in a schism in the empire. Nor is there any reason to think that Prokopios found the goal of total "unity" an attractive one to begin with. In this respect, he should be ranked with the exponents of ancient pagan tradition who argued that universal conformity would be impossible to attain and probably undesirable as well.[53]

In the *Wars*, Prokopios mocked theological ambition and the controversies to which it had given rise:

> I think it is insanely stupid to investigate the nature of God and ask what sort it is. For I do not believe that human beings have a sufficiently exact understanding of merely human things, far less of anything that bears on the nature of God. Therefore, I will keep a safe silence about these things, with the sole intention of not allowing honored teachings to be disbelieved. For I would say nothing else about God than that he is entirely good and holds everything within his power. But let each say about these things whatever he thinks he knows, whether he is a priest or a layman. (5.3.5–9)

In other words, Prokopios' opposition to persecution was not merely pragmatic but based also on an agnostic position regarding human knowledge, a position diametrically opposed to the theological certainties of Justinian. He implied that intolerant religious policies rested on arrogant claims to superhuman knowledge that were, at bottom, delusions. Prokopios was not even willing to admit to any belief about God that was recognizably Christian. A pragmatist

53. Kelsos in Origenes, *Against Kelsos* 5.26, 8.72; cf. N. Siniossoglou, *Plato and Theodoret: The Christian Appropriation of Platonic Philosophy and the Hellenic Intellectual Resistance* (Cambridge: Cambridge University Press, 2008), 105–06, 212.

when it came to social policy, then, he put people's actual lives above metaphysical abstractions just as he put "jobs" and the rights of property ahead of religious unity. And as a historian, he was enough an empiricist to recognize that even the truth about human beings cannot be known adequately. In Book 8 of the *Wars*, two years later, he would write that the truth he was seeking in his own works "was not about intelligible or intellectual matters or other such invisible things, but about rivers and lands" (8.6.9–10). Accordingly, his account of the greatest natural disaster of his times, the Justinianic plague, is aggressively skeptical regarding the causes of the event. Not only is his account of that catastrophe the only one of the many that survive that does not ever mention the "anger of God," he also makes it clear that the plague, to the degree that it was not just random in its movements, tended to spare the worst people and even had a deleterious effect on their morals. This is a total rejection of Justinian's interpretation of such events.[54] In fact, it is unlikely that Prokopios believed in divine providence as a historical agent. While at times he vaguely refers to God—and it was certainly necessary for him to *appear* to be Christian (at least formally)—his discussions of the actual workings of providence are identical to the way in which he believed that "fortune" operated (or chance, *tyche*). Human beings can form plans and attempt to shape the world based on them but they cannot fully determine the outcome of their efforts. At the intersection of so many chains of causation as are involved in politics and war, unpredictable events will always intervene. Prokopios understood that most people like to call this element "God," though for him it was morally random. His notion of chance (*tyche*) undermined Justinian's ideology of Providence just as Tyche herself had wrecked so many of the emperor's plans.[55]

Not only did Prokopios believe that theological speculation was "stupid," he also knew that it could become fundamentally immoral, at least in the way that it was translated into policy by Justinian. The

54. For Prokopios' account of the plague, see related text 8; cf. Kaldellis, *Procopius*, 210–13; and "The Literature of Plague and the Anxieties of Piety in Sixth-Century Byzantium," in F. Mormando and T. Worcester, eds., *Piety and Plague: From Byzantium to the Baroque* (Kirksville, MO: Truman State University Press, 2007), 1–22.

55. This is the position of Kaldellis, *Procopius*, Chap. 5. Many conflicting views have been expressed about Prokopios' religion. Most scholars believe that he was a Christian, albeit an extraordinarily tolerant one for his age, though exponents of this position dismiss his statements about *tyche* as mere rhetorical dressing.

most chilling declaration in *The Secret History* is that Justinian did not consider a killing "murder" if the victim was of a different faith (13.7). Here ideology overrides basic morality, exposing the sinister consequences of the paradox uttered by a zealot of the fifth century that "there is no crime for those who have Christ."[56] Justinian's ideological extremism, in other words, was dehumanizing. This is one of the deeper truths of the demonology of *The Secret History*. Justinian was a power for evil, not quite human in the way that he approached the world. The demonology is not to be taken at face value as a literal expression of Prokopios' religious views (for instance, this section of the text has more disclaimers—"they say," "it is said"—than any other). It was a rhetorical strategy for exposing a ruler's inhumanity and also for directly and ironically reversing his ideology of Christian rule. Whereas Justinian viewed himself as God's highest representative, Prokopios cast him as the Prince of Fiends. The irony consists in the fact that Prokopios deploys Christian terms and images to effect this reversal, invokes the witness of Christian holy men, and possibly draws on contemporary notions regarding the Antichrist to subvert Justinian's image. This was a strategy of invective, not a counter-theology. The historian was well aware that Justinian was only a man; his personality could even be described through Aristotelian theory: he was a man whose own vices were in contradiction with each other. He was malicious yet also naïve and easily duped (8.22–27). And for all his posturing as the champion of the Faith, greed could induce him to take a bribe and look the other way as Christians were oppressed (27.26–33).

The attack on Justinian's ideology in *The Secret History* has a legal aspect as well. Convinced of his right and duty to legislate on all topics, and impelled by the pressing imperative to reshape the entire world, Justinian issued a stream of reformist legislation, especially in the first part of his reign. In principle, anything could be improved: "We do not cease to inquire what needs correction in Our administration."[57] His approach to streamlining the law in the *Digest*

56. The Egyptian abbot Shenute; for a study, see M. Gaddis, *There Is No Crime for Those Who Have Christ: Religious Violence in the Christian Roman Empire* (Berkeley: University of California Press, 2005).

57. *Novella* 114, Preface (of 541), and in many other *Novellae*; see M. Maas, "Roman History and Christian Ideology in Justinianic Reform Legislation," *Dumbarton Oaks Papers* 40 (1986): 17–31. Justinian announced his project of continuous, divinely guided, imperial reform at *Constitutio Tanta* 18 (confirmation of the *Digest*).

exemplified his intentions regarding all aspects of the world that he governed: "There is to be no place for any antinomy . . . but there is to be total concord, total consistency, with no one raising any objection."[58] Justinian's authority, of course, was backed by God, and Justinian did not hesitate to invoke him for even the most minor matters. The price of vegetables, for example, was now to require oaths made on the Scriptures.[59] This was theocratic micromanagement.

Prokopios' concern was not merely to show that continuous reformation threw everything into confusion, for Justinian himself had virtually admitted as much.[60] It was to demonstrate that the emperor, in his revolutionary zeal, had imprudently overturned an established order of things, an order to which many cherished social values were attached. The ancients (and *The Secret History*) called this "innovation," a term with none of the positive connotations that it has today. In this sense, then, Prokopios mounted a conservative attack on Justinian, as did others, such as Ioannes Lydos. It should be noted that Justinian did try to apply a patina of Roman tradition on many of his reforms,[61] but Prokopios and Lydos were apparently not deceived by these specious efforts. The emperor had overridden tradition in favor of his dubious ideals, behind which often lurked his own interests, mostly financial. And a ruler who is not bound by human conventions cannot truly belong to the same moral community as his subjects; he is anchored in a different world. The demonology of *The Secret History* focalizes this notion as well, by removing Justinian from the traditions that bind together the world of men such as Prokopios and Lydos.

Justinian was notorious for eating and sleeping very little: "Such things seemed to him like a distraction imposed on him by Nature" (13.28–29). The new protocol for imperial audiences that he introduced further set him off not only from the mass of his subjects but from his own highest officials as well (30.21–26). Conversely, Justinian was also less than human in that he had no sense of humor. According to *The Secret History*, he was so caught up in himself and weighed down by the gravity of his faith that he failed to recognize when people were manipulating him or pulling his leg (13.10–12,

58. *Constitutio Deo auctore* 8 (prefacing the *Digest*).

59. *Novella* 64.1 (of 538).

60. See T. Honoré, *Tribonian* (Ithaca, NY: Cornell University Press, 1978), 27–28.

61. See Maas, "Roman History and Christian Ideology."

22.29). This lack of nuance and human sensitivity in his "piety," so typical of men who champion such ideologies, made him even less fit to govern in Prokopios' eyes.

The tension that propels *The Secret History* is more political than religious. Justinian juggled different and even competing political notions in his edicts, but the view of the hierarchy of the world that came most naturally to him was as follows: God—Justinian—the subjects of Justinian. This squeezed out the basic component of Roman political thought, the *politeia* (Greek for Latin *respublica*), the national and lawful political community of free Romans that authorized the emperor to rule in their name. The concept of this ancient, dignified, and autonomous "polity" is central to *The Secret History*, especially the second half of the text. While it appears also in Justinian's edicts, it does so more as putty to be shaped by the emperor. For example, Justinian terminated the consulship, an office that Prokopios regarded as providing crucial welfare to the poor through its largess and that Lydos viewed as the last remnant of the ancient freedom of the Romans.[62] Justinian canceled and invented other offices at will, changing the structure and balance of the political sphere. He was the first emperor to claim in an edict that by divine authority the emperor was a kind of incarnate law and therefore not bound even to his own laws.[63] There was, in fact, an opposite way of looking at the imperial office, which Justinian hinted at when he cited the legal fiction of *lex regia*, according to which "all legal capacity and all the power of the Roman people were transferred to the imperial authority."[64] The conclusion that Justinian drew from this law was that he was now the sole repository of Roman political power, but it was possible to view the transfer as a theoretical validation of continued popular sovereignty. According to this interpretation, had the Nika rioters and their senatorial instigators managed to remove Justinian, they would have been acting within their political rights as Romans.

Prokopios does not, to be sure, offer any such radical political theory. In fact, it was not the purpose of *The Secret History* to offer any systematic theory. But his constant references to the *politeia* as the victim of Justinian's greed and innovations bring that concept back

62. *Secret History* 26.12–15; Ioannes Lydos, *On the Magistracies of the Roman State* 1.29, 2.8.

63. *Novella* 105.2.4 (of 537).

64. *Constitutio Deo Auctore* 7 (prefacing the *Digest*).

into focus and reveal what that emperor had tried to obscure. The emperor was not himself the state but the servant of the state of the Roman people. Justinian may have viewed himself as "the least of God's servants,"[65] but for Prokopios and others the emphasis lay more on the emperor's responsibility for the welfare of the Roman people. He was free to legislate but not to violate the laws on a whim or to alter them except for the benefit of that people. The *politeia* was not his instrument but coextensive with the national political community to which, in fact, he belonged and had to answer. It was impersonal and had to be staffed by men of merit whose sole responsibility was to enforce the laws and promote the interests of the Romans. To be sure, Prokopios had in mind here mostly educated landowners and other men of talent like himself whose interests, status, and discretionary power were being threatened by Justinian's reforms, by his micromanagement of the administration, and by his reliance on types like Ioannes the Kappadokian. Still, this class could only govern effectively in an environment of legality; otherwise private and even sinister interests would prevail. They were not supposed to be the emperor's "own men" or his servants. Far less were they supposed to be the servants of the *empress*, especially of one such as her.

This is the political ideology that underlies *The Secret History*'s attack on the regime. It consistently exposes how private interests undermined the *politeia*, in particular how the court implicated Roman magistrates in its personal politics, exposing the impotence of the traditionalist, right-thinking classes that Prokopios might have wished to see in power. Theodora was the worst offender. This was a woman who had no *policy* for the state beyond the satisfaction of her whims and hatreds. Even in the *Wars*, her famous speech during the Nika riots is a pure expression of will-to-power without any awareness of political responsibility.[66] "She insisted on presiding over every branch of the state [*politeia*] and on always having her way. She appointed both magistrates and priests" based on one criterion: how well they would serve her (17.27). Having lost all shame during her years as a prostitute along with, probably, all respect for the games that men like to play, she "had no regard for the dignity of office or the rights of the state, nor did she care about anything else at all so long as she got her way" (17.15). She treated officials as her

65. *Codex Iustinianus* 1.27.1.5.

66. For Prokopios' account of the Nika riots, see related text 2.

instruments and relished it. "The state was thereby reduced to a slave-pen and she was our teacher in servility" (15.16). The most striking image of this servility was the demeaning ceremony of prostration that the imperial couple introduced, which, for Prokopios, symbolized the new despotism: the emperor was now to be called "Master" and officials had to refer to themselves as his "slaves" (30.21–26). Prokopios was here describing the erosion of a public sphere defined by law that used to protect subjects from the whims of their rulers. Justinian presented himself as the protector of his subjects from the abuses of his own higher officials, but he seems to have been unaware that the *politeia*—the state—was not an instrument of his will but a relatively autonomous political culture. Public functions were now performed in the palace, whereas "in the past, it was permitted for magistrates to exercise their own independent judgment in making decisions about what was just and lawful" (30.28). Nor would Prokopios allow that this shift benefited the bulk of the population that lay (well) below the class of magistrates. That is what *The Secret History* aims to prove as well.

We have here an archetypical conflict between a classical conservative-liberal on the one hand and a revolutionary ideologue on the other. The ancient world had not yet seen the likes of Justinian. His was a form of tyranny with no precedent in the known history of Greece and Rome, and, in fact, with almost no direct progeny (the Roman *politeia* was to be much stronger in Byzantium than under Justinian). Regimes premised on doctrinal certainties, governed by totalitarian bureaucracies that mask deep corruption and private interests, and have at their disposal an apparatus of enforcement and propaganda comparable to those of the late Roman state, would not appear again until modern times. *The Secret History* represents an innovative, bold, and subtle effort to come to terms with this type of regime. The text's strengths lie in the analysis of personalities and the exposition of the effects of their crimes against an ancient and so far quite resilient political system. The text does not, however, directly confront its target in a sustained theoretical critique or articulate the alternatives that it upholds. It is a powerful rhetorical and literary invective, but it is not explicit about political philosophy, either its own or its target's. Justinian's ideology is reflected in his edicts and recognizable as the motivating force of the monster targeted in *The Secret History*, but the position of Prokopios himself has to be inferred. For this, the history of political ideas is the poorer.

The Reliability of *The Secret History* and the Case of Theodora

The testimony of *The Secret History* has fascinated, frustrated, and scandalized historians ever since the text was discovered in the seventeenth century. Even today opinions are divided as to its trustworthiness, though sometimes scholars are talking at cross-purposes. Gender historians who have tried to rehabilitate Theodora have predictably accused Prokopios of gross prejudice and distortion whereas political and legal historians find the text reliable, "with allowance for bias and exaggeration."[67] In the case of Prokopios versus Justinian and Theodora we must, of course, keep an open mind. For example, the workings of the Roman administration and the reforms of Ioannes the Kappadokian are still imperfectly understood. Even if those reforms had the effects that Prokopios alleges, their motivation and the problems that they were meant to address cannot always or easily be inferred from *The Secret History*.[68] It is also difficult to situate Justinian's policies within the context of the imperial economy because too much is still unclear about how it worked. This does not exculpate Justinian. It means only that we cannot rely on Prokopios' *interpretation* of his policies even when he is reporting the facts more or less accurately. On the other hand, like Prokopios, most historians today view Justinian's wars as destructive rather than liberating, and agree that he failed to adequately defend the eastern and Balkan frontiers. We do not need to accept Prokopios' fantastic figures for the number of people who died because of the wars (11.29, 18.4), but his analysis of Justinian's failures in postconflict reconstruction is astute and always relevant: "he made no provision to establish and consolidate his governance of the land nor thought ahead about how to secure control over its resources by winning over the goodwill of its inhabitants" (18.9).

The Secret History may be biased and even hyperbolic, but its testimony is confirmed so often and sometimes so stunningly by independent sources that it cannot be dismissed. Most famously, in his *Lives of the Saints*, the Syrian Monophysite missionary Yuhannan of Amida (or John of Ephesos, as he is called by modern historians) casually mentions that Theodora "came from the brothel." Certainly, no one would have believed that Prokopios had completely invented

67. Honoré, *Tribonian*, 6 n. 42.

68. C. Kelly, *Ruling the Later Roman Empire* (Cambridge, MA: Harvard University Press, 2004) is a groundbreaking study in this regard.

all the material in Chapter 9 of *The Secret History*, but this testimony by an independent writer who otherwise mostly praised Theodora for supporting the Monophysite cause reveals that Prokopios' pornographic narrative is only a rhetorical elaboration of what was in fact Theodora's occupation before she became a high-class courtesan.[69] Besides, even without Yuhannan's evidence, we would still have to explain Justin's law, the one that allowed senators to marry former "actresses." Prokopios' account of that law is also accurate.[70] Independent sources likewise confirm Justin's humble origins, his illiteracy, and Theodora's role in the deposition of Pope Silverius.[71] Many sources confirm that the late Roman stage was a venue for precisely the kinds of lewd acts that Prokopios describes.

In some cases, Justinian's own edicts confirm the accuracy of Prokopios' reports. That Justinian did not issue a general cancelation of tax arrears (*Secret History* 23.1) was admitted three years later by the emperor himself in *Novella* 147 (of 553). It was a fact that no consuls were appointed after 541, and in reporting this at *Secret History* 26.12–15 Prokopios savaged Justinian's *Novella* 105 (of 537), whose failed intention was to make the office "immortal." Besides, about matters such as tax relief Prokopios could not easily have lied because his readers would have immediately known it. This probably applies also to the decommissioning of the *limitanei* and the failure to pay donatives (24.12–13, 24.27–29), which some historians have doubted, though Prokopios may have misrepresented what the emperor had attempted to do. In other cases, *The Secret History* gives us the inside scoop, allowing us to understand events and legal reforms that would otherwise remain unintelligible. The story of Priskos the forger (28.1–5) explains the bizarre change between *Codex Iustinianus* 1.2.23 (of 530) and *Novella* 9 (of 535) on the one hand and *Novella* 111 (of 541) on the other. This is a significant gotcha moment for Prokopian reporting. The fate of the secretary

69. For Yuhannan's testimony, see related text 3: "Theodora Helps Monophysite Saints."

70. See related text 1 for the law; for a discussion, see D. Daube, "The Marriage of Justinian and Theodora: Legal and Theological Reflections," *Catholic University of America Law Review* 16 (1966): 380–99. For Prokopios' narrative, see the analysis at p. xxxvi.

71. Respectively: the Syriac *Chronicle* of pseudo-Zacharias (8.1), tr. F. J. Hamilton and E. W. Brooks, *The Syriac Chronicle known as that of Zachariah of Mitylene* (London: Methuen & Co., 1899), 189; the *Chronicle* of Ioannes Malalas (17.1); and *The Book of Pontiffs* (60: Silverius), tr. R. Davis (Liverpool: Liverpool University Press, 1989), 55.

Priskos (a different man) at *Secret History* 16.7–10, is confirmed by Malalas, except that Malalas, echoing imperial propaganda, has him banished for (inexplicably) insulting Theodora, whereas in Prokopios it is, more plausibly, Theodora who attacks Priskos.[72]

These specific instances of outside confirmation (and there are others) create reserves of trust for *The Secret History* that can be spent elsewhere. We may be skeptical of its report that some of the prostitutes whom Theodora locked up in the Convent of Repentance jumped from the walls to escape (17.5–6), but the exact same thing has been reported from modern Thailand in connection with the activities of Christian groups who want to save the country's prostitutes.[73] Moreover, Prokopios distances himself from some of the most vicious rumors by the use of phrases such as "they say" or "it is said" (e.g., at 1.27 and especially in the demonology of 12.14–32). Such phrases mark what journalists today call "unconfirmed reports." Still, it is possible that Prokopios misunderstood or deliberately misrepresented Justinian's policies in some instances. The burden of proof here lies, on balance, with those who would question the accusations of *The Secret History*, and we still lack a detailed and up-to-date institutional history that would explain the changes taking place in this period. But the text's rhetoric does sometimes get ahead of its factual reporting, and this is when the reader must be cautious. For example, Prokopios accuses Justinian of selling provincial posts in the first part of his reign, which naturally led to corruption and the exploitation of the provincials (21.9–25). Justinian himself, in *Novella* 8 (of 535), confirmed that this was the case and sought to curb this practice by instituting salaried positions instead. So far so good. But Prokopios savages the later policy too (21.20–25), only his denunciation is so uncharacteristically vague that we must remain suspicious. There are none of the names and specifics that we find elsewhere in the text. This is the closest that the text comes to being purely rhetorical, in the bad sense. We need, in other words, to be on the lookout for such transitions. Consider the story of Antonina's affair. The facts that Prokopios reports about her relationship with Theodosios are plausible, but the accusation that she meant to cheat on Belisarios from the start of their

72. Ioannes Malalas, *Chronicle* 18.43, a fuller version of which entry survives in *De insidiis* 3.45; C. de Boor, ed., *Excerpta historica iussu imp. Constantini Porphyrogeniti confecta*, vol. 3, *Excerpta de insidiis* (Berlin: Weidmann, 1905), 171–72.

73. "Thailand's Brothel Busters," *Mother Jones*, November–December 2003, 19–20.

marriage (1.13) sounds like rhetorical invective. Prokopios really knows of only one affair.

The portrayal of Theodora requires separate discussion, because it has always been regarded as one of *The Secret History*'s highlights and has probably attracted more attention than any other aspect of the text. In particular, a stream of revisionist publications since the late 1970s have rejected Prokopios' testimony about Theodora as an expression of his misogyny and patriarchal attitudes. An alternative image was then constructed based on Monophysite sources that depict her favorably as the "believing queen." However, far from contradicting the image of the empress in *The Secret History*, these sources actually reinforce it, for Prokopios insists that she acted as the Monophysites' patron while her husband acted as their enemy. In addition, strong criticisms of her are found in these very Monophysite sources alongside the praise,[74] and Chalcedonian sources were naturally hostile. Besides, just because she is presented as pious in some of those sources hardly contradicts Prokopios' image of her. His Justinian is pious, and also cruel and murderous. Great piety in *The Secret History* is normally associated with great crime. Finally, some of these revisionist efforts relied on much later and legendary material about Theodora without noting that it was fundamentally unhistorical. *The Secret History* remains our most reliable contemporary source. Its testimony on specific points has been confirmed, and its character portrait of Theodora as empress is coherent, plausible, and consistent with outside evidence.[75] It cannot be dismissed simply because it is hostile.

When it came to most women, Prokopios adhered to conventional values, for example, as when he says that Justinian could "have married a woman who was the most well-born among all women and had been raised outside the public gaze, who had learned the ways of modesty and lived discreetly; moreover, she could have been exceedingly beautiful and still a virgin and even, as they say, with perky breasts" (10.2). On the other hand, like most classical historians he was entirely willing to accept and even praise powerful women if they ruled with justice. He had nothing but admiration for Amalasountha, the Gothic queen of Italy whom, he claims, Theodora had murdered. In his view, she was noble, magnificent, clever, wise, just, manly, *and* beautiful (16.1; *Wars* 5.2.3–5); perhaps

74. See related text 3: "Theodora Helps Monophysite Saints."

75. The best recent study is by C. Foss, "The Empress Theodora," *Byzantion* 72 (2002): 141–76.

he holds her out as a kind of anti-Theodora. Prokopios, then, did not attack Theodora because she was a powerful woman but because she was unfit to wield the kind of power that Fortune bestowed upon her. We should not forget that in writing up his notes for what would become *The Secret History* he was risking his life. *She* was the one with the power, not he, except of course when it came to shaping the perceptions of posterity, which is why he composed the work only after her death. This is the dynamic in the Preface of *The Secret History* (1.2–10).

That *The Secret History* is our most reliable source does not, of course, mean that it offers a perfect or full picture of Theodora (or, indeed, of any topic). For example, it would be easy for most readers to overlook the fact that it actually paints two different pictures of Theodora, the so-called pornography in Chapter 9 and the account of her deeds as empress in the later chapters. Both images are carefully constructed but along different rhetorical axes. The imperial section, as we saw, is based on a specific *political* ideology. Its overarching accusation is that Theodora treated affairs of state as personal matters subject to her whims. We do not, of course, hear her view. Even if everything that Prokopios alleges were true, she might have been able, based on her experiences as a prostitute, to adduce valid reasons for despising the so-called honor and dignity of high-ranking men. This is a hypothetical response, to be sure, but it underscores that ultimately we are dealing with interpretations of actions. Moreover, while Prokopios provides some vague links between the pornography and the imperial sections, he does not quite account for the transition between them. To give an example of this discontinuity, he never accuses Theodora of infidelity after her marriage to Justinian, except for one rumored episode in which nothing seems to have happened (16.11). Had she undergone a conversion of some kind in the meantime? This does not necessarily mean that she became a good person, but it points to a missing element in the overall portrait. Here was something interesting that, for whatever reason, Prokopios did not wish to discuss. Nor does he help us understand Justinian's unconventional decision to publicly court, marry, and elevate a woman with her past, and even acknowledge her in his legislation as a partner in his deliberations.[76] Prokopios attributes it to erotic infatuation (9.30–32), which actually

76. C. F. Pazdernik, "'Our Most Pious Consort Given Us by God': Dissident Reactions to the Partnership of Justinian and Theodora, A.D. 525–548," *Classical Antiquity* 13 (1994): 256–81.

makes Justinian seem a more interesting person to us, but does not help us to understand how policy was formulated.

The pornography, on the other hand, is a superb invective narrative that draws on a long tradition of sexual slander. Much of this narrative undoubtedly consists of rhetorical invention, which does not mean that Prokopios necessarily meant to deceive: elaboration highlighted essential truths and made them clearer and more persuasive. Besides, the modern study of gendered narratives has largely outgrown the words *patriarchy* and *misogyny* and has turned to literary criticism. How did Prokopios rework traditional motifs and adopt them to his specific purposes? It turns out that the pornography is a smorgasbord of classical allusions. Aristophanes and even Juvenal have been implicated.[77] I will discuss here the literary pedigree of only one brief passage, the most notorious in the entire text, 9.18: "Even though she put three of her orifices to work she would impatiently reproach Nature for not making the holes in her nipples bigger than they were so that she could devise additional sexual positions involving them as well." This is, of course, not something that Prokopios could really have *known*. He made it up to illustrate Theodora's depravity, and the passage has accordingly gained much attention in modern times. It resonated with previous sexual invective, placing Theodora in a line of ancient whores precisely in order to make her seem worse than them. In his classic rhetorical textbook *On Types of Style*, which Prokopios probably knew, the theorist Hermogenes (late second century AD) reported that one version of the Demosthenic speech *Against Neaira* contained the statement that "she plied her trade through three orifices." Hermogenes reports that some critics rejected this passage as too vulgar to be authentic.[78] Prokopios seems to have one-upped the charge (whether he knew it from the speech itself or from the quotation in Hermogenes' textbook). But its prehistory is even longer. The twelfth-century classicist Ioannes Tzetzes claimed, in fact, that the speech *Against Neaira* was plagiarizing and shamefully amplifying an accusation made by Lysias against the whore Antiope,

77. See F. Bornmann, "Su alcuni passi di Procopio," *Studi Italiani di filologia classica* 50 (1978): 27–37; B. Baldwin, "Sexual Rhetoric in Procopius," *Mnemosyne* 40 (1987): 150–52.

78. Hermogenes, *On Types of Style* 2.3 (325); tr. C. W. Wooten (Chapel Hill: University of North Carolina Press, 1987), 73. The speech was probably wrongly attributed to Demosthenes.

namely that she used *both* of her holes in intercourse.[79] The rhetoric, as often happens, had to keep getting stronger and stronger to have an effect.

The Contemporary Context of *The Secret History*

Many studies of the reign of Justinian give the impression that Roman society was now solidly Christian and that there were no alternatives to the emperor's imperial and theocratic ideology. This mirage has been constructed partly by taking Justinian as ideologically representative of the society that he ruled and, more recently, by assuming that the fifth-rate chronicler Ioannes Malalas spoke for the majority of his contemporaries (when in fact he was simply echoing Justinian himself). If we look more closely at intellectual life in the sixth-century empire, we find a diversity of religious and political views that were chaffing under the authority of a ruler whom most writers repudiated. Justinian was not a popular emperor. *The Secret History* was but one expression of widespread discontent. At the cost, then, of simplifying the nuances of some of these texts, this final section will sample the diversity of opinion that must be considered when situating *The Secret History* in its contemporary intellectual background.

It was around AD 500, under Anastasios, that the last openly pagan and anti-Christian history was written. The civil functionary Zosimos covered the history of the empire from Augustus to the early fifth century in order to argue that the adoption of Christianity and the abandonment of pagan cults had led to decline and fall. In his preface, moreover, he also took aim at the imperial regime itself, claiming that the Roman Republic had been more vigorous and less corrupt.[80] In the early years of the reign of Justinian, Hesychios of Miletos wrote a chronicle of world history from the Assyrians to 517 with an emphasis on Roman history, which he presented from a pagan point of view. Hesychios seems to have omitted Christianity altogether.[81] Justinian's reign also witnessed (and partly caused) the final phase of pagan Neoplatonism. Damaskios led his six colleagues into Persia when the emperor moved against the Athenian schools, and possibly authored the clause of protection that Chosroes

79. Ioannes Tzetzes, *Histories or Chiliades* 6.42–48; P. A. Leone, ed., *Ioannis Tzetzae Historiae* (Naples: Libreria Scientifica Editrice, 1968), 209.

80. F. Paschoud, "La digression antimonarchique de préambule de l'*Histoire Nouvelle*," *Cinq études sur Zosime* (Paris: Les Belles Lettres, 1975), 1–23.

forced Justinian to sign in 532.[82] His student Simplikios wrote a number of commentaries after that, including one on Epiktetos which denounced tyranny in terms that are strikingly reminiscent of the language of *The Secret History*.[83] Olympiodoros in Alexandria subtly criticized Christian doctrines in his lectures. For all we know, Prokopios, who exhibits signs of philosophical learning in the *Wars*, may have studied with men like these.

At some point in the 550s, Ioannes Lydos, a functionary in the office of the prefecture and a professor of Latin in Constantinople, published his antiquarian work *On the Magistracies of the Roman State*. This exalted the Roman Republic as a period of freedom and the consulship as its guarantee (he drew attention to the fact that Justinian had abolished the consulship). Like Zosimos, he viewed the empire as an oppressive regime that had deteriorated over the centuries into a despotism (he too, like Prokopios, drew attention to the fact that Justinian had himself addressed as "despot"). This work contains both platitudinous praise of Justinian (it was, after all not a secret work) as well as biting, covert criticism of the same emperor that aligns the work with *The Secret History* on many points (praise of Anastasios and hatred for Ioannes the Kappadokian being only two of them). It is possible that Lydos was among the original readers of *The Secret History*. His religion was an antiquarian and occult form of Neoplatonism, syncretistic except that Christianity seems to have played a small role in it. Lydos was a student of one of the early-sixth-century pagan Neoplatonists.[84] It was likewise during the reign of Justinian that an anonymous *Dialogue on Political Science* was written, which is only partially preserved. It draws on Greek and Latin theorists to advocate a form of limited constitutional

81. A. Kaldellis, "The Works and Days of Hesychios the Illoustrios of Miletos," *Greek, Roman, and Byzantine Studies* 45 (2005): 381–403.

82. The story is told in Agathias, *Histories* 2.30–31.

83. See related text 6: "A Contemporary Philosopher's View of Justinian's Tyranny."

84. A. Kaldellis, "Republican Theory and Political Dissidence in Ioannes Lydos," *Byzantine and Modern Greek Studies* 29 (2005): 1–16; "Identifying Dissident Circles" (see note 27); "The Religion of Ioannes Lydos," *Phoenix* 57 (2003): 300–16. Some scholars believe that Lydos was a Christian, but there is no evidence for that. That he had read *The Secret History* was also suspected by M. Hendy, *Studies in the Byzantine Monetary Economy c. 300–1450* (Cambridge: Cambridge University Press, 1985), 295. W. Treadgold calls the evidence "slight": *The Early Byzantine Historians* (New York: Palgrave, 2007), 264 n. 117, but it is in fact quite strong.

monarchy, which it accommodates to a Christian world (for example, priests are more prominent in it than they are in the dialogue's classical sources). This work has often been read as an aristocratic reaction to Justinian.[85]

Monophysites, of course, hated Justinian. Their hagiographies have choice words for "the impious Justinian."[86] The "pit of the abyss," some believed, "was opened again in the days of the emperor Justinian. Again that soul-destroying madness, again the torrents of lawlessness flowed in their ravines to shake the house of the faithful."[87] We need not rehearse here all the sources to that effect. It is, however, important to note that whereas texts produced by Prokopios' class of intellectuals expressed idiosyncratic political and philosophical ideologies that were accessible to a few, in the case of religious polemic we are dealing with a mass opposition to (and hatred of) the emperor grounded in his persecution of beliefs that were different than his own. There was nothing in the actual content of Monophysite thought that Prokopios found useful, being a man who found theological speculation pointless, but it was perhaps crucial for his political purposes that by 550 approximately a third of the empire's Christian population hated Justinian on religious grounds (to say nothing of the abundance of other grounds for hating him that they may have had).

The Monophysites were not alone. In his efforts to enforce a compromise, Justinian alienated many Chalcedonians as well, certainly those in the West. When he threatened Pope Agapetus, he received this reply: "Sinner that I am, I have long wanted to come to the most Christian emperor Justinian—but now I have encountered Diocletian; yet I am not in the least afraid of your threats."[88]

85. See A. Cameron, *Procopius and the Sixth Century* (London: Duckworth, 1985), 248–50; also A. S. Fotiou, "Dicaearchus and the Mixed Constitution in Sixth-Century Byzantium: New Evidence from a Treatise on 'Political Science,'" *Byzantion* 51 (1981): 533–47; and D. O'Meara, "The Justinianic Dialogue *On Political Science* and Its Neoplatonic Sources," in K. Ierodiakonou, ed., *Byzantine Philosophy and Its Ancient Sources* (Oxford: Clarendon Press, 2002), 49–62.

86. E.g., L. S. B. MacCoull, "'When Justinian Was Upsetting the World': A Note on Soldiers and Religious Coercion in Sixth-Century Egypt," in T. S. Miller and J. Nesbitt, eds., *Peace and War in Byzantium: Essays in Honor of George T. Dennis, S.J.* (Washington, DC: Catholic University of America Press, 1995), 106–13.

87. Quotation and discussion in J. Moorhead, *Justinian* (Harlow: Longman, 1994), 129.

88. *The Book of Pontiffs* 59 (see note 71), 53.

(Diocletian was the early Church's fiercest persecutor). Similar attitudes can be found among the emperor's eastern subjects. Most striking is the hostility of this period's ecclesiastical historian Euagrios, a Chalcedonian who claimed that Justinian went to hell. He also criticized the emperor for avarice, cowardice, and cruelty. Euagrios knew the *Wars*, which he quotes extensively. Some have suspected that he knew *The Secret History* as well, but the parallels are not exact.[89] It is more likely that his hatred was part of the mainstream of popular opinion after the reign. Theodora's Monophysite sympathies were also a liability when it came to dealing with Chalcedonians. Granted an audience before Justinian, Saint Sabbas refused to pray, as he was asked to do, that God grant Theodora a child. "Believe me, fathers," he told his companions afterward, "fruit will never come forth from her womb, lest it suck in the doctrines of Severos [a leading Monophysite theologian] and cause worse upheaval to the Church than Anastasios [an emperor who supported the Monophysites]."[90] There is more such direct evidence of hostility to the emperor's policies. It has recently been suggested that even the liturgical poet Romanos Melodos covertly compared Justinian to the Antichrist (formerly it was believed that he was one of the emperor's propagandists).[91] In short, the *Ecclesiastical History* that Prokopios was planning to write would have found a large and receptive audience.

No other reign provoked the same degree of bloody resistance among the subjects of the Roman Empire. The Montanists in Asia Minor preferred to commit mass suicide in their churches than submit to Justinian's demands. Samaritans in Palestine twice resorted to separatist warfare that devastated the province. The Arians in North Africa rebelled and joined a mutiny. Leading senators, including the admired prefect Phokas, committed suicide in the antipagan purges. Roman soldiers defected to the enemy in record

89. See especially Euagrios, *Ecclesiastical History* 4.30, 4.32, 4.41, 5.1; for discussion, see M. Whitby, *The Ecclesiastical History of Evagrius Scholasticus* (Liverpool: Liverpool University Press, 2000), esp. 233, n. 86.

90. Kyrillos of Skythopolis, *Life of Sabbas* 71; tr. R. M. Price, *Lives of the Monks of Palestine by Cyril of Scythopolis* (Kalamazoo, MI: Cistercian Publications, 1991), 183.

91. A. Varghese, "Kaiserkritik in Two Kontakia of Romanos," in J. Burke et al., eds., *Byzantine Narrative: Papers in Honour of Roger Scott* (Melbourne: Australian Association for Byzantine Studies, 2006), 392–403; see also Moorhead, *Justinian*, 59, n. 59; and M. Papoutsakis, "The Making of a Syriac Fable: From Ephrem to Romanos," *Le Muséon* 120 (2007), 29–75, here 65–74.

numbers and on all fronts. The people of Constantinople staged the most destructive riot in Roman history, which was put down by force and resulted in the slaughter of some thirty thousand people. Justinian's officials were hated both by the people, who demanded their resignation, and by the midlevel functionaries who had to work under them. Conquered peoples in Italy, Lazike, and Armenia seethed with discontent and aided or joined the empire's enemies. The list goes on. *The Secret History* documents the failures of Justinian's reign and its many victims. However, it is always worth considering that without this text modern historians might have idolized this ruler, dazzled as they often are by buildings, authoritarian rule and legal tomes, and especially by wars of conquest. To judge from Justinian's ambiguous reputation in modern times, Prokopios' treatise, more than any of the sources mentioned above, succeeded in undermining the force of imperial propaganda. It is probably to *The Secret History* that we owe the absence of a "Justinian the Great" in our histories.

A Note on the Translation and the Spelling of Names

The following translation of *The Secret History* is based on the text published by J. Haury in 1906 and revised by G. Wirth in 1963.[92] It aims to adhere closely to the dry style of Prokopios' prose and so differs from the two most widely used English translations by H. B. Dewing in the Loeb Classical Library (1935) and by G. A. Williamson in the Penguin Classics (1966; revised by P. Sarris in 2007). In terms of style, the Loeb translation is the least faithful to the text. Its verbosity, syntactical complexity, and archaic obscurity are invented by the translator, presumably on the assumption that all Attic Greek must read like this. On the other hand, the Penguin translation often tends to infer the rhetorical flavor of Prokopios' accusations and convey it through English idioms, which makes it slightly more colorful, if too idiomatic at times. This is legitimate as a practice of translation, but I have kept the prose blunt and precise, as it is in the original. There are also places where my translation differs in substance from the others, but I have not drawn attention to this in the notes.

Byzantium is one of the few remaining cultures that some scholars in the English-speaking world continue to distort by the Latinization and Anglicization of its personal names. Thankfully, this redundant form of affectation is gradually ending. We would, as a rule, not call an Italian, French, Russian, or Arab "John," even if that is what his name "means." There is no reason to continue to do so for the Byzantines. With a few exceptions, the names in *The Secret History* are spelled here according to their Greek form. This is not an attempt to capture the *sound* of these names, as is done in the transcription of modern Greek names for example, but only their spelling. The exceptions include well-known figures such as John the Apostle and Justinian, who might not even be recognized if their names were spelled correctly, and individuals from the Latin West. Place-names are given in their English form if they are still in use (e.g., Sicily, Beirut), otherwise they are spelled as in the text (e.g.,

92. J. Haury, ed., *Procopii Caesariensis opera omnia*, vol. 3, *Historia qvae dicitvr arcana*, rev. G. Wirth (Leipzig: Teubner, 1963).

Kappadokia, Kilikia). Byzantion is Prokopios' way of referring to the city of Constantinople; Byzantium is how I refer to the entire Roman Empire of his time (and afterward). Latin offices and terms have generally been left in Latin and italicized (e.g., *referendarius*), which effectively conveys the sense of foreignness that Prokopios intended when using and glossing them. Greek terms are simply transliterated and italicized (e.g., *logothetai*). It is, however, impossible to make any spelling system entirely consistent.

Acknowledgments

The idea for this volume was Rick Todhunter's. He also guided it to completion gently and professionally. Rick has additional ideas about what I can do with my time, namely to translate the *Wars*. Having worked with him so far, I am far more inclined to take that on than before I met him, but other texts are ahead in line, just now. Michael Kulikowski, Chuck Pazdernik, and a third anonymous reader for the Hackett Publishing Company gave me detailed and valuable suggestions for the improvement of the book's structure, presentation, and accuracy. I am grateful for all their work and advice, which has led to many improvements. Ian Mladjov did a fantastic job with the maps (as always), patiently putting up with my inconsistencies. Kasia Jazdzewska helped me understand passages and aspects of the text better than I would have on my own.

Timeline

518	Justin becomes emperor
520–524 (?)	Justinian marries Theodora
527	Justinian proclaimed coemperor Death of Justin I; Justinian becomes sole emperor
528–529	Persecution of pagans, Manicheans, heretics, homosexuals
528–534	Work of law commission on *Corpus iuris civilis*
529	Philosophical schools closed in Athens Samaritan revolt in Palestine
530	Belisarios defeats Persians at Daras
531	Persians defeat Belisarios at Kallinikos Chosroes becomes king of Persia
532	Nika riots Eternal Peace signed with Persia
532–537	Rebuilding of Hagia Sophia
533–534	Reconquest of North Africa Belisarios returns to Constantinople in triumph
534	Death of the boy-king Athalaric in Italy
535	Theodahad murders Amalasountha in Italy, seizes throne Belisarios reconquers Sicily
536	Belisarios invades Italy Vitigis elected king of the Goths in Italy
537–538	Siege of Rome
537	Pope Silverius deposed, replaced with Vigilius
540	Vitigis surrenders Ravenna to Belisarios Belisarios returns to Constantinople in triumph Persians invade Syria, capture Antioch
541	Plague in Egypt Chosroes captures Lazike Belisarios campaigns in Mesopotamia Downfall of Ioannes the Kappadokian Totila king of the Goths in Italy

542	Plague in Constantinople and surrounding regions
543	Plague continues to ravage Constantinople
544	Belisarios sent to Italy
	Solomon killed in North Africa
	Chosroes invades Roman provinces
545	Five-year truce agreed with Persia (excluding Lazike)
546	Revolt and murder of Gontharis in Carthage
	Totila recaptures Rome
547	Belisarios recaptures Rome
548	Death of Theodora
	Antonina returns to Constantinople from Italy
549	Belisarios recalled from Italy
	Plot by Artabanes and Arsakes against Justinian
550	Totila recaptures Rome
550/551	Prokopios finishes *The Secret History*
552	Battle of Busta Gallorum; death of Gothic king Totila
552/553	Silkworms brought to the Roman Empire
565	Death of Justinian; Justin II becomes emperor

Glossary of Offices and Administrative Terms

This glossary explains offices and technical Roman terms that appear more than twice in the text or notes.

comes: a high imperial official, usually placed in charge of military units smaller than a field army or of various offices of the administration (English *count*).

kentenarion: one hundred Roman pounds of gold (from Latin *centum*); each pound corresponded to seventy-two gold coins.

magister officiorum (Greek *magistros*): this official directed aspects of the civil bureaucracy, diplomacy, court ceremony, and commanded the palace guard.

patrician (Latin *patricius;* Greek *patrikios*): this was the highest honorary court dignity, and it did not carry any administrative duties.

praetorian prefect (Latin *praefectus praetorio;* Greek *eparchos tôn praitôriôn*): this office controlled many aspects of the civil administration, especially taxation and the budget. The empire was divided into vast regional prefectures, but with the loss of the West in the fifth century, that of the East (*Oriens*) became by far the most powerful. That prefect was based in Constantinople and was effectively second in command of the empire. Justinian had prefects also for Illyricum (the Balkans) as well as for Italy and North Africa (after their reconquest).

quaestor (full Latin title: *quaestor sacri palatii;* Greek *kouaistor*): this was the emperor's legal advisor and public spokesman, a minister of justice of sorts (see *Secret History* 6.13, 9.41, 14.3, 20.15).

referendarius (Greek *repherendarios*): these officials ushered petitioners into the imperial presence and spoke for the emperor after he had made a decision in their case; see *Wars* 2.23.6 (translated in related text 8) and *Novella* 10 of 535 (there were fourteen *referendarii;* Justinian wanted only eight).

urban prefect (Latin *praefectus urbis;* Greek *eparchos tês poleôs*): The urban prefect of Constantinople (there was another for Rome) was the president of the Senate and entrusted with keeping order, provisioning, and administrating the imperial capital.

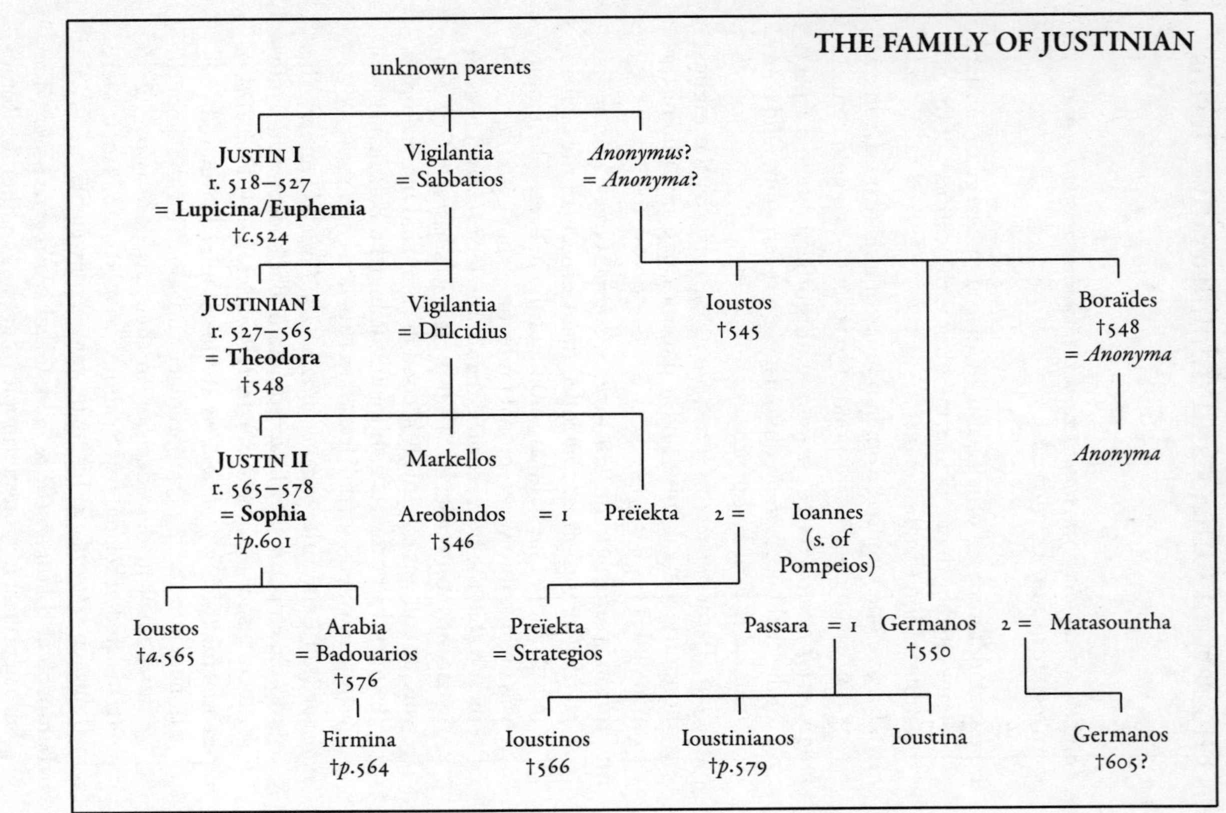
THE FAMILY OF JUSTINIAN
unknown parents
JUSTIN I
r. 518–527
= Lupicina/Euphemia
†c.524
Vigilantia
= Sabbatios
Anonymus?
= Anonyma?
JUSTINIAN I
r. 527–565
= Theodora
†548
Vigilantia
= Dulcidius
Ioustos
†545
Boraïdes
†548
= Anonyma
Anonyma
JUSTIN II
r. 565–578
= Sophia
†p.601
Markellos
Areobindos
†546
= 1
Preïekta
2 =
Ioannes
(s. of
Pompeios)
Ioustos
†a.565
Arabia
= Badouarios
†576
Firmina
†p.564
Preïekta
= Strategios
Passara
= 1
Germanos
†550
2 =
Matasountha
Ioustinos
†566
Ioustinianos
†p.579
Ioustina
Germanos
†605?

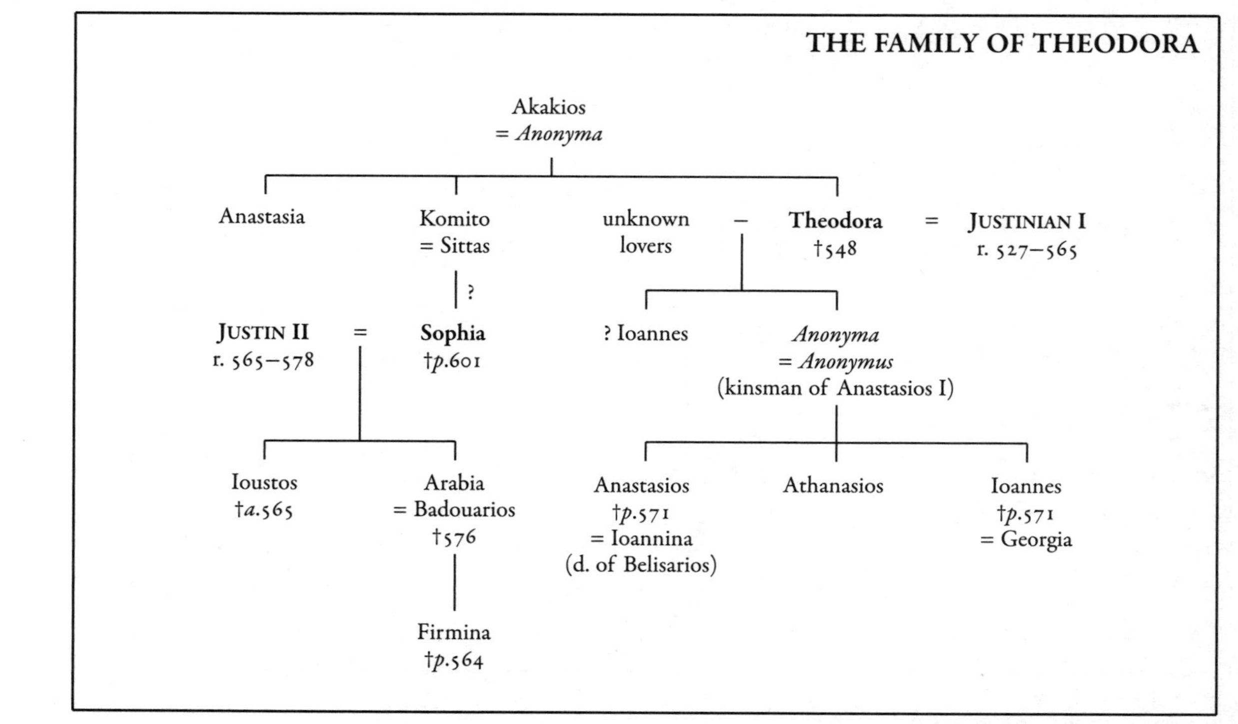
THE FAMILY OF THEODORA
Akakios
= Anonyma
Anastasia
Komito
= Sittas
unknown
lovers
–
Theodora
†548
=
JUSTINIAN I
r. 527–565
?
JUSTIN II
r. 565–578
=
Sophia
†p.601
? Ioannes
Anonyma
= Anonymus
(kinsman of Anastasios I)
Ioustos
†a.565
Arabia
= Badouarios
†576
Anastasios
†p.571
= Ioannina
(d. of Belisarios)
Athanasios
Ioannes
†p.571
= Georgia
Firmina
†p.564

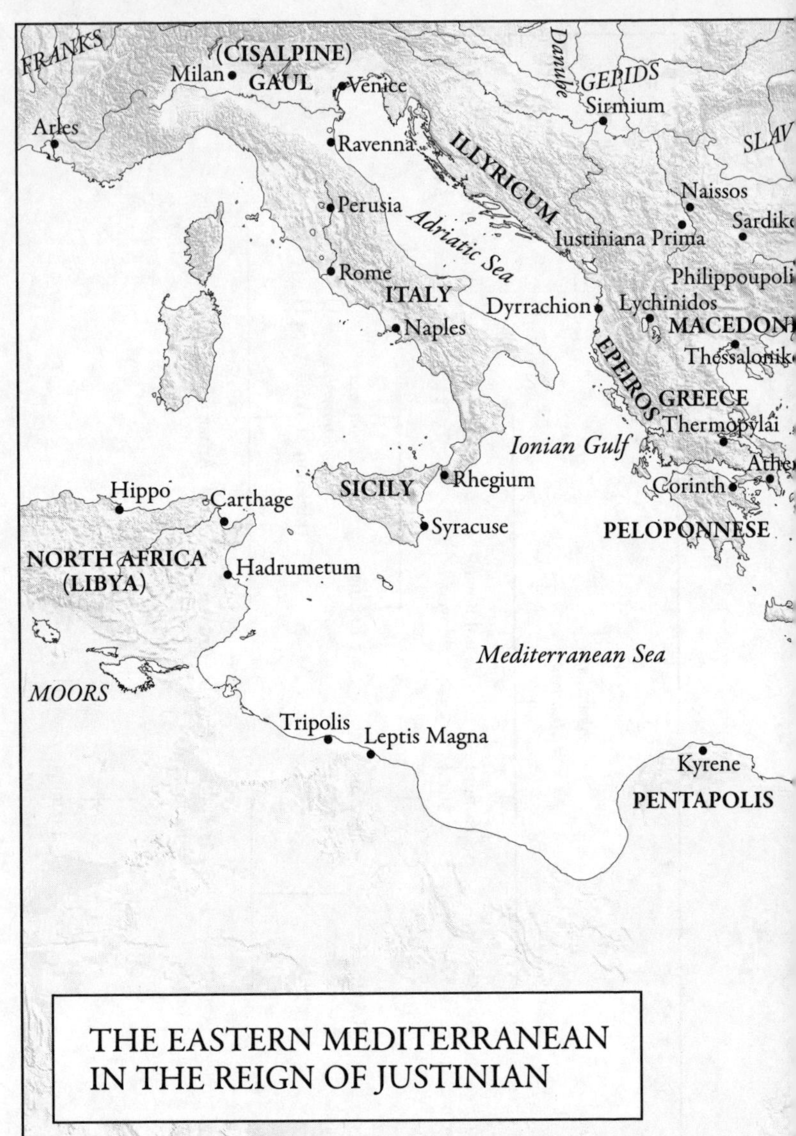
FRANKS
(CISALPINE)
GAUL
Milan
Venice
Danube
GEPIDS
Sirmium
Arles
Ravenna
ILLYRICUM
SLAV
Naissos
Perusia
Adriatic Sea
Iustiniana Prima
Rome
ITALY
Dyrrachion
Lychinidos
MACEDON
Naples
Thessalonik
EPEIROS
GREECE
Thermopylai
Ionian Gulf
Rhegium
Corinth
Hippo
Carthage
SICILY
Syracuse
PELOPONNESE
NORTH AFRICA
(LIBYA)
Hadrumetum
Mediterranean Sea
MOORS
Tripolis
Leptis Magna
Kyrene
PENTAPOLIS
THE EASTERN MEDITERRANEAN
IN THE REIGN OF JUSTINIAN

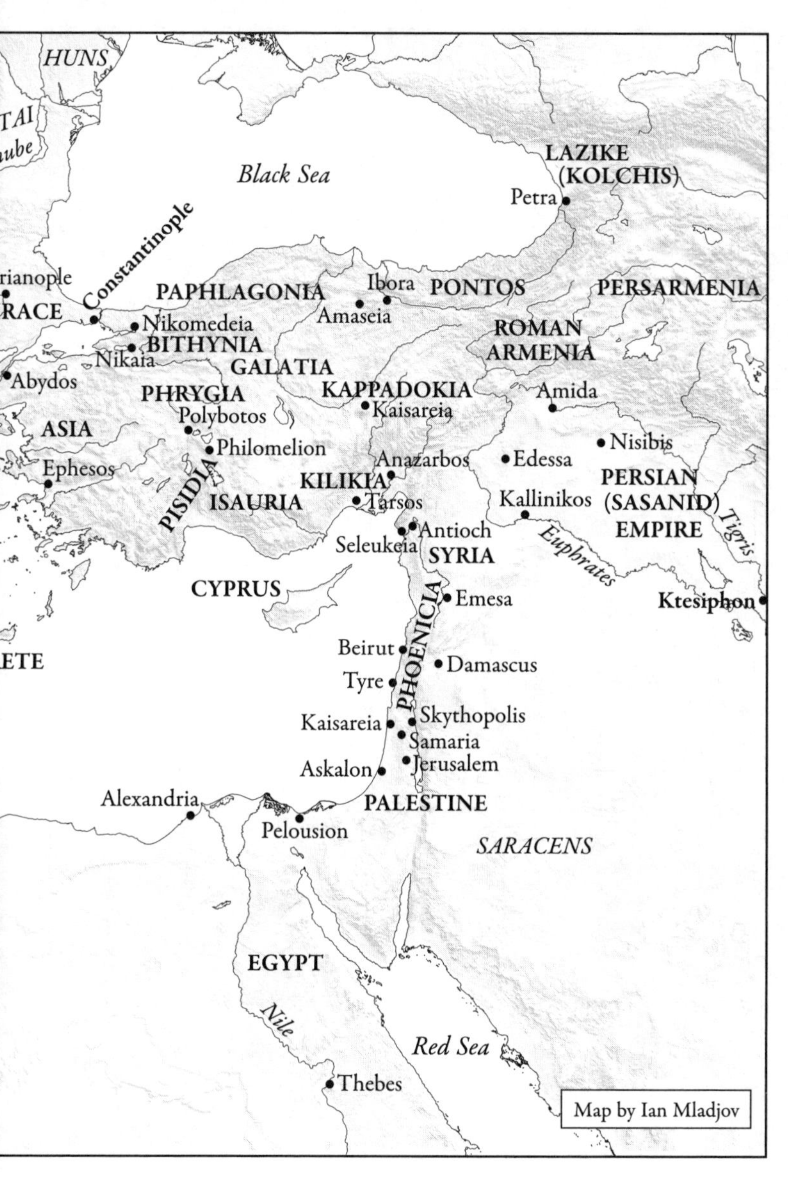
HUNS
Black Sea
LAZIKE
(KOLCHIS)
Petra
Constantinople
PAPHLAGONIA
Ibora
PONTOS
PERSARMENIA
Amaseia
Nikomedeia
BITHYNIA
Nikaia
ROMAN
ARMENIA
GALATIA
Abydos
PHRYGIA
KAPPADOKIA
Amida
Polybotos
Kaisareia
ASIA
Philomelion
Nisibis
Ephesos
Anazarbos
Edessa
KILIKIA
PERSIAN
(SASANID)
EMPIRE
PISIDIA
ISAURIA
Tarsos
Kallinikos
Antioch
Seleukeia
SYRIA
Euphrates
Tigris
CYPRUS
PHOENICIA
Emesa
Ktesiphon
Beirut
Damascus
Tyre
Kaisareia
Skythopolis
Samaria
Askalon
Jerusalem
Alexandria
PALESTINE
Pelousion
SARACENS
EGYPT
Nile
Red Sea
Thebes
Map by Ian Mladjov

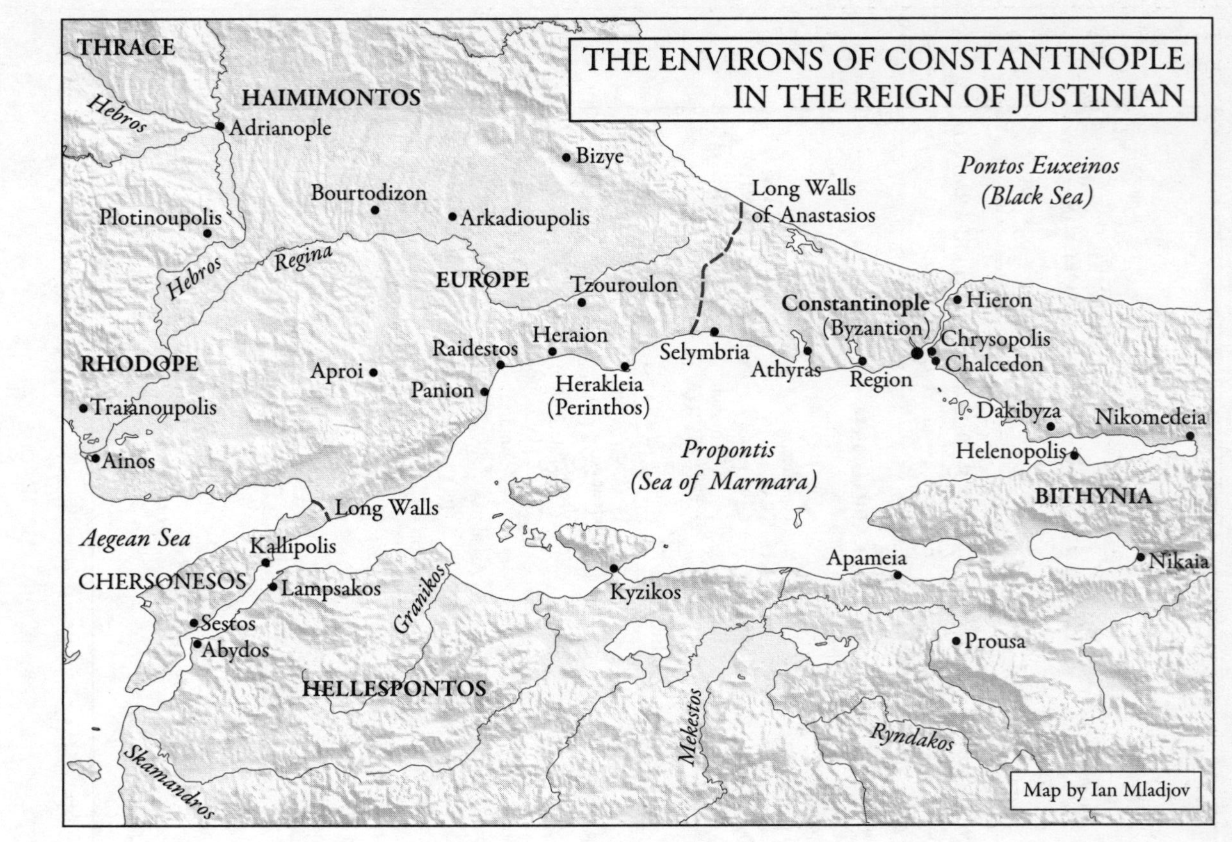
THE ENVIRONS OF CONSTANTINOPLE
IN THE REIGN OF JUSTINIAN
THRACE
HAIMIMONTOS
Hebros
Adrianople
Bizye
Pontos Euxeinos
(Black Sea)
Long Walls
of Anastasios
Bourtodizon
Plotinoupolis
Arkadioupolis
Hebros
Regina
EUROPE
Tzouroulon
Constantinople
(Byzantion)
Hieron
Chrysopolis
Chalcedon
Heraion
Raidestos
Selymbria
Athyras
Region
RHODOPE
Aproi
Panion
Herakleia
(Perinthos)
Trajanoupolis
Dakibyza
Nikomedeia
Ainos
Propontis
(Sea of Marmara)
Helenopolis
BITHYNIA
Long Walls
Aegean Sea
Kallipolis
Apameia
Nikaia
CHERSONESOS
Lampsakos
Kyzikos
Granikos
Sestos
Abydos
Prousa
HELLESPONTOS
Mekestos
Ryndakos
Skamandros
Map by Ian Mladjov

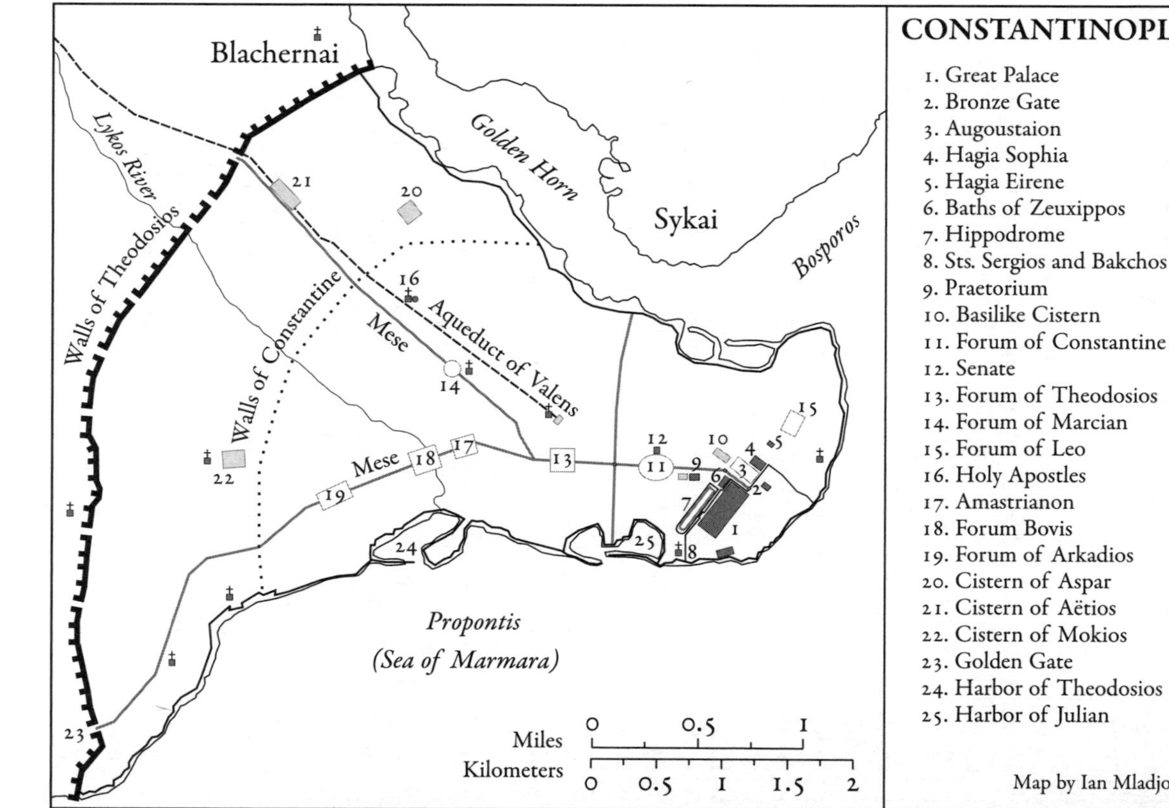
CONSTANTINOPLE
1. Great Palace
2. Bronze Gate
3. Augoustaion
4. Hagia Sophia
5. Hagia Eirene
6. Baths of Zeuxippos
7. Hippodrome
8. Sts. Sergios and Bakchos
9. Praetorium
10. Basilike Cistern
11. Forum of Constantine
12. Senate
13. Forum of Theodosios
14. Forum of Marcian
15. Forum of Leo
16. Holy Apostles
17. Amastrianon
18. Forum Bovis
19. Forum of Arkadios
20. Cistern of Aspar
21. Cistern of Aëtios
22. Cistern of Mokios
23. Golden Gate
24. Harbor of Theodosios
25. Harbor of Julian
Map by Ian Mladjov
Blachernai
Golden Horn
Sykai
Bosporos
Lykos River
Walls of Theodosios
Walls of Constantine
Aqueduct of Valens
Mese
Mese
Propontis
(Sea of Marmara)
Miles
Kilometers
0
0.5
1
0
0.5
1
1.5
2

A Guide to the Main Sources

Compared to any other period of the Roman Empire's existence, the sixth century was extraordinarily prolific in terms of literary and scholarly activity. That is especially true when we compare it to the relative dearth of activity presented by the fifth century (a still unexplained phenomenon for the eastern empire, which prospered materially at this time and was largely free of war) and to the almost total (and perfectly understandable) collapse of literary activity that followed the Arab conquests of the early seventh century. The sixth century witnessed literary creativity *and* a consolidation of knowledge into encyclopedic compilations, both movements affecting many literary genres and scientific disciplines.

Setting aside the philosophical, theological, and medical productions of the period, the present guide will concentrate on works that are most relevant to *The Secret History* (and that are available in English translation). Perhaps the most important contemporary sources for studying *The Secret History* are the edicts of Justinian, which are found in two places. The *Codex Iustinianus*, a component of the codification of Roman law that Justinian commissioned (which, in modern times, is called the *Corpus iuris civilis*), contains a selection of abbreviated imperial edicts from the second century AD to 534, so many of its headings end with edicts of Justin and Justinian. The edicts that Justinian issued after 534, his *Novellae*, form a separate collection. It is from the *Novellae* that we learn about many officeholders in Justinian's administration (as the edicts are either addressed or copied to them). S. P. Scott translated the *Codex* and the *Novellae* in his seventeen-volume *The Civil Law* (Cincinnati: Central Trust Co., 1932), but he omitted certain edicts, sections of edicts that he found uninteresting, and the subscriptions (with the dates). His translations have to be checked against the original, but they are usually reliable. They have been posted in the *Roman Law Library* maintained online by A. Koptev and Y. Lassard. The best study of the legal activity of this period is T. Honoré's *Tribonian* (Ithaca, NY: Cornell University Press, 1978). Another source of Justinian's ideology are the texts that preface the ***Digest***, a huge anthology of legal interpretations and clarifications edited by A. Watson (*The Digest of Justinian* [Philadelphia: University of Pennsylvania Press, 1985]).

The works of only two historians survive who wrote about the reign of Justinian in what has been called a classicizing format, that is, focusing on war, diplomacy, and ethnography in an elevated form of classical Greek. **Prokopios** is one; a complete translation of his works by H. B. Dewing can be found in the Loeb Classical Library. There are currently two strongly contrasting interpretations of this author: A. Cameron's *Procopius and the Sixth Century* (London: Duckworth, 1985) and A. Kaldellis' *Procopius of Caesarea: Tyranny, History, and Philosophy at the End of Antiquity* (Philadelphia: University of Pennsylvania Press, 2004). **Agathias** is the other, who wrote around 580 and continued the narrative of Prokopios for the years 552–559. He focused on the final stages of the war in Italy and the continued hostilities with the Persians. A good translation was made by J. D. Frendo in *Agathias: The Histories* (Berlin and New York: W. de Gruyter, 1976). For contrasting readings of Agathias, see A. Cameron's *Agathias* (Oxford: Clarendon Press, 1970) and A. Kaldellis' "The Historical and Religious Views of Agathias: A Reinterpretation," *Byzantion: Revue internationale des études Byzantines* 69 (1999): 206–52.

An alternative historiographical tradition was that of the Christian world chronicle. These chronicles began with the Creation and reached to historical times, recording the events of each year of Roman imperial history in brief entries. **Marcellinus** (a *comes* at Justinian's court) produced a Latin chronicle covering the years 379–534, favorably toward Justinian for the final years. A translation (with commentary) was made by B. Croke, *The Chronicle of Marcellinus* (Sydney: Australian Association of Byzantine Studies, 1995). An excellent study is B. Croke's *Count Marcellinus and His Chronicle* (Oxford: Oxford University Press, 2001). A Greek chronicle from Adam to the end of the reign of Justinian was produced by **Ioannes Malalas**, though only an abbreviated version survives: E. Jeffreys (and many others), *The Chronicle of John Malalas* (Melbourne: Australian Association of Byzantine Studies, 1986). Malalas has been touted recently as an alternative and perhaps more authentic picture of the sixth century than that found in Prokopios, but he must be used with extreme caution. It has recently been shown that he plagiarized and made up material for the period before the fifth century, inventing dozens of sources for which to attribute his wild stories; see W. Treadgold, *The Early Byzantine Historians* (New York: Palgrave, 2007), 246–56. Also, for the events of the reign of Justinian, he tended to copy the emperor's own propaganda uncritically. This makes him a useful source for Justinian's proclamations but hardly an authentic image of any historical period. Useful information on the reign of Justinian can also be found in the early-seventh-century ***Paschal Chronicle*** in M. and M. Whitby, *Chronicon Paschale 284–628 AD* (Liverpool: Liverpool University Press, 1989). Finally, the early ninth-century chronicler **Theophanes** relied on Prokopios and Malalas in his coverage of the sixth century but also made use of other, now lost, sources. There is a superb translation and commentary by C. Mango and R. Scott, *The Chronicle of Theophanes Confessor: Byzantine and Near Eastern History, AD 284–813* (Oxford: Clarendon Press, 1997).

Two curious, albeit largely neglected, historiographical works written in Constantinople at the very same time that Prokopios finished *The Secret History* were **Ioannes Lydos'** *On the Magistracies of the Roman State* and Iordanes' *Getica*. Lydos was a functionary in the office of the praetorian prefecture and a professor of Latin in the University of Constantinople, though he wrote in Greek. *On the Magistracies* is an antiquarian work that focuses on offices, titles, and insignia but also contains a pro-Republican view of history and, if read carefully, supports the accusations of *The Secret History;* the text and a translation can be found in A. C. Bandy, *Ioannes Lydus: On Powers or The Magistracies of the Roman State* (Philadelphia: American Philosophical Society, 1983); for Lydos and *The Secret History*, see A. Kaldellis, "Identifying Dissident Circles in Sixth-Century Byzantium: The Friendship of Prokopios and Ioannes Lydos," *Florilegium* 21 (2004): 1–17. **Iordanes**' *Getica* is a fabulous history (in Latin) of the Gothic nation to 551, which is amalgamated with the histories of other ancient peoples such as the Skythians and Amazons. Iordanes claimed Gothic ancestry and so is the only barbarian historian of late antiquity, though he was writing within the classical tradition. He praises Justinian at the very end, but his view of history is generally pro-Gothic (at a moment when Justinian was still warring against the Goths in Italy). See C. C. Mierow, *The Gothic History of Iordanes* (Princeton, NJ: Princeton University Press, 1915); the most recent discussion is by B. Croke, "Jordanes and the Immediate Past," *Historia* 54 (2005): 473–94.

Though Greek was by far the dominant language in the eastern Roman Empire of the sixth century, the last secular Latin epic poems of antiquity were written by a poet from North Africa, **Corippus**, who moved to Constantinople. One of his two poems concerned the North African campaigns of the general Ioannes Troglita (in the late 540s); see G. W. Shea's *The* Iohannis *or* De bellis Libycis *of Flavius Cresconius Corippus* (Lewiston, NY: Edwin Mellen Press, 1998). (The other poem was about the accession of Justin II in 565.) A number of **epigrams** (erotic and otherwise) that were written during Justinian's reign were collected by Agathias, and his collection was later incorporated in what is called the *Greek Anthology*, of which there is a complete translation in the Loeb Classical Library series. For the evolution of this collection, see A. Cameron, *The Greek Anthology: From Meleager to Planudes* (Oxford: Clarendon Press, 1993). The greatest liturgical poet in the Byzantine tradition was **Romanos Melodos**, whose career basically overlapped with the reign of Justinian, and some historians have detected in his works allusions to that emperor. They are translated by M. Carpenter, *Kontakia of Romanos: Byzantine Melodist* (Columbia: University of Missouri Press, 1970–1972).

The ecclesiastical historiography of the period may be mentioned briefly as *The Secret History* does not touch much on affairs of the Church. At the end of the century **Euagrios**, a lawyer of the Church of Antioch, wrote a history of the years 428–592, in fact the main history of the Church in Greek for this period; see M. Whitby, *The Ecclesiastical History of Evagrius Scholasticus* (Liverpool: Liverpool University Press, 2000). Despite being orthodox, Euagrios was hostile to Justinian, so much so that some scholars have detected the influence of *The Secret History*. Another important ecclesiastical author of this period was **Yuhannan of Amida**, who after 558 was the (titular) Monophysite bishop of Ephesos (he is usually called John of Ephesos, even though his name was not John and he had little to do with the city of Ephesos). Later in life he wrote an ecclesiastical history (in Syriac) that has mostly been lost, though sections of it were used in a Syriac chronicle written toward the end of the eighth century; see W. Witakowski, *Pseudo-Dionysius of Tel-Mahre: Chronicle Part III* (Liverpool: Liverpool University Press, 1996). It features a long account of the Justinianic plague. Yuhannan also wrote a series of fifty-eight *Saints' Lives* with valuable historical information about the sixth century (including confirmation that Theodora was a prostitute), which were translated by E. W. Brooks, *John of Ephesus: Lives of the Eastern Saints*, in *Patrologia Orientalis* 17 (1923): 1–307; 18 (1924): 513–698; 19 (1926): 153–285. For a good study of the latter text, see S. Ashbrook Harvey, *Asceticism and Society in Crisis: John of Ephesus and the* Lives of the Eastern Saints (Berkeley: University of California Press, 1990).

Many of the commentaries of the **philosophers** of the early sixth century, especially Simplikios and Ioannes Philoponos of Alexandria, are translated in the series *Ancient Commentators on Aristotle* published by Cornell University Press. A fascinating anonymous (albeit fragmentary) *Dialogue on Political Science* has not yet been published in translation, but its contents are discussed by A. S. Fotiou, "Dicaearchus and the Mixed Constitution in Sixth-Century Byzantium: New Evidence from a Treatise on 'Political Science,'" *Byzantion* 51 (1981): 533–47; and D. O'Meara, "The Justinianic Dialogue *On Political Science* and Its Neoplatonic Sources," in K. Ierodiakonou, ed., *Byzantine Philosophy and Its Ancient Sources* (Oxford: Clarendon Press, 2002), 49–62. A work on geometry by **Anthemios**, the architect of Hagia Sophia, was published without translation by G. L. Huxley, *Anthemius of Tralles: A Study in Later Greek Geometry* (Cambridge, MA: Eaton Press, 1959).

A Guide to Scholarship in English

For a concise **narrative history** of the later Roman Empire followed by a magisterial analysis of its governance and society, see A. H. M. Jones, *The Later Roman Empire 284–602: A Social, Economic, and Administrative Survey* (Oxford: Blackwell, 1964; reprinted by Johns Hopkins University Press, 1986). For an insightful and sympathetic study of the tensions and contradictions within the late Roman bureaucracy, focusing on the career of Prokopios' fellow traveler Ioannes Lydos, see C. Kelly, *Ruling the Later Roman Empire* (Cambridge, MA: Harvard University Press, 2004). For the reign of Anastasios, who is mentioned often in *The Secret History*, see F. Haarer, *Anastasius I: Politics and Empire in the Late Roman World* (Cambridge: Francis Cairns, 2006). For a study of the reign of Justin I, outdated in some respects, see A. A. Vasiliev, *Justin the First: An Introduction to the Epoch of Justinian the Great* (Cambridge, MA: Harvard University Press, 1950). In *The Secret History*, Prokopios presents Justinian as the power behind the throne of his uncle Justin; this notion has been questioned by B. Croke, "Justinian under Justin: Reconfiguring a Reign," *Byzantinische Zeitschrift* 100 (2007): 13–56. The most accessible and insightful surveys in English of Justinian's reign are J. Moorhead, *Justinian* (Harlow: Longman, 1994), and J. A. S. Evans, *The Age of Justinian: The Circumstances of Imperial Power* (London and New York: Routledge, 1996).

Much of *The Secret History* focuses on the **careers** and deeds of specific individuals. Basic information about these men and women, excluding monks and churchmen, is presented in the volumes of what scholars call the *PLRE*: J. R. Martindale, ed., *The Prosopography of the Later Roman Empire*, vol. 2: *A.D. 395–527* (Cambridge: Cambridge University Press, 1980) and vol. 3: *A.D. 527–641* (1992). Prokopios' portrait of Theodora has generated much scholarship and fiction over the centuries. The best scholarly biography is J. A. Evans, *The Empress Theodora: Partner of Justinian* (Austin: University of Texas Press, 2002). A partly scholarly, partly fictional, but certainly readable biography can be found in P. Cesaretti, *Theodora: Empress of Byzantium* (New York: Vendome Press, 2004; tr. by R. M. Giammanco Frongia). T. Honoré, *Tribonian* (Ithaca, NY: Cornell University Press, 1978) is indispensible not only for the famous *quaestor* but for the legal culture of the period and the ambitions of

Justinian in general. For the historians who wrote about the reign, see W. Treadgold, *The Early Byzantine Historians* (New York: Palgrave, 2007).

Specialized studies have been written on the **events of the reign**. For the Nika riots, see G. Greatrex, "The Nika Riot: A Reappraisal," *Journal of Hellenic Studies* 117 (1997): 60–86. A. Cameron's *Circus Factions: Blues and Greens at Rome and Byzantium* (Oxford: Clarendon Press, 1976) remains a classic study of the *demoi*, proving that they were sporting clubs (or guilds) that did not directly take sides in religious or economic conflicts. For the natural disasters of the reign, see the catalog and analysis in D. C. Stathakopoulos, *Famine and Pestilence in the Late Roman and Early Byzantine Empire: A Systematic Survey of Subsistence Crises and Epidemics* (Birmingham, UK: Ashgate, 2004). The papers in L. K. Little, ed., *Plague and the End of Antiquity: The Pandemic of 541–750* (Cambridge: Cambridge University Press, 2007) present the latest findings about the so-called Justinianic plague. That plague, however, is known only from literary sources; these are surveyed in A. Kaldellis, "The Literature of Plague and the Anxieties of Piety in Sixth-Century Byzantium," in F. Mormando and T. Worcester, eds., *Piety and Plague: From Byzantium to the Baroque* (Kirksville, MO: Truman State University Press, 2007), 1–22. For the incredibly complicated theological controversies, a good survey is P. T. R. Gray's *The Defense of Chalcedon in the East (451–553)* (Leiden: Brill, 1979); for ecclesiastical politics in the East, see V.-L. Menze, *Justinian and the Making of the Syrian Orthodox Church* (Oxford, Oxford University Press, 2008).

Justinian's **wars** have attracted less specialized attention, and are normally covered in the surveys of the reign (see above). One exception is G. Greatrex, *Rome and Persia at War, 502–530* (Cambridge: Francis Cairns, 2006). There is need for a new study of the war in Italy in particular; for the period of Gothic rule there and Theodoric, who is mentioned in a few places in *The Secret History*, see J. Moorhead, *Theoderic in Italy* (Oxford: Clarendon Press, 1997). For war in general in this period, see the excellent survey by A. D. Lee, *War in Late Antiquity: A Social History* (Oxford: Blackwell, 2007). For numbers, structures, and pay, see W. Treadgold, *Byzantium and Its Army, 284–1081* (Stanford, CA: Stanford University Press, 1995). Obviously, we know more about the Roman state and its armies than those of the **peoples** who surrounded it. For an accessible survey of the Sasanian Persian state, see J. Wiesehöfer, *Ancient Persia from 550 BC to 650 AD*, tr. A. Azodi (London: I.B. Tauris 1996), Part 4. For other people whom Prokopios mentions along the eastern frontier, see I. Shahîd, *Byzantium and the Arabs in the Sixth Century* (Washington, DC: Dumbarton Oaks Research Library and Collection, 1995), and D. Braund, *Georgia in Antiquity: A History of Colchis and Transcaucasian Iberia 550 BC–AD 562* (Oxford: Clarendon Press, 1994). The Germanic people who appear most frequently in the text are the Goths, about whom see H. Wolfram, *History of the Goths*, tr. T. J. Dunlap (Berkeley: University of California Press, 1988) and the Vandals, about whom see A. H. Merrills, ed., *Vandals, Romans and Berbers: New Perspectives on Late Antique North Africa* (Aldershot, UK: Ashgate, 2004).

The **economy** is usefully surveyed by C. Morrisson and J.-P. Sodini, "The Sixth-Century Economy," in A. E. Laiou, ed., *The Economic History of Byzantium from the Seventh through the Fifteenth Century* (Washington, DC: Dumbarton Oaks Research Library and Collection, 2002), 1:171–220. For a fascinating analysis of the inner workings of the great estates of Egypt, coupled with a theory about class conflict, see P. Sarris, *Economy and Society in the Age of Justinian* (Cambridge: Cambridge University Press, 2006). A great deal of material has recently come to light regarding the state of the cities of the eastern empire in the sixth century; see H. Saradi, *The Byzantine City in the Sixth Century: Literary Images and Historical Reality* (Athens: Society of Messenian Archaeological Studies, 2006). Oddly, there has been no study of Justinian's **Constantinople** since G. Downey's brief and now outdated *Constantinople in the Age of Justinian* (Norman: University of Oklahoma Press, 1960). A far more interesting approach is taken by B. Croke, "Justinian's Constantinople," in M. Maas, ed., *The Cambridge Companion to the Age of Justinian* (Cambridge: Cambridge University Press, 2005), 60–86.

There are many historical novels set in the early sixth century, but none can be recommended that are both historically accurate and well written. R. Graves' *Count Belisarius* (London: Penguin Books, 1954; originally 1938) is at least well written.

PROKOPIOS OF KAISAREIA

The Secret History

Preface

1. When I recounted all that befell the Roman nation in its foreign wars up to the present, I made an effort to arrange my narrative according to the particular time and place in which each event occurred. But from this point onward I will no longer follow this plan of composition because I intend to tell all that has happened in every part of the empire of the Romans.[1] [2] The reason for this decision is that I could not at that time give a candid report concerning certain events so long as the people who were responsible for them were still alive.[2] It would have been impossible either to evade detection by the legions of their spies and informers or, having been caught, not to suffer a most cruel death. I could not even trust my closest relatives.[3] [3] Moreover, I was forced to conceal the causes of many of the events that I narrated in earlier books. It is therefore incumbent on me here to reveal what had previously remained concealed as well as to disclose the causes of those events that I did report there.

[4] But as I face this new challenge, namely the difficult and discouraging task of explaining the kind of life that Justinian and Theodora actually led, I find myself at a loss for words and ready to turn back and abandon the effort, as I can predict that the things that I am about to write will not seem trustworthy or even plausible to posterity. Besides, the long passage of time dulls the immediacy of events and I fear that I may earn the reputation of being a mere storyteller or be regarded as one of those who put on tragic plays. [5] And yet what gives me the confidence not to shrink back from the enormity of this task is that my testimony will not lack for witnesses. My contemporaries, who have exact and firsthand knowledge of the deeds that were committed, will be trustworthy references in the eyes of posterity for the accuracy of my report.[4]

1. For the relation between *The Secret History* and the *Wars*, in terms of their structure and contents, refer to "The Works of Prokopios," p. xxvi.

2. Chiefly Theodora (who died in 548); Justinian and Belisarios were still alive.

3. See also 16.13–14 below, which reveals that Prokopios has Theodora primarily in mind here.

4. It is possible that more writings hostile to the regime survive from the reign of Justinian than from the reign of any other Roman emperor; see the Introduction, p. lv.

[6] There was something else too that for a long time held me back on many occasions when I grew eager to write this book. I reasoned that it might not be advantageous for future generations were I to do so, given that it would be more in their interests if they remained ignorant of the most wicked deeds recounted herein than that future tyrants should learn about them and be aroused to imitate them. [7] For most rulers, being uneducated, always find it convenient to imitate the evil deeds of their predecessors; and so as not to exert themselves, they are always facilely repeating the mistakes of the past. [8] And yet in the end I was moved to write the history of these deeds by the following consideration, namely that it would also be made perfectly clear to future tyrants that punishment was almost certainly going to befall them on account of their wickedness, just as it did those in my narrative.[5] In addition, their deeds and characters would be publicized in writing for all time, which might give some pause to their illegalities. [9] For who in later times would have known about the shameful lifestyle of Semiramis or the lunacy of Sardanapalos and Nero had the memory of them not been preserved by contemporary writers?[6] Besides, my account will not be entirely useless to those who suffer similar things at the hands of future tyrants, if it should come to that, [10] for there is consolation in knowing that you are not the only one to have experienced such terrible things. I will, therefore, proceed to relate first all the wretched deeds that were done by Belisarios; then I will testify to all the wretched deeds done by Justinian and Theodora.

5. *The Secret History* does show that many of the emperor's associates came to ruin through their involvement in the regime's illegalities, but the same cannot be said for Justinian himself, and Prokopios passes up the chance to cast Theodora's death as punishment for her crimes.

6. In Greek legend, Semiramis was a dynamic oriental queen who built Babylon but slept with her soldiers (a garbled memory, perhaps, of the Assyrian queen Sammu-ramat of the late ninth century BC). Sardanapalos, an Assyrian king (Ashurbanipal), became notorious for his love of luxury. By Prokopios' time, Nero (r. AD 54–68) was the archetypal "bad emperor."

Part I

The Gynocracy

The Affair of Antonina

[11] Belisarios had a wife, whom I have mentioned in the earlier books.[7] Her father and grandfather were both charioteers who had performed professionally in Byzantion and Thessalonike.[8] Her mother, on the other hand, had been one of those types who whore themselves on the stage.[9] [12] Before marrying Belisarios, then, this woman had lived a wanton life and had never learned to show any restraint. She had also spent time with those people from her parents' world who knew all about poisons and magic herbs and had learned from them many things that were useful to her.[10] Later she became the lawful wife of Belisarios, though she was already the mother of many children.[11] [13] She had every intention of cheating on him from the start but took precautions to practice her adultery in secret, not because she felt any qualms about her habits, and certainly not because she had any fear of the man with whom she now lived given that, firstly, she never felt shame for anything that she did and, secondly, she had quite overpowered her husband with her charms and philters of seduction. No, it was because she was terrified that the empress might punish her. Theodora, you see,

7. Antonina appears prominently in the downfall of the prefect Ioannes the Kappadokian (*Wars* 1.25, translated in related text 7), in the expedition to Africa in the *Vandal War*, and at various moments of the *Gothic War*. She usually accompanied Belisarios on campaign.

8. Chariot racing was hugely popular in the Roman Empire, and hippodromes could be found in most major cities. Charioteers were celebrities and often popular heroes but of low social status and so despised in polite society.

9. Acting and prostitution were considered overlapping or interchangeable professions.

10. Herb lore, poison, medicine, and magic are all evoked by the Greek term *pharmakeia*.

11. In addition to her son Photios (see below), Antonina had a daughter who married the general Ildiger (*Wars* 4.8.24, 2.7.15), and a granddaughter old enough to be courted by Sergios in 544–545 (see 5.33 below).

used to yell at her savagely and, as they say, to bare her teeth at her.[12] [14] But Antonina managed to tame Theodora by serving her whenever there was a crisis, first by getting rid of Pope Silverius in the way that I will describe in a later book,[13] and then by plotting the downfall of Ioannes the Kappadokian, which I have described in an earlier book.[14] After that Antonina had no fear left at all and no longer even bothered to conceal all the crimes that she committed.

[15] There was a young man from Thrace in Belisarios' household named Theodosios, who belonged, through the tradition of his ancestors, to the sect of the so-called Eunomians.[15] [16] When the expedition was about to sail for Africa, Belisarios purified him in the holy immersion of baptism.[16] Raising him up from the font with his own hands, he formally accepted him into his family as the son of himself and his wife, according to the custom of adoption among Christians. From that moment on Antonina, as was only to be expected, loved Theodosios for he was her son according to sacred law, and cared for him greatly, keeping him by her side. [17] But during that voyage she quickly became immoderately infatuated with him, and was seized by an insatiable passion. She shook off all fear and

12. An allusion to Aristophanes, *Peace* 620. The same at 13.3 below.

13. Prokopios never divulges the details of Silverius' fall; this may be a forward reference to an *Ecclesiastical History* that he was planning to write (see the Introduction, p. xxvii). Pope Silverius was the son of Pope Hormisdas (514–523); he was appointed in June 536 by the Gothic king Theodahad and deposed in March 537 by Belisarios and Antonina. According to the *Book of Pontiffs* (a series of papal biographies), Theodora hated Silverius because he refused to restore the bishop of Constantinople Anthimos, who had been deposed for heresy by Pope Agapetus at a council in Constantinople in 536. She instructed Belisarios to find some pretext on which to depose him and replace him with the deacon Vigilius, whom she sent along. The pretext was that Silverius was in communication with the Goths during the siege of Rome. Prokopios and the *Book of Pontiffs* agree that Antonina was heavily implicated in these intrigues. Her agent in the matter was the eunuch Eugenios (see 1.27 below). Note the neutral way in which Prokopios recounts the matter at *Wars* 5.25.13: "A suspicion fell upon Silverius, the archpriest of the city, that he was plotting a betrayal to the Goths, so that Belisarios dispatched him immediately to Greece and soon replaced him with another archpriest, named Vigilius."

14. For the downfall of Ioannes (in 541), see Prokopios' account (*Wars* 1.25) translated in related text 7.

15. Eunomios was a fourth-century Arian theologian who argued that the substance (*ousia*) of the Son (Christ) was different from that of the God the Father.

16. The expedition to North Africa set sail from Constantinople in June 533. Other soldiers were baptized at the embarkation ceremony by the patriarch Epiphanios to ensure divine favor (*Wars* 1.12.2). The voyage lasted three months.

respect for both human convention and divine authority and had sex with him, at first secretly but finally even before the household servants and handmaidens. [18] Smitten with desire and obviously driven by erotic passion, she did not see any further reason why she should refrain from the deed. When Belisarios once caught them in the act when they were in Carthage,[17] he willingly allowed his wife to pull the wool over his eyes. [19] For even though he was furious at finding them together in a basement room, she was not overcome with shame nor even flinched at her compromising situation. "I came down here," she said, "with the boy to hide the most precious spoils of war so that the emperor doesn't find out about them."[18] [20] That was her excuse, and he let on that he had bought it, even though he could see that the belt around Theodosios' pants had been loosened in the part closest to his genitals. He was so infatuated with this person, his wife, that he could not bring himself to believe the evidence of his own eyes.

[21] Her lust kept getting stronger until it was unspeakably disgusting. Others saw what was going on but kept quiet, except for a slave named Makedonia. In Syracuse, when Belisarios had taken Sicily,[19] she bound her master with the most powerful oaths never to reveal her identity to the mistress and then told him everything. She produced two slave-boys as witnesses, whose job it was to tend to the couple's bedchamber. [22] When Belisarios understood the situation he ordered some of his men to kill Theodosios. [23] But the latter was warned and fled to Ephesos. This happened because most of Belisarios' men, considering how unsteady the man's mood was, were more careful to be in the good graces of the wife than to appear to be devoted to her husband. And so they treacherously betrayed their instructions regarding Theodosios. [24] But Konstantinos, seeing how depressed Belisarios was because of these events, took his side in all matters and was even heard to say, "I would sooner have done away with the wife than with the young man."[20]

17. This was between September 533 and mid 534; for Belisarios in Carthage, see *Wars* 3.20, 3.23.

18. The vast treasure captured from the Vandals, including spoils from the Temple of Jerusalem taken to Rome by Titus in 70 and from there to Carthage by Gaiseric in 455, was paraded in a triumph before Justinian in 534 (*Wars* 4.9). Antonina and her husband seem to have agreed on their right to defraud the imperial treasury.

19. This was during the winter of 535–536, at the beginning of the war in Italy against the Goths.

20. Konstantinos was one of Belisarios' most able commanders in the Italian War; for his demise, see below.

[25] When Antonina learned this, she began to hate Konstantinos, albeit in secret, so that her hatred for him could strike out all the more spitefully at an opportune moment. [26] Her fury lurked like a scorpion in the shadows.[21] Not long afterward she persuaded her husband, by using magic charms or soothing flatteries, that the slave's accusation was not sound. And so he immediately recalled Theodosios and even consented to turn Makedonia and the slave-boys over to his wife. [27] They say that first she cut out all their tongues, then cut their bodies into little pieces, which she put into sacks and threw into the sea without the slightest hesitation. In this whole horrid business she was assisted by one of her creatures named Eugenios, who had also carried out the outrage against Silverius. [28] Not long afterward, Belisarios executed Konstantinos at his wife's instigation, for it happened that the affair of Praesidius and the daggers transpired just then, as I related in an earlier book. [29] Even though the man would surely have been acquitted, Antonina did not relent until he had been punished for the remark that I just mentioned. [30] And because of this, Belisarios earned the hatred of both the emperor and all the best men among the Romans.[22]

[31] That was the outcome of those events. Theodosios, on the other hand, said that he was unable to come to Italy, where Belisarios and Antonina were then residing, unless Photios were first removed.[23] [32] For Photios was by nature quick to turn against those who had more influence than he with any person. Of course, in this business with Theodosios he had good reason to choke with rage insofar as he, who was after all a biological son, had been marginalized, while Theodosios was wielding power and amassing piles of money. [33] It is said that Theodosios had plundered up to a hundred *kentenaria* from the palaces of Carthage and Ravenna, and had

21. An allusion to a lost tragic play.

22. Konstantinos had stolen two precious daggers from Praesidius, a wealthy Italian refugee, who complained to Belisarios at Rome in the winter of 537–538. Belisarios ordered Konstantinos to return the daggers, but he refused; when Belisarios summoned his guards, Konstantinos thought that he was about to be killed and tried to stab Belisarios. He was arrested and executed "at a later time" (*Wars* 6.8). The point when "he would have been acquitted" was between his arrest and execution. In the account in the *Wars*, no mention is made of Antonina's role.

23. Photios was Antonina's son by a former liaison (possibly marriage), who was adopted by Belisarios. He had a distinguished military and political career under his stepfather's patronage.

been able to do so because they were placed under his sole command.[24] [34] When Antonina heard what was holding Theodosios back, she began to plot against her own son and set murderous traps for him, and did not relent until she had prevailed in forcing him, when he could no longer put up with her schemes, to leave from there and go to Byzantion. And so Theodosios joined her in Italy, [35] where she fully enjoyed both her lover's presence and her husband's foolishness. Later she returned to Byzantion with both of them.[25] [36] But there Theodosios became self-conscious and lost his nerve. His mind twisted this way and that as he reasoned that the affair couldn't stay secret forever, and he saw that the woman was no longer able to dissimulate her infatuation or indulge in it secretly. She was apparently unconcerned that she was behaving openly as an adulteress or even that she was being called one. [37] So again he fled to Ephesos, taking the tonsure as is the custom for those who wish to enroll among the "monks" (as they are known), which is what he did. [38] Antonina then became quite hysterical, changing her clothes and comportment to make it seem as though she were in mourning, and wandered throughout the house shrieking and wailing right in front of her husband. She lamented about what a good thing she had lost; how loyal; how charming; how kind; how vigorous! [39] She went so far as to draw her husband into these laments and make him join in. So he too, pathetic fool, wept and cried out for his beloved Theodosios. [40] Later he even went before the emperor and, entreating both him and the empress, persuaded them to recall him on the grounds that he was indispensable to his household and always would be. [41] But Theodosios absolutely refused to leave Ephesos, insisting that he had every intention of following the monastic rule. [42] This excuse, however, was but a pretense, for his intention was to come secretly to Antonina the very moment that Belisarios departed from Byzantion. And this is exactly what happened.

24. I.e., 720,000 coins worth of plunder (see the Glossary). However, there is a problem in this story. Ravenna fell in May 540, and Belisarios and Antonina were recalled to the capital later that year, taking Theodosios with them (see 1.35 below). Therefore, Theodosios could have plundered Ravenna only during the summer of 540, and so Photios could not have hated him for that *before* his return to Italy. Prokopios was writing with hindsight, but the story may be accepted as an illustration of Theodosios' character, to explain the general grounds of Photios' resentment.

25. In late 540.

2. Immediately afterward Belisarios set out to war against Chosroes, taking Photios with him,[26] but Antonina stayed put, which was unusual for her. [2] For in order that the man should never be left by himself, at which time he might come to his senses, cast off her enchantments, and form a more realistic opinion of her, she made a point of accompanying him to the ends of the earth. [3] And in order for Theodosios to have easy access to her yet again, she did everything she could to get Photios out of the way. [4] She persuaded some of Belisarios' men to taunt and harass him to no end and not to ease up on him for even a moment. Meanwhile, she wrote some libel against him virtually every day, slandering him ceaselessly and moving heaven and earth against her son. [5] These things forced the young man to retaliate with slanders of his own against his mother. When a certain person arrived from Byzantion with news that Theodosios was secretly consorting with Antonina, Photios immediately presented this man to Belisarios, bidding him to tell the whole story. [6] When Belisarios learned the truth he choked with rage. He fell on his face before Photios' feet and begged him to punish, on his behalf, those people who had caused him such grief, people who least of all should have committed such unholy acts. "O son," he said, "dearest boy, you never knew what sort of man your father was, as he left you, departing from this life, while you were still a baby in the wet nurse's arms. Not only that, he didn't benefit you materially either as he was not especially favored at making money. [7] No, you were raised by *me*, even though I am only your stepfather, and now you have reached that age when it is your duty to avenge me when I am treated most unjustly. You have attained the rank of consul[27] and have amassed such vast wealth that I might with justice be called your father and your mother and your entire family; indeed, my good boy, I might just as well actually *be* all that for you. [8] For it is in fact not blood but deeds that typically determine how much affection people will have for each other. [9] This, then, is not a time for you to stand aloof, when you see that in addition to the ruin of my family I have lost vast amounts of wealth while your mother has brought such great opprobrium upon herself in the eyes of all people. [10] Remember that the sins of

26. In early 541. In 540, Chosroes I (Khusrow), king of Persia (r. 531–579), had violated the Eternal Peace between the two states (signed in 532) and invaded the eastern provinces, capturing and plundering the metropolis of Antioch (see 2.25 below).

27. Photios' title was only honorary.

women do not fall only upon husbands but taint their children all the more, as children are generally believed to resemble by nature the character of the women who bore them. [11] Believe this about me: I greatly love my own wife, and if there is some way in which I can be avenged against the one who ruined my family, I will do her no harm. But so long as Theodosios remains alive, I cannot turn a deaf ear to this accusation against her."

[12] Upon hearing these things, Photios did agree to help in all ways but admitted that he was apprehensive lest it turn out badly for him, as he did not feel at all confident that Belisarios' mood regarding his wife would remain steady. He could not discount how Makedonia had been mistreated, and many other things troubled him as well. [13] Because of this concern, the two men swore to each other all the most dreadful oaths that exist among Christians and are recognized as the most binding, to the effect that they would never betray each other, not even in the most perilous of dangers. [14] But it did not seem to them expedient to attempt the deed immediately; rather, when Antonina arrived from Byzantion and Theodosios went to Ephesos, Photios then would travel to Ephesos and seize both Theodosios and the money without any difficulty. [15] This was all happening at the time when they were invading Persian territory with the entire army and also while, back in Byzantion, that business regarding Ioannes the Kappadokian was taking place, events that I narrated in the earlier books.[28] [16] There is only one fact that I covered up in that account out of fear, namely that it was not easy for Antonina to deceive Ioannes and his daughter; no, she had to swear a multitude of oaths to them of the kind that are regarded as the most terrifying among Christians, to the effect that she was not planning any deceit against them. [17] Having achieved her purpose and feeling even more confident of the empress' favor,[29] she sent Theodosios to Ephesos and set out for the East, not expecting to encounter any opposition.

[18] Belisarios had just taken the fort of Sisauranon when it was reported to him that she was on the way. Disregarding all other cares and responsibilities, he marched the army back. [19] For it happened that certain other things had also occurred during this campaign, as I related in the earlier book, which had predisposed him

28. For Belisarios' invasion of Persia in 541, see *Wars* 2.16–19. For the downfall of Ioannes, see Prokopios' account (*Wars* 1.25), translated in related text 7.

29. As explained at 1.14 above.

to retreat.[30] But this caused him to implement it all the sooner. [20] As I said at the beginning of this book, I then deemed it too dangerous for me to reveal all the causes of those events.[31] [21] At any rate, because of what happened, Belisarios was reviled by all the Romans for sacrificing the most critical needs of the state to his paltry domestic affairs. [22] At first he was so distraught over this business with his wife that he was unwilling to march far from Roman territory so that he would be able to retreat swiftly as soon as he found out that she had arrived from Byzantion, and arrest and punish her. [23] Therefore, he ordered the men under the command of Arethas to cross the Tigris river, but they accomplished nothing even worth mentioning and went home.[32] He himself, however, was careful never to go farther than a day's march from the Roman boundaries. [24] Now the fort of Sisauranon is more than a day's march from the Roman boundaries by the Nisibis route for an unencumbered traveler, but by a different route it is half that distance. [25] And yet if he had been willing from the beginning to cross the Tigris River with his entire army, I believe that he would have been able to plunder all the regions of Assyria, and could even have reached the city of Ktesiphon without meeting any resistance.[33] He could have then liberated the prisoners from Antioch and any other Romans who happened to be there,[34] and restored them to their old lives. Moreover, it was he who more than anyone else enabled Chosroes to return home from Kolchis with impunity. How this came about I will now explain.

[26] When Chosroes, the son of Kavades, invaded the land of Kolchis and did all the things that I narrated earlier—this was when

30. Namely, a contingent of Arab allies and Romans that had been sent across the Tigris had not reported back in a while (see below); Belisarios' army was suffering from fever; and his soldiers from Syria feared that the Arab allies of Persia would attack their lands (*Wars* 2.19.26–46).

31. See 1.3 above.

32. Arethas (al-Harith ibn Jabalah, r. 528–569) ruled the Ghassanid Arabs, allies of the Romans. Prokopios claims that Arethas did not report back to Belisarios because he did not want to share the loot that he had gathered after crossing the Tigris into Persian territory (*Wars* 2.19.26–29).

33. Ktesiphon was the capital of the Persian empire, sixty kilometers north of Babylon by the confluence of the Tigris and the Euphrates.

34. When Chosroes captured Antioch the previous year (540), he settled his many captives in a city near Ktesiphon that he called "Chosroes' Antioch" (*Wars* 2.14).

he captured Petra[35]—it happened that many soldiers in the army of the Medes perished in battle as well as because of the difficult terrain. For Lazike, as I explained, has many sheer cliffs and few good roads.[36] [27] As if this were not enough, an epidemic then fell upon them and carried away the majority of the soldiers, and many of them perished also due to lack of supplies.[37] [28] In the midst of all this some people who had just arrived there from Persia announced that Belisarios had defeated Nabedes in a battle by the city of Nisibis and was advancing further;[38] that he had captured the fort of Sisauranon after a siege and taken Bleschames and eight hundred Persian cavalry prisoner;[39] also that he had dispatched a separate Roman army under Arethas, the commander of the Saracens, who had crossed the Tigris River and plundered all those regions which had never before been touched. [29] It happened as well that Chosroes had sent a force of Huns against those Armenians who were subject to the Romans, hoping to keep the Romans there busy with troubles of their own and unaware of what was transpiring in Lazike. [30] But others now reported that Valerianos and the Romans had intercepted these barbarians and defeated them overwhelmingly in hand-to-hand combat, killing almost all of them.[40] [31] When the Persians heard this news, worn down by the hardships that they had endured among the Lazoi and fearing that they would encounter an enemy army during their return march in the steep and densely overgrown passes of that region, in which case they would all be destroyed in their disarray; and driven by anxiety for the safety of their children, wives, and even of their own country, whatever units remained in the army of the Medes that were fit for service began to

35. Chosroes invaded Kolchis (or Lazike, in modern Georgia) in 541 at the invitation of the local king Goubazes, capturing the Roman fort of Petra on the Black Sea (*Wars* 2.15, 2.17).

36. *Wars* 2.15.32–34, 2.17.1, 2.29.24–25.

37. This cannot have been the Justinianic plague, which was, in 541, just spreading out from Egypt (*Wars* 2.22–23; see related text 8). Prokopios alludes to this predicament of the Persian army at *Wars* 8.7.4.

38. The Persians had held Nisibis since 363 (when it was surrendered to them after Julian's failed campaign). Belisarios defeated the Persians who came out against him from the city but decided not to besiege it (*Wars* 2.18–19).

39. Bleschames and his Persian soldiers were sent by Justinian to fight in Italy (*Wars* 2.19.25, 7.3.11).

40. Valerianos, who had served with Belisarios in North Africa and Italy, had just been appointed to command the field armies in Roman Armenia. Armenia was by now entirely divided between Roman and Persian spheres of authority.

rail against Chosroes, accusing him of breaking his oaths and the conventions of all mankind when he invaded the land of the Romans in a time of peace without having any just reason to do so, and that he was committing an injustice against a state that was ancient and more worthy of respect than any other, a state, moreover, that he would not be able to overcome in war. They were on the verge of forming a mutiny.

[32] Chosroes was thrown off balance by this turn of events, but devised the following solution to his troubles. He had some official correspondence read aloud to them, which the empress had recently sent to Zaberganes.[41] [33] The letter said this: "You know well, O Zaberganes, from your recent embassy to our court, that I esteem you highly, believing that you are favorably disposed toward us. [34] You would, then, be acting in accordance with the high opinion I have formed of you if you persuaded Chosroes your king to adopt a peaceful policy toward our state. [35] I can assure you that you will, in such a case, be richly rewarded by my husband, who does nothing without my consent." [36] This was what Chosroes read out to them, mocking the leading Persians if they thought that there can be a true state that is governed by a woman. And so he dampened the indignation of his men. [37] Even so he departed in great distress, as he was fully expecting the army of Belisarios to oppose him. But not a single enemy sought to contest his passage, and so he arrived in his native land with great relief.

3. When Belisarios returned to Roman territory he found that his wife had arrived, and so he placed her under guard and in disgrace. And though he tried to do away with her many times, he was unmanned, in my view, overcome by a burning erotic passion. [2] They say that his wife used magic to subdue him and that she could break his will in but a moment. Meanwhile, Photios hastened to Ephesos taking one of her eunuchs with him as a prisoner, a certain Kalligonos, who had played the part of the pimp in his mistress' affairs. He tortured him along the way and extracted all his secrets from him. [3] Theodosios, informed in advance, fled to the sanctuary of John the Apostle, the holiest in that place and held in high regard.[42] [4] But Andreas, the archpriest of Ephesos, was bribed to turn the man over. While this was happening, Theodora became concerned on Antonina's behalf, hearing about all that had befallen

41. A Persian high official and diplomat.

42. Justinian had the small church of Saint John the Theologian at Ephesos torn down and erected a magnificent basilica in its place (*Buildings* 5.1.4–6).

her, and so she recalled Belisarios along with his wife to Byzantion.[43] [5] When Photios heard this, he sent Theodosios to Kilikia, where the personal guards and field marshals of Belisarios were quartering for the winter,[44] with instructions that this man was to be conveyed with the utmost discretion and that when they arrived in Kilikia they were to keep him under guard in a most secret location, leaving no clues for anyone to know where on earth he was. He himself came to Byzantion, bringing with him Kalligonos and the money of Theodosios, a substantial sum. [6] There the empress was parading before all of mankind the fact that she knew how to repay gifts of murder with even greater and more polluted rewards. [7] Whereas Antonina had just recently entrapped only one enemy, the Kappadokian, and betrayed him to her, Theodora rounded up an entire throng of men and, without formally charging them, turned them over to Antonina to be destroyed. [8] She subjected some of the friends of Belisarios and Photios to torture for the sole reason that they were on good terms with those two men. Such was her treatment of them that we still do not know what their ultimate fate was. She sent others into exile, bringing that same charge of friendship against them too.

[9] In fact, one of the men who had accompanied Photios to Ephesos (his name was Theodosios) she deprived of his property even though he had attained senatorial rank, and forced him to stand on the sideboard of a feeding-trough for animals in a pitch-black dungeon cell with a noose tied around his neck attached to the ceiling by a rope so short that he had to stretch his body and never relax. [10] So the poor wretch had to stand continuously on this manger, eating there and sleeping and performing all the other needs of nature, and was lacking in resemblance to an ass only in that he did not bray. [11] The man was forced to spend no less than four months in this condition, at which point he succumbed to the affliction of melancholy and went raving mad. In this sorry state of mind he was released from captivity, and died.

[12] Theodora also forced Belisarios, quite against his will, to reconcile with his wife Antonina. Upon Photios, on the other hand, she

43. Belisarios spent the winter of 541–542 in Constantinople (*Wars* 2.19.49). Prokopios there says that it was the *emperor* who recalled him from the eastern front.

44. Belisarios employed a large corps of personal guards and field marshals (the *bucellarii*), which, in 540, numbered seven thousand (*Wars* 7.1.20). Other generals had similar retinues, though not as large.

inflicted tortures normally reserved for slaves, mangling his back and shoulders with many lashes while demanding that he reveal where on earth Theodosios was and where the pimp was. [13] But he, even though he was racked by torture, resolved to keep to his sworn word. Despite his sickly constitution and easy lifestyle—for he was most attentive to the care of his body and was utterly without experience of hardship or injustice—[14] he nevertheless revealed not one of Belisarios' secrets. But later all the secrets came to light. [15] The empress found Kalligonos there and handed him over to Antonina. As for Theodosios, she recalled him to Byzantion and hid him in the palace as soon as he arrived. The next day she summoned Antonina and said to her cryptically, [16] "O dearest patrician, a pearl fell into my hands yesterday the likes of which no one has ever set eyes on. If you like, I would not begrudge you the spectacle of it out of spite; on the contrary, I would willingly make an exhibition of it for your pleasure." [17] The other woman, not entirely understanding what was going on, begged her earnestly to show her the pearl. So the empress had Theodosios brought out from one of the niches in which the palace eunuchs lurk and unveiled him before her. [18] Antonina was at first so overwhelmed with joy that she was too happy even to speak, but then thanked Theodora profusely for all the favors she had done her, calling her Savior and Benefactor and her True Mistress. [19] The empress then kept this Theodosios in the luxury and other enjoyments of the palace and even threatened to make him a general of the Romans in the near future. [20] But some kind of justice reached him first: an illness of dysentery removed him from the world of men.[45]

[21] Now Theodora had some secret cells, dark and isolated, that no one knew about and where it was impossible to tell whether it was night or day. [22] She kept Photios imprisoned in one of them for a long time. By some luck he managed to escape from there not just once but twice. [23] The first time he sought sanctuary in the temple of the Mother of God, which is the most holy in Byzantion and is in fact so named.[46] There he sat down by the holy altar as a suppliant. Theodora had him pulled up from there with all necessary force, and locked him up again. [24] The second time he went to Hagia Sophia and, before anyone could stop him, he sat down

45. Theodosios died in 542 or 543.

46. This may have been the church of the Theotokos at Blachernai (by the coast of the Golden Horn just outside the city walls to the northwest); it too had been embellished by Justinian (*Buildings* 1.3.3, 1.6.3).

within the divine basin itself, where baptisms are performed, a place that Christians revere above all others.[47] [25] But that woman prevailed in having him dragged away from there too. For there was no inviolable place that she would ever hesitate to desecrate, as she thought nothing of violating all sacred things.[48] [26] Along with the common people, the priests of the Christians were likewise too scared of her and so they stood aside and let her do whatever she pleased. [27] Three more years passed for Photios in this condition, at which point the prophet Zacharias appeared to him in a dream and bid him to flee, promising with oaths to facilitate his escape. [28] Trusting in this apparition, he emerged from that hole and reached Jerusalem, evading capture even though myriads of people were searching for him. Yet none of them actually noticed the young man, even when they were right next to him. [29] He there took the tonsure and adopted the habit of the men who are called "monks," managing in this way to escape the wrath of Theodora.[49]

The Emasculation of Belisarios

[30] As for Belisarios, he disregarded his oaths, preferring not to offer Photios any assistance at all, even though the latter was suffering such unholy things as have been mentioned. It therefore makes perfect sense that Belisarios found the will of God ranged against him in all his subsequent undertakings. For when he was soon sent out against Chosroes and the Medes—this was during their third invasion of Roman land[50]—he earned a reputation for cowardice. [31] And yet he did seem to have accomplished something noteworthy, namely to have relieved that region of war. But when Chosroes crossed the Euphrates River, he captured Kallinikos, a densely populated city, without encountering any resistance, and enslaved many myriads of Romans. Belisarios did not care so much

47. Hagia Sophia was rebuilt by Justinian between 532–537, as the original building was destroyed in the Nika riots of 532 (*Wars* 1.24; translated in related text 2).

48. See also 17.10 below for the same idea, and an example.

49. Photios eventually became abbot Photeinos of the New Monastery at Jerusalem. Justin II (r. 565–578) sent him to quell ecclesiastical disturbances in Egypt and suppress a Samaritan-Jewish revolt, in the execution of which tasks he is said to have displayed exceptional brutality.

50. In 542; see *Wars* 2.20–21 (for the number of Persian invasions see 18.23 below and *Wars* 2.26.1). For God being opposed to Belisarios from now on, see 4.42 below.

as to even pursue the enemy, leaving but two possibilities regarding his character, namely that he willfully neglected his duty or that he was too afraid. For he stayed put.

4. Around the same time, something else befell him as well. When the plague, which I described in a previous book, was cutting down the people of Byzantion, it happened that the emperor Justinian fell so grievously ill that it was even said that he had died.[51] [2] This rumor was spread about by hearsay until it reached the camp of the Romans. Some of the officers there began to declare that if the Romans in Byzantion foisted another emperor like that upon them all, they would never allow it. [3] But shortly afterward it happened that the emperor recovered and the officers of the Roman army began to slander each other. [4] The general Petros and Ioannes (whom they called by the nickname "the Eater") insisted that they had heard Belisarios and Bouzes saying those things which I just reported. [5] The empress Theodora now interpreted these things as having been directed by those who said them against *her* specifically, and she became indignant. [6] She immediately summoned them all to Byzantion and began to inquire into the circumstances of that statement. All of a sudden she had Bouzes brought to the women's quarters of the palace, alleging that she had something of the utmost importance to tell him.[52] [7] Now, the palace has an underground wing, basically a maze with guards that you might confuse with Tartaros. It was her general policy to keep imprisoned there any people whose actions had clashed against her will. [8] Bouzes too was thrown into this pit, where he, a man descended from consuls, remained utterly unaware of the passage of time. [9] Sitting in the dark, he could neither determine for himself whether it was night or day nor could he come into contact with anyone else, [10] for the person who flung food at him every day treated him as one beast does another, mute to mute. [11] Meanwhile, everyone had simply assumed that he had been immediately killed and so no one dared to speak of him or even mention his name. Yet two years and four months later she took pity on the man and let him go. [12] He seemed to everyone like a man

51. For the Justinianic plague, which struck Constantinople in 542, see Prokopios' account (*Wars* 2.22–23) translated in related text 8. Justinian's illness is mentioned at *Wars* 2.23.20.

52. Bouzes was a general whose career had been spent fighting on the eastern front. At this time he shared the command of the eastern armies with Belisarios.

brought back from the dead, but ever after this experience he was nearsighted and generally sickly of body.[53]

[13] This, then, was what happened to Bouzes. As for Belisarios, though he had not been convicted of a single charge, the empress leaned on the emperor to strip him of his command and appoint Martinos instead as general in the East.[54] The emperor also instructed that Belisarios' personal guards and field marshals as well as any of his retinue who had displayed military skill were to be scattered among the units commanded by other officers and the palace eunuchs. [14] So the latter cast lots over them, men and weapons alike, to distribute them all among themselves, as chance would have it for each one. [15] He also forbade many of Belisarios' friends or men who had previously served him in another capacity to visit him any longer. [16] What a bitter spectacle and incredible sight it was to see Belisarios going about in Byzantion as a private citizen: virtually alone, always gloomy and sullen, in constant terror of a murderer's knife. [17] And when the empress discovered that he had much money stashed away in the East, she sent one of the palace eunuchs to haul it all in. [18] Now it happened that Antonina, as I explained, was estranged from her husband but was on excellent terms with the empress, who regarded her as an indispensable instrument given that she had recently ruined Ioannes the Kappadokian.[55] [19] The empress, therefore, contrived to gratify Antonina by doing everything to create the impression that it was the *wife* who had interceded on the *husband's* behalf and had delivered him from this crushing adversity. Her goal was not only to reconcile Antonina in all ways with that miserable man but that it should be known to all that it was Antonina who had saved him, just as if he were a prisoner of war who had been ransomed by her.

[20] It happened in the following way. One morning Belisarios went to the palace as was his custom, accompanied by a meager and pitiful retinue. [21] But when he realized that both the emperor and the empress were not favorably disposed toward him and found,

53. Bouzes is not heard from again until he was given a minor command in 549, which was the year after Theodora's death. He was appointed general again in 554 (in Lazike).

54. At *Wars* 2.21.34, Prokopios says that Belisarios was recalled *by the emperor* in order to be sent to Italy, but he was not sent there until 544.

55. For the downfall of Ioannes (in 541), see Prokopios' account (*Wars* 1.25) translated in related text 7. He has already alluded to this service performed by Antonina at 1.14 and 2.15 above.

moreover, that he was being insulted there by men of a vulgar and common sort, he departed for his home late in the evening, looking over his shoulder every few minutes as he was walking and scanning the streets all around to see from what direction his killers would come. [22] In this state of terror he went up to his room and sat alone upon his bed, having no intention of doing anything brave, not even remembering that he had once been a man. His sweat ran in streams. He felt light-headed. He could not even think straight in his panic, worn out by servile fears and the worries of an impotent coward. [23] All the while, Antonina, as if she were not fully aware of what was going on or as if she were not eagerly expecting what was to come, was fussing about the room pretending to have heartburn; for they were still suspicious of each other. [24] Meanwhile, a man, Kouadratos by name, arrived from the palace when the sun had already set. He passed through the courtyard gate and suddenly appeared by the door that led into the man's quarters, saying that he had been sent by the empress. [25] Upon hearing this, Belisarios drew his arms and legs up onto the bed and lay there on his back, serving himself up to be slaughtered, so completely had his manliness deserted him. [26] Without entering the room, Kouadratos presented him with a letter from the empress. And this letter said the following. [27] "Noble sir, you know how you have treated us. But I, for my part, owe so much to your wife that I have decided to disregard all these accusations against you, giving her a gift of your life. [28] So from now on you may feel confident regarding your survival and property, but as to how you intend to treat her we will judge based on your behavior." [29] When Belisarios read these words, he was ecstatic with joy and wished at that very moment to make an immediate declaration of his gratitude. He jumped up from the bed and fell on his face before his wife's feet. [30] Placing a hand behind each of her calves, he began to lick the soles of his wife's feet with his tongue, one after the other, calling her the Cause of his Life and Salvation, promising that henceforth he would be her devoted slave and not her husband. [31] Of his property the empress gave thirty *kentenaria* of gold to the emperor,[56] and the rest she returned to Belisarios.

[32] This, then, was what happened to Belisarios—to Belisarios *the general*, the man to whom Fortune had shortly before delivered

56. I.e., she confiscated 216,000 coins (see the Glossary).

Gelimer and Vitigis as captives of war.[57] [33] The man's great wealth had long grated on Justinian and Theodora, as it was excessive and more suited to a royal court. [34] They kept saying that he had treacherously hidden away the majority of the public funds of Gelimer and Vitigis and given only a small and insignificant portion of them to the emperor. [35] But they weighed the man's hard work against the defamation that they would incur from others,[58] and besides they could concoct no credible accusation to use against him, and so they made no move. [36] But at the time of the events I have been relating, the empress had him under her thumb, as he was terrified and altogether cringing, and a single act sufficed to make her the owner of his entire property. [37] For the two of them became in-laws when Ioannina, the daughter of Belisarios and his only child, was engaged to Anastasios, the son of the empress' daughter.[59]

[38] Belisarios now requested to be restored to his old post as general of the East and, having been reassigned there, to lead the Roman army against Chosroes and the Medes. But Antonina was utterly opposed to the idea. She said that she had been grossly insulted by him in that region and so, she reasoned, he should never see it again. [39] He was appointed instead as Commander of the Imperial Grooms and sent for the second time to Italy, promising the emperor, some say, that he would never request funds for the prosecution of this war but that he himself would finance the operations entirely from his own money.[60] [40] Everyone was thinking that in settling his affairs with that wife of his in the way that I described, and in making the promise to the emperor regarding the war that I just mentioned, Belisarios' plan was to stop wasting his time in Byzantion,

57. Gelimer was the last king of the Vandals in North Africa (r. 530–534); he surrendered to Belisarios after losing two battles and enduring a siege with his remaining followers. Vitigis was king of the Goths in Italy (r. 536–540); he spent his entire reign fighting the Romans in Italy, until he surrendered himself and Ravenna to Belisarios.

58. I.e., if they moved against him.

59. Anastasios was the son of Theodora's daughter (not by Justinian). For his relationship (possibly marriage) to Ioannina in 548, and its dissolution after Theodora's death, see 5.18–24 below.

60. This was in 544. The war was not going well in Italy, where the Goths were resurgent under their new king Totila. Moreover, the effects of the Justinianic plague were being felt on military recruitment, and Justinian was short of both cash and men. As Belisarios' household troops were serving in the East, he had to recruit four thousand men in Thrace (*Wars* 7.10.1–3). The name of his new office, *comes stabuli*, survives in the English "constable."

and that as soon as he found himself outside the city walls he would without delay take up arms and do something noble and befitting a man against his wife and against those who had violated him.[61] [41] But it was not to be. He cared not at all for what had happened, entirely forgetting and disregarding the oaths that he had sworn to Photios and his other friends, and simply obeyed that woman. He was so extraordinarily infatuated with her, and this despite the fact that she was already past sixty years old.[62] [42] While he was in Italy, every day things went wrong for him, because the will of God was manifestly opposed to him.[63] [43] In fact, the plans that this general had once improvised against both Theodahad and Vitigis, even though they seemed not to be well thought-out for dealing with those circumstances, did in large part have their desired results;[64] but later, after he had gained a reputation for devising the best strategies, given that he was now experienced in prosecuting this particular war, events would still turn out badly for him, which was then generally ascribed to his bad planning. [44] This is what it means when we say that human affairs are governed not by our own plans but by the impulsion of God, which people tend to call *chance* because they do not know why events turn out the way that they do, when their full course becomes manifest. [45] The word *chance*, then, tends to be invoked when events seem to make no sense. But let each person think about these things as he likes.[65]

5. So Belisarios, campaigning in Italy for the second time, departed from there in total disgrace. For a full five years he was unable to even set foot on the mainland, as I related in an earlier book,[66] unless there happened to be a fort somewhere. During that entire time he used the fleet to sail along the coasts. [2] Totila was franti-

61. It seems that many were hoping that Belisarios would overthrow Justinian.

62. Belisarios was not yet fifty at the time.

63. For a similar statement, see 3.30 above; see also, in connection with Belisarios in Italy in 544, the long exposition of this idea at *Wars* 7.13.14–18, where Prokopios jumbles together God and the Greek concept of "chance" (or "fortune").

64. Theodahad (r. 534–536) and Vitigis (r. 536–540) were the kings of the Goths whom Belisarios faced during the first phase of the war in Italy. He prevailed over them despite (or because of) his bold and even reckless tactics and strategies.

65. In many passages, Prokopios mixes together the notions of God and chance (or fortune, Greek *tyche*), e.g., 10.9–10 below and *Wars* 8.12.34–35. His own beliefs on the matter remain elusive, and the end of this passage invites us to think more carefully about them.

66. *Wars* 7.35.1; the years were 544–549.

cally trying to catch him outside the walls,[67] but Belisarios was never out in the open because he and the entire army of the Romans were simply too terrified. [3] So not only did he fail to recover anything that had been lost, he lost Rome into the bargain,[68] and indeed just about everything else as well. [4] At this time he also became the most greedy person in the world, carefully devising ways to turn a profit, no matter how disgraceful, on the pretext that he had been given no financial resources by the emperor. It is a fact that he plundered nearly all the Italians who lived in Ravenna and Sicily, indeed in any place that he was lucky enough to bring under his power. He scarcely put a veneer of legality on all this, other than to allege that he was now holding them accountable for their past conduct.[69] [5] In this way he even went after Herodianos, requesting funds and shaking him down with threats. [6] This so angered the other man that he detached himself from the Roman army and immediately pledged himself, his followers, and Spoleto to Totila and the Goths.[70]

[7] I will now explain how it was that Belisarios quarreled with Ioannes, the nephew of Vitalianos, an incident that greatly harmed Roman interests. [8] The empress so hated Germanos, and made her hatred of him so obvious to all others, that no one would dare enter into a marriage relationship with him even though he was the emperor's cousin.[71] His sons remained without brides until her death and his daughter Ioustina was still unwed at the age of eighteen. [9] For this reason, when Ioannes arrived at Byzantion, having been

67. Totila (also Baduila), king of the Goths in Italy (r. 541–552), restored the fortunes of his people and managed to wrest most of the peninsula from Roman control. He was finally defeated and killed by the army of Narses at the battle of Busta Gallorum, effectively ending the Gothic dominion in Italy.

68. The Romans (Byzantines) lost control of Rome in December 546 (*Wars* 7.20) but Belisarios recaptured it in April 547 in a bold attack (*Wars* 7.24).

69. Presumably for assisting the Goths at some juncture of the war, or for acquiescing in their rule before it (see 24.9 below).

70. Herodianos was a Roman officer who accompanied Belisarios to Italy in 535. In 545 he was in command of the garrison when Spoleto was besieged by the Goths; he promised to surrender the city if no help arrived in thirty days, which is what happened. Prokopios mentions the hatred that existed between him and Belisarios also at *Wars* 7.12.16. Herodianos was still serving with the Goths in 552.

71. Germanos was the nephew of Justin I (r. 518–527), therefore the cousin of Justinian. At this point he had a distinguished military and administrative career; from his first wife Passara he had two sons (Ioustinos and Ioustinianos) and one daughter (Ioustina). For his refusal to participate in a plot against Justinian, see related text 10.

sent there by Belisarios,[72] Germanos was so desperate that he entered into negotiations with him regarding a possible marriage, even though Ioannes was far beneath his rank. [10] Since the prospect was pleasing to both, they decided to exchange the most dreadful oaths to the effect that they would do everything in their power to make the marriage happen since each had little trust in the other, the one being all-too-aware that he was reaching above his rank, the other being otherwise unable to secure a son-in-law. [11] The empress was furious beyond belief and applied pressure on both of them, using every possible approach to frustrate this transaction. No tactic was beneath her. [12] But even though she alarmed them she did not dissuade either one, so she resorted to explicit threats against Ioannes' life. [13] Because of this, when Ioannes returned to Italy he did not dare to contact Belisarios, fearing the plotting of Antonina, at least until she returned to Byzantion.[73] [14] For one might quite reasonably suspect that the empress would commission her to arrange his murder; and so, weighing the character of Antonina and knowing that Belisarios always let her have her way, a great fear was born in him that shook him to his core. [15] This dashed Roman fortunes to the ground, which even before that were on their last legs.[74]

[16] This was how the Gothic war turned out for Belisarios. In despair, he begged the emperor for permission to depart from there as quickly as possible. [17] When he found that the emperor accepted this request, he left happily and swiftly, bidding a "fond" farewell to both the Roman army and the Italians, abandoning most of the country into the hands of the enemy at a time when Perusia was being hammered by a siege. In fact, the city was captured by storm while he was still on his way back and it suffered every kind of misfortune, as I recounted earlier.[75] It happened then that he suffered the following domestic misfortune as well.

72. Ioannes was the nephew of Vitalianos (who rebelled against Emperor Anastasios in 513 and was murdered in the palace in 520, possibly on Justinian's orders; see 6.27–28 below). Ioannes had a military career, most of it spent fighting in Italy. He was on bad terms with Belisarios, who sent him to Constantinople in 545 for money and reinforcements. He obtained neither (*Wars* 7.12).

73. Ioannes returned to Italy the next year (i.e., 546). Prokopios refers to the hatred between him and Belisarios in a speech that he attributes to Totila, the king of the Goths, at *Wars* 7.25.22.

74. Ioannes refused to obey Belisarios' order to march from the south of Italy to Rome (*Wars* 7.18.29), and the city was taken in December 546.

75. *Wars* 7.35.2. This was in 549. At *Wars* 7.30.25, Prokopios states that it was Antonina who went to Constantinople and begged for Belisarios' recall.

[18] The empress Theodora pressed hard to hasten the marriage between Belisarios' daughter and her own grandson by harassing the girl's parents with constant letters.[76] [19] But they, desiring to back out of the arrangement, put off the wedding until such a time as they could be in attendance. When the empress summoned them to Byzantion, they pretended that they were unable at just that moment to leave Italy. [20] But because she was eager to make her grandson the master of Belisarios' wealth—for she knew that his daughter would be his only heir, as he had no other children—and yet had little confidence in the loyalty of Antonina, fearing lest Antonina betray the interests of the empress' family after Theodora's death by calling off the arrangement—and this despite the fact that the empress had supported her so generously at critical moments—considering all this, then, she devised an unholy deed: [21] she arranged for the cohabitation of the boy and girl outside legal bounds.[77] They even say that she secretly forced the girl, who was not willing, to lie with him and only then, after she had lost her virginity, arranged for the wedding ceremony in order that the emperor not put an end to all this business. [22] In fact, when the deed was done, Anastasios and the girl conceived a burning passion for each other, and the time that they passed in this way was no less than eight months. [23] Yet when Antonina arrived in Byzantion after the empress had died,[78] she willingly forgot all that the other woman had recently done for her. Not caring at all that, if she were now to marry the girl off to someone else, it would mean that her previous conduct was effectively that of a prostitute, she nevertheless thought little of Theodora's grandson as a potential son-in-law and forced the girl quite against her will to separate from her beloved husband. [24] This deed earned her the reputation, in the eyes of all people, for immense ingratitude, and when her husband arrived she had no difficulty in persuading him to share in the responsibility for this outrage. It was now easy to see exactly what kind of a person he was. [25] For even though he had previously sworn oaths to Photios and certain other friends and yet had in no way remained true to his word,[79] nevertheless he was universally forgiven for it. [26] This was

76. For the engagement of Ioannina and Anastasios, see 4.37 above.

77. Illegal because Theodora had presumably not obtained permission from the girl's parents for this cohabitation; or because the girl was (at first) unwilling; and perhaps she was still also under the legal of age of twelve.

78. In 548 (see *Wars* 7.30.25).

79. See 2.13 and 3.30 above.

because everyone suspected that the cause of his faithlessness was not that he was governed by his wife but that he was afraid of the empress. [27] But after the empress' death, which I just mentioned, he took no thought for Photios or for any of those other friends. It was now transparent that his wife was his true mistress and Kalligonos, the pimp, was his master. Everyone now repudiated him. He was mocked in the streets and reviled as a confirmed fool. Such, then, were the crimes of Belisarios, if one were to state them more or less without concealment.

The Crimes of Sergios and Solomon

[28] As for the crimes committed by Sergios, the son of Bakchos, in North Africa, I have sufficiently described them in the relevant place, namely how he was the person chiefly responsible for the collapse of Roman interests in that region by disregarding the oaths that he had sworn on the Gospels to the Leuathai and by doing away with the eighty ambassadors for no good reason.[80] I must at this point add only this to my previous account, that these men had no treacherous intention when they came to Sergios nor did Sergios have any pretext to suspect deceit on their part; rather, having sworn as to their safety and having invited these men to a feast, he killed them shamefully.[81] [29] It was this that caused the destruction of Solomon, the Roman army, and all the North Africans, [30] and it was because of him, especially after Solomon's death, which I have already recounted, that not a single officer and not a single soldier was willing to face the dangers of war.[82] [31] Worst of all in this regard was

80. In 543, Sergios was appointed military governor of Tripolis. Swearing an oath as to their safety, he invited eighty leaders of the Leuathai (a tribe of Moors) to a banquet in Leptis Magna where, after an altercation, his guards killed all of them but one (who escaped). Sergios defeated the tribe in battle but war continued in 544, culminating in a battle in which the Romans were defeated and their great general Solomon was killed (*Wars* 4.21). Sergios, Solomon's nephew, was appointed to govern North Africa, but with disastrous results (*Wars* 4.22). He was recalled in 545 but was still alive (and a patrician) in 559.

81. At *Wars* 4.21.4, Prokopios had recorded that "it was said" that the eighty Leuathai approached Sergios with treasonous intent. *The Secret History* here directly gives the lie to that report.

82. Solomon had served under Belisarios during the conquest of North Africa (533–534) and had then governed the region in 534–536 and 539–544, defeating the Moors in 540 and establishing peace and relative prosperity. Prokopios praised his courage and wisdom (*Wars* 4.20.33), but it seems that he was unpopular with many of his soldiers.

Ioannes, the son of Sisinniolos, who removed himself from the fighting on account of his hatred for this man, until Areobindos arrived in North Africa.[83] [32] For Sergios was soft and unwarlike, quite young in years and immature of character, envious and hugely arrogant toward all people, emasculated by his tender lifestyle yet blown up with pride. [33] But because he also happened to be a suitor for the granddaughter of Antonina, Belisarios' wife, the empress was altogether unwilling to impose any kind of punishment on him or depose him from his command, though she saw that North Africa was being continually ruined. She and the emperor even let Solomon, Sergios' brother,[84] get away with the murder of Pegasios. What this episode was I will now explain.

[34] When Pegasios had ransomed Solomon from the Leuathai and the barbarians had gone home,[85] Solomon set out for Carthage along with his ransomer Pegasios and a small number of soldiers. Along the way Pegasios caught Solomon committing some injustice or another and remarked that he ought to remember that God had only recently delivered him from the enemy. [35] This sat heavily with Solomon, who took it as an insult about being captured in battle and immediately killed Pegasios. This was how he reimbursed the man for the ransom that he had paid on his behalf. [36] When Solomon arrived in Byzantion, the emperor cleared him of the murder on the grounds that he had killed an enemy of the Roman empire. [37] He even gave him an official document granting immunity from prosecution on this count. And so Solomon escaped punishment and, in good spirits, traveled to the East to see his native land and family back home. [38] But the punishment that comes from God overtook him along the way and removed him from the world of men. This, then, was what happened with Solomon and Pegasios.

83. *Wars* 4.23.32. Areobindos, a senator, arrived in 545 to share the military command of North Africa with Sergios. This Ioannes obeyed Areobindos in a joint campaign but Sergios did not, costing Ioannes his life.

84. Not the general mentioned above (who was Sergios' uncle).

85. Solomon (the younger) had been captured by the Moors in the battle in which his uncle (the general Solomon) was killed; he pretended to be a Vandal and was ransomed by the doctor Pegasios (*Wars* 4.22.12–20).

Part II

Justinian and Theodora

The Origin of Justinian

6. I turn now to explain what kind of people Justinian and Theodora were, the two of them as a pair, and how they ruined the affairs of the Romans. [2] When Leon held imperial power in Byzantion,[1] three young Illyrian farmers named Zimarchos, Ditybistos, and Justin (who was from Bederiana),[2] set out to join the army because at home they had to struggle constantly against poverty and all its attendant hardships, and they wanted to be rid of all that. [3] They even walked on foot all the way to Byzantion carrying on their own shoulders sacks made of goat's hair that, by the time they arrived, contained only some baked bread that they had packed at home. They enlisted in the military rolls and were selected by the emperor to serve in the palace guard, for all three were tall and brawny.[3] [4] Some time later, when Anastasios had succeeded to the throne, a war broke out with the nation of the Isaurians, who had taken up arms against the emperor.[4] [5] He sent a formidable army against them under the command of Ioannes, who was nicknamed the Hunchback. This Ioannes imprisoned Justin in a holding cell for some offense and would have executed him the next day, had a dream-vision not appeared to him in the meantime and prevented it. [6] The

1. Leon I (r. 457–474).

2. Bederiana was in the province of Dacia Mediterranea, near the city of Naissos (modern Niš) in the north-central Balkans, a region that had supplied the empire with soldiers for centuries. Its inhabitants could be called Illyrians or Thracians, which were only vague geographical labels. Justin (who was born around 450) is called a Thracian in other sources, and his companions have Thracian names. All were basically Romans.

3. Probably the palace guard known as the *excubitores*.

4. Anastasios (r. 491–518). Isauria, in southern Asia Minor, was not fully pacified. Also, Anastasios' predecessor Zenon (r. 474–475, 476–491) had been an Isaurian and had appointed other Isaurians to high office. Many resented their loss of power and influence under Anastasios. The Isaurian War lasted throughout the 490s.

general revealed that an entity had appeared to him in the dream that was too vast of body and too awesome in other respects to be likened to a human being. [7] This entity called upon him to release the man whom he had imprisoned that day. When the general arose, however, he disregarded the dream-vision. [8] Yet when the next night came, he dreamed again that he heard the same words that he had heard the previous night. But still he was unwilling to do what it bid.[5] [9] A third time, then, did the dream-vision loom before him, vowing that his fate would indeed be grim if he did not do as he was told, adding that in the future, in a moment of great anger, he would actually have need of this man and his relatives.[6]

[10] This, then, was how Justin managed to survive at that moment, and as time passed he rose to great power. [11] The emperor Anastasios promoted him to captain of the palace guard and, when Anastasios passed away, Justin, by virtue of this command, rose to the imperial throne, even though he already had one foot in the grave and was utterly without learning when it came to letters; in fact, he was what we call an illiterate, something that has never before happened to the Romans.[7] [12] The custom, after all, is for the emperor to authorize with letters of his own writing all the documents that contain his official orders, but this one was incapable either of authorizing his own orders or of understanding what any official act was all about. [13] Rather, the man who happened to be his executive assistant handled everything on his own initiative (he was named Proklos and held the position that is called *quaestor*).[8] [14] But in order to obtain formal ratification by the imperial hand, those who supervise this matter devised the following scheme.

5. Yet the general had intended to execute Justin after the *first* night (according to 6.5 above).

6. That is, the dream-entity itself would make use of Justin's family in the future (presumably in order to wreak havoc among human beings).

7. Justin was almost seventy when he came to the throne in July 518. The *Chronicle* of Ioannes Malalas confirms that Justin was "unlettered" (17.1). He was not, however, senile, at least not in 518. According to one version, Justin was given money by Amantios, the director of the palace staff (see 6.26 below), with instructions to secure the soldiers' support for the accession of his associate Theokritos, but Justin used it to secure their support for himself instead. Amantios and Theokritos were executed in the disturbances that followed.

8. An epigram for Proklos calls him "the mouth of the emperor" (*Greek Anthology* 16.48). Prokopios calls him a just and unbribable man (*Wars* 1.11.11; see also 9.41 below). The professor of Latin and civil functionary Ioannes Lydos calls him "most just" (*On the Magistracies of the Roman State* 3.20). He held office between 522/523 and 525/526.

[15] Onto a small strip of polished wood they carved the shape of four letters that spelled, in the Latin language, the word "I have read."[9] They dipped the pen into the special ink that is used for imperial subscriptions and put it into the hands of this emperor. [16] Then they placed the slat of wood that I mentioned upon the document and, holding the emperor's hand, traced the pattern of the four letters with the pen, following the curving lines that were cut into the wood.[10] And so they would complete their business with the emperor in this way, having obtained his handwritten letters, such as they were.

[17] That was how the Romans coped with Justin. The wife that he lived with was named Lupicina; she had previously been a slave and a barbarian, a concubine of a man who had bought her. She too, along with Justin, attained the throne in the sunset of her life.[11] [18] Generally speaking, Justin neither benefited his subjects nor did them harm. He was good-natured in a simpleminded way, entirely inarticulate and boorish in the extreme. [19] But his nephew Justinian, who began to govern the entire state while he was still young, was the cause of disasters for the Romans the sheer number and magnitude of which no one had even heard of in all of prior history.[12] [20] The murder of innocent people and the seizure of property that was not his were casual matters for him. The death of countless thousands was nothing to him, even though these people had given him neither cause nor pretext. [21] He had no interest in maintaining established institutions but constantly wanted to innovate in all fields; in a word, he was the greatest destroyer of good

9. I.e., the stencil *LEGI*.

10. The imperial chancery had developed a special handwriting to be used in imperial documents, to prevent forgery (*Codex Theodosianus* 9.19.3). The imperial signature, moreover, was written in a special purple ink (*Codex Iustinianus* 1.23.6). The only surviving sample of the handwriting of an ancient Roman emperor appears on a papyrus containing an order from Theodosios II (r. 408–450) to a commander in Egypt.

11. Lupicina is a diminutive of *lupa* ("little wolf girl"), a name common among prostitutes in the Graeco-Roman world (cf. Lycisca in Juvenal, *Satire* 6.123). An independent contemporary source confirms Lupicina's servile and barbarian origins. Upon becoming empress, she took the name Euphemia (see 9.49 and note 56).

12. Justinian was from the village of Taurision, near Justin's village of Bederiana, where he later built the city of Iustiniana Prima (*Buildings* 4.1.17–28). Born in 482, he was a son of Justin's sister and a certain Sabbatios (see 12.18 below); his full imperial name was Flavius Petrus Sabbatius Iustinianus.

institutions. [22] Consider, by contrast, the plague, which I described in an earlier book: even though it fell upon the entire earth, at least as many people survived it as perished in it, either because they were not infected at all or because they recovered after their infection.[13] [23] Compared to that, however, not a single person, at least no Roman, managed to escape from this man. Like some new calamity sent from heaven to fall upon the whole of mankind, it left no one entirely unscathed. [24] Some people he killed for no good reason while others were left in his wake to struggle with poverty after being reduced to an even more wretched state than those who had died. They begged to be put out of their present misery, even if it meant a most cruel death. But in some cases he was happy to take their lives along with their money.[14]

[25] As if it were not enough for him to subvert the Roman empire, he conquered North Africa and Italy as well for no other reason than to be able to destroy the people there in addition to those who were already under his power. [26] He had not held power for ten days before he killed Amantios, the overseer of the palace eunuchs, along with certain others, for no cause whatsoever. He accused that person of nothing other than saying something rash about Ioannes, the archpriest of the city. [27] This action made him the most feared of all people.[15] He also immediately summoned the rebel Vitalianos, to whom he had previously given a guarantee of safety by partaking with him in the Christian sacraments. [28] But soon afterward he clashed with Vitalianos and killed him in the palace along with his associates, based purely on his suspicions and in no way mindful of the most binding guarantees that he had given.[16]

13. Prokopios' account of the Justinianic plague (*Wars* 2.22–23) is translated in related text 8.

14. This passage itemizes the main accusations against Justinian in *The Secret History:* innovation in government, murder, and theft.

15. Amantios attempted to seize power when Anastasios died in 518 by placing his own protégé Theokritos on the throne. It seems that he continued to plot against Justin after his accession, but there was a religious dimension to his fall, for before his execution he was vilified as a heretic at a church service and was perceived as an enemy of Justin's pro-Chalcedonian policy. Within days of Justin's accession the patriarch Ioannes II (518–520) had recognized Chalcedon. Prokopios may be alluding here to a pretext given out by Justin's regime for the execution.

16. Vitalianos rebelled against Emperor Anastasios in 513 and maintained his independence in Thrace. Justin attempted to win him over with titles and promises. Vitalianos was murdered in the palace in 520.

Unleashing the Hippodrome Fan-Clubs

7. The populace had long been divided into two rival fan-clubs, as I explained in an earlier book.[17] Justinian sided with one of them, the Blues, which he had enthusiastically supported also before his rise to power, and by doing so he shook up and confused everything. This was another way by which he brought the Roman state to its knees in defeat. [2] Of course, it was not *all* the Blues who agreed to go along with this man's plans, only the militant ones, [3] and even they, as the rot progressively worsened, were shown to be the most restrained of all people. [4] For they were given power to do worse than they actually did.[18] Nor did the militant partisans among the Greens remain quiet, of course. They too were perpetually committing crimes, to whatever degree lay within their power, though they were constantly being punished, one at a time. [5] Yet this very fact made them even more reckless every time, for when people are treated unjustly they tend to become desperate. [6] So as Justinian fanned the flames and openly agitated the Blues, the entire Roman Empire shook from side to side as if it had been hit by an earthquake or a flood, or as if each of its cities had been captured by an enemy army. [7] All things in all places convulsed and nothing was left standing. In the confusion that ensued, the laws were toppled to the ground and social order collapsed.[19]

[8] The first thing that the militants did was to invent a new hairstyle, cutting it in no way as other Romans did. [9] They did not touch the moustache or beard at all, wanting the hair to grow out as long as possible, as is the custom among the Persians. [10] But the hair on the head they cut in the front as far as the temples, while

17. The Blues and the Greens were imperially sponsored guilds (called "factions" in much of the scholarship) that organized entertainments and acclamations in many cities of the empire. They hired charioteers, mimes, and provided halftime shows, featuring dancers and "wild" beasts (see 1.11 above and 9.2–8 below). The population was divided in its loyalties between them but only about one thousand people were officially registered with each guild, including sons of the aristocracy. Their partisans wore distinctive, frightening clothes and hairstyles and engaged in hooliganism and criminal activity, and could even stir up sedition when government policy was unpopular, as happened in 532 in the so-called Nika riots (*Wars* 1.24, translated in related text 2).

18. See also 9.43–44 and 10.19 below.

19. Prokopios is here countering the regime's own propaganda, reflected in the *Chronicle* of Ioannes Malalas 17.18, that Justinian established peace and security in all the cities by requiring the punishment of all militants no matter their fan color.

letting it hang out long in the back for no particular reason, as among the Massagetai. So they called this look "Hunnish."[20] [11] Then, when it came to their dress, they all wanted to be stylish and each wore clothes that were too ostentatious for his class. [12] But then again they were in a position to acquire them at no cost to themselves. The part of the tunic that covers the arms they wrapped very tightly around the wrist but from there until the shoulders it hung loose like an immense flap. [13] And so whenever they waved their arms as they chanted in the theaters or hippodromes or shouted support for their favorites, as was their habit, this part of the tunic would flutter up and out and give any fool the impression that the bodies of these men were so strong and brawny that they had to cover themselves with such garments, not thinking that in fact a loosely hanging and mostly empty tunic reveals how scrawny the body underneath is. [14] Their cloaks and barbarian trousers along with most of their shoes were also classified as Hunnish by name and style.

[15] At night almost all the militants carried steel on them openly, but during the day they would conceal two-edged daggers strapped to their thighs under their cloaks. When night fell they would gather into gangs and mug their social betters both in the open marketplace and in the alleys, robbing any whom they met of clothes, belts, golden brooches, and anything else they had on them. [16] Some they killed after robbing, lest they report to anyone what had befallen them. [17] These crimes were detested by everyone, especially by those among the Blues who were not militants, given that they too were not spared. [18] And because of this most people wore only bronze belts and brooches from then on as well as clothes that were well beneath their station, for being stylish was no reason to lose your life. Even before the sun had set they all went home and hid there. [19] As this disorder dragged out and there was no response to the crimes on the part of the urban authorities, the audacity of these men continuously reached new heights.[21] [20] For it is in the nature of wrongdoing to grow without limit when it is given free rein; even when crimes are punished, that is hardly the end of them. [21] It is by their very nature that most people turn readily to crime.

20. According to the classical historian Herodotos, the Massagetai were a Skythian tribe. Prokopios and his contemporaries often used those classical ethnonyms to refer to barbarian peoples of their own time, in this case the Huns.

21. The audacity of the militants for Prokopios grows whether the authorities take no action (as here) or whether the authorities crack down on them (see 7.5 above).

[22] That is how things were for the Blues. As for the militants of the rival fan-club, some switched over to their side, desiring to join in the Blues' crimes and not have to face justice, while others fled and lay low in other lands. But many who were caught in the city were destroyed by their rivals or executed by the authorities. [23] Many young men now poured in to join the ranks of this team, men who had never before shown an interest in its activities but were drawn to it now by the prospect of power and insolence coupled with impunity. [24] There was not a single offense to which man has given a name that was not committed at this time and left unpunished. [25] The first thing that they did was to destroy the militants of the rival fan-club; then they moved on to killing even those who did not stand in their way. [26] Many even bribed them with money to strike against their own personal enemies, whom the militants would label Greens and swiftly murder, despite being utterly ignorant about who they were. [27] These things were not taking place in the dark or in secret but in the full light of day, in every part of the city, and even when by some chance prominent men were present and witnessed what was being done. [28] There was no need for them to cover up the crimes because they had no fear of punishment. To the contrary, there was even a kind of rivalry among them for putting on displays of strength and manliness, for example to see who could, with a single blow, kill any unarmed man whom they chanced upon in the streets. No one had any hope of surviving for long in these perilous circumstances of daily life. [29] Due to this state of terror, everyone suspected that death was lurking around the corner: no place seemed secure and no occasion seemed to offer a guarantee of safety, since people were being killed senselessly even in the most revered shrines and during religious celebrations. No trust remained among friends and relatives, for many were dying because their own people were treacherously scheming against them.

[30] Yet there was no official inquiry into these crimes. Ruin fell upon each person without warning, and no one avenged the fallen. [31] Laws and contracts had lost any power they may have derived from the security of social order, and all things were now governed by violence and so were fundamentally unstable. The state was virtually indistinguishable from a tyranny, not even a tyranny that was long set in its ways but one that kept changing every day, in the turmoil of a continuous renewal. [32] The magistrates' decisions seemed to issue from minds that were in shock, enslaved by the fear of a single man, while judges issued their verdicts in settling disputes between rival parties not based on what seemed to them to be just

and in accordance with the law but depending on whether each of the disputants was on good or bad terms with the militants. For any judge who disregarded their prior instructions about a case, the fine was death.

[33] In addition, many creditors were violently pressured to return notes of receipt to their debtors, having collected nothing of what was owed, and many were required against their will to set their servants free. [34] It is even said that some women were compelled by their own slaves to do many things that they did not want to do. [35] It had reached the point where the sons of prominent men, who would hang out with these young men, were forcing their fathers to do many things against their will, particularly to hand over their money to them. [36] Conversely, many boys were forced against their will into unholy sexual acts with the militants—with their fathers' complicity. [37] The very same thing befell women who were living with their husbands. It is said that one woman wearing opulent attire was sailing in the company of her husband to one of the suburbs on the opposite continent.[22] They were boarded during the crossing by some of the militants who yanked her away from her husband after threatening him and hauled her over to their skiff. But as she was being transferred to the skiff with the young men, she whispered to her husband to take courage and fear not that anything vulgar would befall her. [38] No outrage would be done upon her body. And while the husband was looking upon her in great sorrow, she threw her body into the sea and immediately disappeared from among men.

[39] Such, then, were the outrageous crimes that these militants committed at that time in Byzantion. And yet, in fact, these things distressed their victims less than the crimes that Justinian himself was committing against the state, since the greatest part of the anguish experienced by those who have been severely victimized by criminals in times of incipient social disorder is alleviated by the firm expectation that the laws and the authorities will always inflict punishment. [40] For people find the present more tolerable and easy when they are hopeful for the future, but when they are assaulted by the established government of the state itself it is reasonable that they should be all the more distressed by what they are suffering and always fall into despair because they do not expect justice to come to their aid. [41] Justinian was guilty not only because he lacked the slightest inclination to stand by the victims in these cases but because

22. I.e., Asia, so across the Bosporus.

he had no qualms about being openly known as the militants' patron. [42] He handed over large sums of money to these young men and kept many of them by his side, promoting some of them to magistracies and handing out other court titles.

Justinian's Governance and Physical Appearance

8. These things were taking place in Byzantion and every city. For the evil began there and, like any other disease, spread to every corner of the Roman Empire. [2] The crimes, however, were of no concern whatever to the emperor,[23] as the man was unaware of what was going on around him, even though he was constantly witnessing such scenes in the hippodrome. [3] He was extraordinarily dumb and more like a stupid donkey than anything, following whoever pulled on his reins, waving his ears about.

[4] Justinian was responsible for these things, and threw everything else into confusion as well. As soon as he succeeded to his uncle's position,[24] he rushed to squander the public funds for no other reason than that he was now their master, but he lacked a rationale for this spending. [5] The Huns whom he kept encountering in his foreign policy he paid handsomely on the state's behalf, which resulted in multiple raids being made against Roman lands. [6] For once these barbarians had tasted the wealth of the Romans, they could no longer stay off the road that led here.[25] [7] He also poured many funds into constructions along the coasts in an attempt to check, through brute force, the constant surging of the waves. [8] By piling up blocks he kept moving forward from the coast, competing against the onrush of the ocean as though the power of his money could rival the strength of the sea.[26] [9] He gathered to himself the private wealth of all Romans from every part of the world,

23. We are still under Justin I. For his stupidity, see also 9.50 below.

24. In 527.

25. Prokopios criticized Justinian for paying barbarians (especially those north of the Danube) *not* to raid Roman territory, because this merely induced them to raid it even more in order to qualify for these subsidies, in addition to being a shameful policy of appeasement for a state that had an army and (for Prokopios) a sense of pride. For more detail, see 11.5–11 and 19.13–17 below, and in Books 8–9 of the *Wars* (e.g., 8.5.16–17, 8.18.19). Some modern historians defend this policy through a cost-benefit analysis.

26. Prokopios documents Justinian's building programs in the *Buildings*, albeit from a panegyrical point of view, especially 1.5–9 and 1.11 for his coastal constructions by Constantinople.

accusing some of them of this crime or that even if it had not actually been committed by anyone, while twisting the intentions of others to make it seem as though they had donated their money to him. [10] Many who were convicted of murder and other like crimes could, by turning over their entire property to him, escape without paying the just penalty that they owed.[27] [11] Still others who happened at the time to be laying claim, without justification, to lands that belonged to their neighbors and were making no progress in arbitration against their opponents because they had no legal case, finagled themselves out of the matter by simply making a gift to the emperor of the very properties that were in dispute. In this way, through a favor that cost them nothing they were introduced to the man and through a most unlawful method prevailed over their opponents in the eyes of the law.

[12] I think that now would also be a good time to give a sense of the man's physical appearance. He was neither tall nor too short, but of medium height, not thin at all but slightly fleshy. His face was round and not unshapely. He retained a ruddy complexion even after two days of fasting.[28] [13] If I had to capture his whole appearance in one image I would say that he was most similar to Domitian, the son of Vespasian, whose foul character the Romans so enjoyed that their rage against him, they decided, was not satisfied even when they had hacked him into pieces, so that the Senate passed a decree that the name of this emperor should never again be carved in an inscription and no image of him should be allowed to survive. [14] In fact, one can see that this name alone has been chiseled out of all the inscriptions in Rome as well as out of any place where it happened to be written, and this was done in such a way that it left the words around it intact.[29] It seems that no image of him survives in the Roman Empire,[30] except for a single one of bronze, whose story is as follows. [15] Domitian had a wife, a

27. I.e., capital punishment.

28. For the possible significance of this complexion, see the Introduction, p. xxxviii.

29. Historians call this erasure of memory *damnatio memoriae*. Titus Flavius Domitianus (r. 81–96) was hated by the Senate by the end of his reign and suffered this fate after he was stabbed to death. Suetonius says that he had a ruddy complexion and unassuming expression. Prokopios had visited Rome in the company of Belisarios and had experienced the siege of 536–538. His account of the war in Italy reveals an interest in Roman antiquities.

30. This may sound like an exaggeration, but it may have been difficult for anyone in the sixth century to find a bust of Domitian and correctly identify it, there being no iconographic manuals.

dignified and otherwise discreet woman who had never done anything bad to anyone, nor were any of her husband's actions to her liking.[31] [16] As she was well loved, the Senate summoned her and asked her if there was anything it could do for her now. [17] She begged for one thing only, namely to be given Domitian's body for burial and to be allowed to set up one bronze statue in his honor, wherever she designated. [18] And the Senate allowed it. The woman's intention was to leave for posterity a memorial of the inhumanity of those who had butchered her husband, and so she devised the following. [19] She gathered up all the carvings of Domitian's flesh, fitted them together by placing each in its exact position in relation to the others, and then sewed up the whole body. She showed it to the sculptors and bid them to produce a bronze imitation of the fate that befell her husband. [20] The craftsmen quickly made the image, which she took and set up on the road that leads up to the Capitoline, on the right-hand side as you go up from the forum. From that time on it has depicted both the appearance and the fate of Domitian. [21] One could imagine that the body and the very appearance itself of Justinian as well as the expressions of his face were perfectly mirrored in this statue.[32]

[22] That is what he looked like. I could not, however, accurately describe his character. This man was both prone to evil and simultaneously easy to lead around by the nose, a type that they called a "fool and villain in one." On the one hand, he himself never spoke the truth to anyone in his presence, always saying and doing everything with treacherous intent; yet at the same time he was easy prey for those who wished to deceive him. [23] An unusual kind of mixture had taken place within him, a fusion of foolishness and malice. Perhaps this was what one of the Aristotelian philosophers was referring to in past times when he said that the most opposite qualities are found together in the nature of man just as in the blending of colors. [24] But I am writing here about lofty matters that I have

31. Domitian's wife, Domitia Longina (daughter of Nero's general Gnaeus Domitius Corbulo), is said by some sources to have been party to the plots against her husband, but this may be mere insinuation; she appears to have been devoted to his memory after his death.

32. Domitian was not hacked to pieces but stabbed to death, and his body was duly cremated by his nurse Phyllis. It is not clear what Prokopios saw in Rome and what he was told about it, but his use of this macabre image indicates what fate he believed Justinian should suffer. Moreover, it makes his readers think of the living emperor as a ghoul, reinforcing the theme of his demonic nature (see below).

not been able to master.[33] This emperor, then, was ironic in speech, treacherous in his intentions, a hypocrite, secretly vindictive, two-faced, a formidable man in his own way and highly accomplished at hiding his true opinion. When he cried it was not as an expression of genuine joy or sorrow at anything but a strategy to serve the needs of the moment. He was always lying but his lies were prepared. Indeed, he ratified his agreements with his signature and the most dread oaths, even when dealing with his own subjects. [25] But he would immediately depart from what had been agreed on and sworn to, like the most contemptible of slaves who, fearing torture, confess to things that they had denied under oath. [26] He was unreliable as an ally, treacherous as an enemy, craving murder and money like an ardent lover, stirring up strife and obsessively innovating, easily persuaded to commit evil but rejecting all counsel for the good, eager to devise base plans and implement them,[34] a man whose ears were offended by the very mention of the good—[27] how could words, therefore, ever suffice to describe Justinian's character? All the vices I have described along with other, even worse ones that he had seemed to exceed human capacity; it was as though nature had removed every inclination to do wrong from other people and deposited them all together into the soul of this man.

[28] He was, in addition to all that, quite receptive to slander and eager to inflict punishment. He never once decided a matter by investigating the facts but made his decision known as soon as he had heard the slanderer. [29] He had no qualms about writing orders for the sacking of villages, the burning of cities, and the enslavement of entire nations, and all for no good reason. [30] So that if one wanted to weigh these things against everything that has befallen the Romans from the beginning, he would discover, it seems to me, that more people have been slaughtered by this one man than in all of past history put together. [31] As for the money of others, he showed no hesitation in quietly appropriating it. And when he reached out to take possession of things that did not belong to him, he did not even bother to screen what he was doing behind a pretext of legality. Yet once it was his, he was quite capable of squandering it through

33. Prokopios had some familiarity with philosophy, especially political philosophy, but disclaims knowledge of more lofty fields: "I am not talking about intelligible or intellectual matters or other such invisible things, but about rivers and lands" (*Wars* 8.6.9–10).

34. An allusion to Thucydides, *History* 1.70.3; see also 13.33 below and *Wars* 3.9.25.

wasteful generosity and by giving it away to the barbarians, even though there was no good reason to do so. [32] In sum, neither did he himself ever have any money nor would he allow anyone else to have it either, as if the problem was not that he was driven by love of money but rather by envy of those who had it. [33] Prosperity, then, migrated out of the land of the Romans because of him, while he inaugurated an era of poverty for all.

Theodora's Background

9. All that I am able to say about Justinian's character is as I have stated above. As for the woman he married, I will now disclose her origins and the manner of her upbringing as well as how she destroyed the Roman state root and branch after marrying this man.

[2] There was a certain Akakios in Byzantion who kept the amphitheater beasts for the Green fan-club, his position being what they call the keeper of the bears.[35] [3] This man died of illness while Anastasios was emperor and left behind him three children, all girls: Komito, Theodora, and Anastasia, of whom the eldest was not yet seven years old.[36] [4] His widow, facing hardship, married another man and their arrangement was that he would help her in the future to provide for the household and carry on her husband's job. [5] But the dancing-master of the Greens, a certain Asterios, was bribed by another man to remove these two from that position and, without making a fuss, appoint in their place the man who gave him the bribe. For the dancing-masters had the authority to arrange such appointments as they saw fit.[37] [6] So when the woman saw that the entire populace had gathered in the hippodrome, she placed garlands on her children's heads and in their hands and made them sit as suppliants. [7] But the Greens were in no way inclined to accept the supplication. The Blues, however, appointed the woman and her daughters to the equivalent position on their side, as their keeper of the beasts had recently died as well.

35. For the fan-clubs, see note 17 above. Little is known about the location of the amphitheater for wild beast shows in Constantinople (the *kynegion* or *kynegesion*) or the forms that those games took at this time.

36. Komito married the general Sittas in 528 (so after Theodora's marriage to Justinian).

37. They seem to have stood high in the hierarchy of the fan-clubs and to have been in charge of the practical organization of entertainments.

[8] When these children reached puberty, their mother immediately put them on the stage in that place, for they were beautiful to behold. They did not all enter the profession at the same time, but each whenever her mother deemed her suitably attractive. [9] The first, Komito, was already a great success among the call girls of her age. But the second, Theodora, covered by a loose dress with sleeves, the kind that slaves wear, would follow her sister and serve her in many ways but especially by always carrying around on her shoulders the base upon which her sister perched before her audiences. [10] At this time Theodora was hardly ripe enough to sleep with a man or to have sex with him in the way that a woman should. So she would offer herself to certain poor wretches who performed that disgusting act on her that some men do with other men. She did it even with slaves who were attending their owners at the theater and who took the opportunity to step aside for a moment and practice this pestilence. And so she spent much time selling herself in this way, specializing in that unnatural service of the body.

[11] As soon as she reached puberty and was ripe enough, she joined the women on the stage and immediately became a call girl in her own right. She belonged to the lowest rank, which in the old days they called "basic infantry."[38] [12] For she had no skill with the *aulos*,[39] nor could she sing or even perform in the dance troupe: all she had to offer to passing customers was her youth, and she put her whole body to work for them. [13] Later she took up full-time with the mimes in the theater, taking part in their performances by providing backup vulgarity for the comedians. For she had an especially quick and biting wit, and soon became a star feature of the show. [14] There was no shame at all in her, and no one ever saw her embarrassed. She would provide shameful services without the slightest hesitation and was of such a sort that if someone slapped her or even punched her full in the face she would crack a joke about it and then burst out laughing. She would strip down in front for any passers-by and then in back as well, revealing in the nude those parts which custom forbids to be shown to men. [15] She would joke with her lovers lying around in bed with them, and, by toying with new

38. In ancient comedy, this designated the most common type of prostitute. This section on the early career of Theodora is appropriately full of language taken from the comedians.

39. The *aulos* was a wind instrument played by skilled courtesans at the dinner parties of the upper classes (the "flute-girls" of classical literature).

sexual techniques, constantly managed to arouse the souls of those who were debauched. Nor did she wait for her customers to make the first pass at her; quite the contrary, she herself tempted all who came along, flirting and suggestively shaking her hips, especially if they were beardless youths. [16] Never has there been a person so enslaved to lust in all its forms. She often went to the potluck dinner parties in the company of ten young escorts, or even more than that, all at the peak of their physical prowess and skilled at screwing, and she would bed down with her fellow diners in groups all night long. And when all were exhausted from doing this, she would turn to their servants, all thirty of them if that's how many there were, and couple with each of them separately—but even this would not satisfy her lust.

[17] One time when she went to the house of a notable to entertain during drinks, they say that when the eyes of all the diners were upon her she mounted the frame of the couch by their feet and unceremoniously lifted up her clothes right there and then,[40] not caring in the least that she was making a spectacle of her shamelessness. [18] Even though she put three of her orifices to work she would impatiently reproach Nature for not making the holes in her nipples bigger than they were so that she could devise additional sexual positions involving them as well.[41] [19] She was often pregnant, but by using almost all known techniques she could induce immediate abortions.[42]

[20] Often in the theater too, and with the entire populace as her audience, she would strip and stand naked at the very center of attention, having only a loincloth about her genitals and groin—not that she would have been ashamed to flaunt those before the whole city too, but only because it was not permitted for anyone to be entirely naked in the theater, that is without a loincloth about the groin. Wearing this outfit, then, she would lie down on her back and spread herself out on the floor [21] whereupon certain menials, who were hired to do this very job, would sprinkle barley grains all over her genitals. Then the geese, which were trained for this purpose, pecked them off one at a time with their beaks and ate them. [22]

40. Each guest probably still reclined on a couch; Theodora presumably mounted the lower end of the couch, where the guest's feet were, and there performed a form of lap dance.

41. For this passage, see the Introduction, p. liv.

42. In one case, at least, these techniques did not work; see 17.16 below.

When she stood up again not only was she not blushing with shame but seemed rather to be proud of this performance.[43] For she was not just shameless: she was also more accomplished than anyone else at devising shameless acts. [23] Often she would take her clothes off and stand in the middle of the stage by the mimes, alternately bending backwards or drawing attention to her rear, advertising her special brand of gymnastics both to those who had more intimate knowledge of it and to those who did not—yet. [24] Thus did she abuse her own body licentiously, making it seem that she had genitals not in the place where nature ordained for all other women, but in her face! [25] All who were intimate with her were instantly known, by that very fact, to be men who did not have sex according to the laws of nature, while any decent men who came across her in the marketplace would turn back and beat a hasty retreat, lest they should touch a corner of that person's clothes and feel that they had been tainted by the pollution. [26] Those who saw her, especially early in the morning, regarded her as an ill omen. Yet she was in the habit of constantly lashing out viciously, like a scorpion, against her fellow actresses, for she was mad with envy.

[27] When Hekebolos, a man from Tyre, was later appointed to govern the Pentapolis,[44] she followed in order to serve him in the most shameful things. But she offended the man in some way and was thrown out forthwith.[45] And so it came to pass that she was destitute, lacking even necessities which she obtained from then on in her usual manner, by prostituting her body. [28] First she went to Alexandria and then, after touring the entire East, she returned to Byzantion, plying her trade in each city on the way—God would show no mercy upon the man who specified the name of that trade.[46] It was as though some evil force had decreed that no place should be unacquainted with Theodora's lechery.

43. It is possible that Theodora was acting out a version of the story of Leda and the swan (Leda was impregnated by Zeus in the form of a swan; she laid an egg from which Helen was hatched). Juvenal attests that the story of Leda was being pantomimed in c. 100—by a male actor (*Satire* 6.63). Bawdy versions of mythological tales were popular on the stage in late antiquity too. Leda and the swan appear often in late antique Egyptian funerary sculpture.

44. A province in modern Libya. This was probably near the beginning of Justin's reign.

45. The story of Hekebolos continues at 12.30 below.

46. Could Prokopios possibly be more explicit than he has been already?

Taming the Hippodrome Fan-Clubs

[29] Such, then, was the woman's origin and upbringing, which became infamous among common women and all people generally. [30] Soon after she arrived at Byzantion, Justinian was smitten by an extraordinary passion for her. At first he treated her only as a mistress, even though he raised her to the patrician rank. [31] This enabled Theodora to immediately acquire extraordinary power and vast amounts of money. For nothing could please him more—as happens to men who are infatuated—than to grant his mistress every favor and to give her all his money. [32] The state itself became fuel for the fire of his passion. With her at his side he ruined the people even more, not only there but in every part of the Roman Empire. [33] As both of them had long been fans of the Blue fan-club, they gave much power over the management of public affairs to the militants. [34] After a long time, however, most of this evil was mitigated, in the following way.[47]

[35] It so happened that Justinian was ill for many days and in this illness came into such danger that it was even said that he had died.[48] Meanwhile, the militants were causing their usual trouble, doing all the things that I explained above, and they killed a certain Hypatios, a man who was not undistinguished, in full daylight inside the church of Hagia Sophia.[49] [36] When this evil deed was committed, the disturbances it caused were reported to the emperor. Now each of his courtiers, taking advantage of Justinian's absence, made a point of magnifying the outrage of what had been done, itemizing from the beginning everything that had taken place. [37] The emperor then ordered the urban prefect to exact punishment for all that had been committed. This man was named Theodotos, the one whose nickname was the Pumpkin. [38] He investigated everything thoroughly and arrested many of the wrongdoers, whom he executed as the law required. But many others slipped away and saved themselves. [39] [. . .][50] Yet when Justinian recovered suddenly and against expectation, he made it his top priority to kill Theodotos as a poisoner and a magician. [40] But as he lacked a pretext for moving

47. The following story is not about Theodora at all.

48. This was in 523, during the reign of Justin.

49. This was the original church of Hagia Sophia that burned down in the Nika riots of 532 (*Wars* 1.24; translated in related text 2) and was rebuilt by Justinian.

50. One line of the text is too corrupt to translate meaningfully here.

against the man to destroy him, he cruelly tortured some of his friends and forced them to give preposterously false testimony against him. [41] And while everyone else got out of his way and quietly endured their distress at the plot against Theodotos, Proklos alone, who held the office that is called *quaestor*, declared in his legal opinion that the man was innocent of the charge and so not deserving of death.[51] [42] Therefore the emperor decreed that Theodotos be conveyed to Jerusalem. When the latter realized that some men had arrived there to kill him, he hid in the sanctuary for the rest of his days, and died living in this way.[52]

[43] That, then, was what happened to Theodotos. As for the militants, from that time on they became the most self-controlled of all people. [44] They no longer had the nerve to commit the same kinds of crimes as before, though they now had greater license to live lawlessly and with impunity.[53] [45] And here is the proof. When a few of them later dared to take up their old ways, no punishment at all was visited upon them. [46] For those who were at any time invested with the authority to impose punishment granted immunity to the men committing these terrible wrongs, and by this concession incited them to transgress against the laws.

The Marriage of Justinian and Theodora

[47] For as long as the empress still lived,[54] there was no way that Justinian could make Theodora his lawfully wedded wife. In this alone did the empress oppose him, though she objected to nothing else that he did. [48] The woman was utterly lacking in subtlety and guile, being a peasant of barbarian stock, as I stated.[55] [49] She did not exercise any authority and remained throughout utterly without experience in political affairs. She did not even keep her own proper name when she entered the palace, for it was quite ridiculous, and changed it to Euphemia.[56] Some time later it happened that

51. For Proklos, see also 6.13 above.

52. He probably sought refuge in the Church of the Resurrection (Holy Sepulcher).

53. See also 7.3–4 above and 10.19 below.

54. I.e., Justin's empress Lupicina/Euphemia.

55. See 6.17 above.

56. A literal "euphemism" of a name. It belonged to a popular saint and to the daughter of the eastern emperor Markianos (450–457) who married the western emperor Anthemius (r. 467–472) and reigned briefly when Lupicina was young.

she died.[57] [50] Justin was at the outer reaches of old age and very senile now, causing laughter in his subjects. Everyone had contempt for him because he was not aware of anything that was going on and they paid him no attention.[58] Justinian, on the other hand, they courted in great fear for, by always shaking and stirring things up, he was throwing the whole state into a continuous turmoil.[59] [51] It was then that he set into motion his plan for becoming engaged to Theodora. As it was impossible for anyone who had reached the rank of senator to marry a prostitute (this being prohibited from the earliest times by the most ancient of laws),[60] he forced the emperor to annul those laws with another law, and so afterward he lived with Theodora as his lawful wife, effectively making it feasible for anyone else to marry a prostitute.[61] He then illegitimately mounted the imperial throne, offering a fabricated pretext to conceal the high-handedness of his action; [52] namely, he was proclaimed emperor of the Romans alongside his uncle by all the leading men, who were, however, coerced by overwhelming fear to vote in favor.[62] [53] Justinian and Theodora, therefore, effectively succeeded to the imperial position three days before the Easter celebration, at a time when it is not permitted to greet one's friends or even wish them peace.[63] [54] Not many days later Justin died of illness; he had reigned for

57. The date of her death is unknown.

58. For Justin's stupidity, see also 8.2–3 above.

59. An allusion to Aristophanes, *Peace* 320 and *Knights* 692.

60. E.g., *Digest* 23.2.44 (Paulus): "The *lex Julia* [*de maritandis ordinibus*, passed by Augustus in 18 BC] provides that: 'A Senator, his son, or his grandson, or his great-grandson by his son shall not knowingly or fraudulently become betrothed to or marry a freedwoman, or a woman who is or has been an actress or whose father or mother are or have been actors.'" Also *Codex Iustinianus* 5.27.1 (of AD 336); 5.5.7.2 (of AD 454).

61. For the Herodotean model of the narrative here, see the Introduction, p. xxxvi. The "other law" (probably a pun by Prokopios) is *Codex Iustinianus* 5.4.23; for a translation, see related text 1.

62. In theory, an emperor had to be approved by the Senate, the army, and the people, though in practice the choice was often (though not always) made behind closed doors and merely ratified by those "constitutional" elements in a ceremonial way. An emperor could designate a successor, and so Justinian was crowned coemperor four months before Justin died. Prokopios' implication that he was not freely chosen by the leading men of the state is therefore disingenuous.

63. Justinian was proclaimed Augustus by Justin on 1 April 527 in the palace. He was crowned by the patriarch three days later on Easter, 4 April. Easter celebrates the Resurrection of Christ three days after the Crucifixion, so the day of Justinian's proclamation was a day of mourning. "Peace be unto you" was a Christian salutation (Luke 24.36, spoken by the risen Christ).

nine years.[64] So now Justinian alone, together with Theodora of course, held the throne.

10. Thus Theodora, who was born, raised, and educated as I have stated, rose to the imperial rank without encountering any obstacles. [2] The thought never occurred to her husband that his choice was an outrage, given that it was possible for him to have selected a spouse from the whole of the Roman Empire, to have married a woman who was the most well-born among all women and had been raised outside the public gaze, who had learned the ways of modesty and lived discreetly; moreover, she could have been exceedingly beautiful and still a virgin and even, as they say, with perky breasts. [3] But no, he had to take for his own the common stain of all mankind and was not put off by any of the facts that I have stated. He took as his wife a woman adorned with many great abominations, to say nothing of the infanticide that she had regularly practiced in her voluntary abortions. I do not think it necessary to say anything else about the man's character. [4] This marriage suffices to highlight all the many vices of his soul: it became the interpreter, witness, and chronicler of his personality. [5] Whoever disregards the shame of past deeds and is unconcerned if he is known as a disgusting character, well, every path of lawlessness will be open to such a man. As if the word "shamelessness" were written prominently on his forehead, he casually and unscrupulously advances to the most abominable actions.

[6] Nor, indeed, did a single member of the Senate, seeing the state tying itself to this smear of a woman, decide to disapprove the action and denounce it, though all of them would be prostrating themselves before her as if she were a goddess. [7] Nor did any priest make known his displeasure, despite the fact that they would all be addressing her as Mistress.[65] [8] And the populace, who used to be her audience, immediately now and with upturned hands as though in prayer disgracefully demanded both to be in fact, and to be called, her slave. [9] Nor did any soldier rise up in fury now that he would have to be enduring the dangers of campaigning—on behalf of the interests of Theodora. Nor did any other person challenge her; rather, all of them passively let this pollution happen in the belief, I suppose, that it was simply their ordained fate, as though Chance had made a display of her power. In governing all human matters, she neither cares whether what happens is appropriate nor

64. Justin I died on 1 August 527.

65. For the forms of address on which Justinian and Theodora insisted, see 30.25–26 below.

whether it seems to make any kind of sense to people. [10] Suddenly, exercising her irrational power, she will lift someone up to the pinnacle of good fortune who had previously seemed to be entangled in a multitude of troubles. But now she opposes him in nothing that he undertakes; in fact, he is carried along by every opportune contrivance to the goal that she has ordained for him while all men stand aside or withdraw as Chance has her way. But let these matters hold in whatever way pleases God, and let us speak of them accordingly.[66]

[11] Theodora was beautiful of face and otherwise graceful, but too short and sallow, yet not excessively so; one could rather call her pale.[67] Her glance was swift and always intense. [12] As for her life in the theater, the whole of eternity would not suffice to recount even the majority of it. But the few incidents that I selected above should suffice to give future generations a complete picture of the woman's way of life.

Justinian and Theodora Unanimously Sow Dissension

[13] Now we must, in brief, divulge what she and her husband did, for the two of them did nothing independently of each other while they lived together. [14] For a long time it was believed by everyone that their thoughts and policies were diametrically opposed to each other but later it was recognized that this illusion was deliberately crafted by the two of them so as to prevent their subjects from agreeing among themselves to rise up against them, and so to ensure that every opinion about them differed from the others.

[15] The first thing they did was to set the Christians against each other and divided them all into rival fan-clubs by pretending to take opposite paths in the controversies, as I will explain shortly.[68] [16]

66. For Prokopios' view of God and chance (or fortune), see notes 63 and 65 in Part I.

67. At *Buildings* 1.11.8, Prokopios states that it would be entirely impossible to express her beauty with words or to capture it in a statue.

68. Prokopios is alluding to the major theological controversy of his time, namely between those who accepted and those who rejected the Council of Chalcedon (451), especially regarding the precise way in which the human and the divine natures came together in the person of Christ. At *Wars* 5.3.5–9, Prokopios makes clear that he himself regarded these controversies as idiotic. Unless he is referring to 27.13 below, he may be alluding here to the *Ecclesiastical History* of this period that he planned but apparently never wrote (see the Introduction, p. xxvii). The late sixth-century ecclesiastical historian Euagrios also suspected that Justinian and Theodora played both sides of the religious

Then they kept the militants divided too. She put on that she supported the Blues with all her might and by authorizing them to move against their rival militants she enabled them to flout social order in their criminal activities and cruel violence. [17] He, on the other hand, made out that he was offended at all this and even furious but only—so the act went—in secret, as if he were unable to oppose his wife directly. Often they would exchange roles and make as if the balance of power between them was reversed. [18] So *he* would now demand that the Blues be punished as criminals while she would throw a fake fit and complain, as she put it, because she had to submit unwillingly to her husband's wishes. [19] Yet the militants of the Blues, as I said above, seemed to be the most self-controlled, for they did not deem it right to attack their neighbors as fiercely as was possible for them.[69] In legal disputes, each of the pair seemed to be supporting a different side, but the one of them who sided with the unjust case invariably won. In this way they managed to plunder as much money from the disputants as possible.[70] [20] In addition, this emperor would enroll many men among his close associates and elevate them to positions of power from where they could violate the rights of others and offend against the state in whatever way they wished; but then, when they were perceived to have acquired great riches, they immediately ran afoul of Theodora, as if they had offended her in some matter. [21] At first he would not hesitate to claim them as his own and give them his full support, but later he put aside his goodwill for these people and suddenly became quite unpredictable as their patron. [22] And while she worked her ruin on them, he would pretend to perceive nothing of what was happening but would then welcome their entire property as it fell into his grasp through this shameless mode of acquisition. [23] In these schemes they were always working together, but in public they would pretend to disagree with each other in order to divide their subjects and solidify their hold on the throne they had usurped.

---

debate (*Ecclesiastical History* 4.10); he may have known *The Secret History* (see the Introduction, p. lvii). See also 13.9 and 14.8 below.

69. See 7.3–4 and 9.43–44 above for the Blues' self-control.

70. For how this might have worked, see 8.10–11 below.

The Tyranny of Justinian: Botched Foreign Policy and Religious Persecution

11. When Justinian rose to the throne, he quickly managed to throw everything into confusion. For he kept introducing into public life things that had previously been forbidden by law while abolishing firm and established customs all at once. It was as though he had donned the aspect of an emperor for the sole purpose of mutating everything and giving it a different aspect. [2] He abolished existing offices and invented nonexisting ones with which to govern public affairs.[71] He did the same with the laws and the military rolls, not because he was yielding to what was just or compelled to do so by the public interest, but simply in order to innovate in all fields and have everything named after himself. And if there was something that he proved unable to transform instantly, he still renamed it after himself.[72]

[3] He never felt satisfied with the amount of money he had confiscated or the number of people he had killed. No sooner had he plundered to their ruin a multitude of the households of prosperous men than he was casting around for more because he had instantly squandered the loot from his previous victims to gratify some barbarian tribe or for his stupid buildings. [4] And having caused the death of myriads of people for no good reason, he plotted next how to do the same to an even greater number. [5] As the Romans were at peace with all people he could not indulge his lust for murder that way, so he made all the barbarians fight among themselves. For no cause at all he summoned the chiefs of the Huns and gave them huge sums of money, claiming that this absurd act of ostentation in fact secured their alliance. It was said that he began to do this already

71. For the abolition of the consulship, see 26.15 below; for the invention of offices, see 20.7–12 below.

72. In 537, Justinian decreed that all documents be dated by his regnal year in addition to consular and indiction dates (*Novella* 47). First-year law students were henceforth to be called *Iustiniani novi* (*Digest: Constitutio omnem* 2). Other things named after him included the *Codex Iustinianus*; the city of *Iustiniana Prima* (which he built near his native village of Taurision) as well as over twenty other towns renamed *Ioustinianopolis* or *Iustiniana* (many are mentioned in the *Buildings*); the titles of officials, provinces, and ecclesiastical dioceses were changed to accommodate his name (e.g., to *praetor Iustinianus*, *Carthago Iustiniana*) and military units recruited from among barbarians were named *Iustiniani Vandali* (*Wars* 4.14.17), *Numidae Iustiniani*, *Scythai Iustiniani*, and *Bis electi Iustiniani* (attested on papyri), *Perso-Iustiniani* (attested on an inscription), etc.

during Justin's reign.[73] [6] These chiefs, having received a bounty in cash, would then send some of their fellow chieftains and their followers with instructions to overrun the lands of this emperor with sudden raids so that they too could be in a position to sell peace to a man who seemed to want to buy it for no particular reason. [7] So they were subjugating the Roman empire while at the same time being nothing less than in the emperor's employ. And others quickly followed them in this business of plundering the unhappy Romans in order to receive, in addition to their loot, the emperor's generous largesse as a prize for their raid. [8] Thus it came about, in brief, that all of them were taking turns at ravaging and plundering everything all at once, without letting up for any season of the year. [9] For these barbarians have whole gangs of chieftains and the war would pass from one to the next because of this emperor's irrational prodigality. There was no way to get out of it, for it had become a vicious circle. [10] As a result there was not a field, mountain, cave, or other part of Roman land that remained unplundered at this time, and it happened that some places were captured more than five times. [11] Yet these things, along with everything that was done by the Medes, Saracens, Slavs, Antai, and the other barbarians, have been recounted by me in the earlier books.[74] As I said at the beginning of this book, however, my aim here is to state the causes of those events.[75]

[12] And even though he had given Chosroes a huge sum of *kentenaria* in order to secure peace, he himself became the chief cause of breaking the truce by his bullheaded and senseless policy of trying to win over Alamoundaros and the Huns, who were already allies of the Persians, all of which, I believe, is explained without concealment in my book on this subject.[76] [13] Yet while he was

73. For Prokopios' criticism of the policy of buying peace, see 8.5–6 above and note 25.

74. By Medes Prokopios means Persians. For annual payments to the Saracens, see *Wars* 2.10.23. The Slavs and the Antai make their first appearances on the stage of Roman history at this time. Prokopios describes their raids mostly in Book 7 of the *Wars*.

75. See 1.3 above.

76. In 532, Persians and Romans signed the so-called Eternal Peace, which lasted until 540, when Chosroes invaded Syria and captured Antioch and other cities. This certainly made him the main aggressor, but in the *Wars* Prokopios insinuates that Justinian had provoked him by trying to win over Persian allies (2.1.12–15, 2.3.47, 2.4.20, 2.10.16). Justinian had paid 110 *kentenaria* to secure the peace (*Wars* 1.22.4), i.e., 792,000 coins (see the Glossary). Alamoundaros (al-

igniting and fanning the evil flames of war for the Romans and the violence of the fan-clubs, he never lost sight of his ultimate goal, namely to drench the earth with as much human blood as his many schemes could spill and to steal as much money as possible. And so he devised the following way to murder even more of his subjects.

[14] Throughout the Roman empire there are many Christian doctrines that have been officially condemned and which they are accustomed to call "heresies," for example those of the Montanists and the Sabbatians and all the others by which human judgment is misled.[77] [15] All of them he ordered to renounce their traditional beliefs, threatening those who would disobey with many legal punishments, in particular that they would no longer enjoy the right to bequeath their property to their children and relatives.[78] [16] Now it happens that the churches of these so-called heretics, and especially those that followed the doctrine of Areios,[79] possessed unheard-of riches. [17] Not the entire Senate itself nor any other major group within the Roman Empire could be compared to these churches when it came to wealth. [18] For they had treasures of gold and silver ornamented with precious stones beyond anyone's power to describe or count; they owned houses and villages in huge

---

Mundhir, r. 505–554) was the ruler of the Lakhmid Arabs, allies of the Persians who raided Roman territory in times of war.

77. In the pre-Christian empire, *heresy* referred to the choice that one made among a variety of philosophical positions and, by extension, to the schools that professed those positions (e.g., the Stoics, the Platonists, etc.). Christians used the term to designate *false* theological views held by other Christians (the opposite being *orthodoxy*). These terms were obviously relative, depending on who held power within the Church at any time. Prokopios probably considered all such views misleading or false (*Wars* 5.3.5–9). Montanos preached an ascetic, ecstatic brand of Christianity in the late second century; his followers survived in Asia Minor into the eighth century. Sabbatios was a Novatian priest in late-fourth-century Constantinople who decided to celebrate Easter on the Jewish calendar (the Novatians constituted a rigorous schismatic, but not heretical, Church). His followers survived into the seventh century.

78. For Justinian's laws against heretics, imposing a variety of social and economic sanctions, see *Codex Iustinianus* 1.5.12–22; *Novellae* 37, 42, 45, 109, 115.3.14, 131.14, and 132.

79. Anyone who believed that the Son (Christ) was not of the same substance (*ousia*) as God the Father could be labeled an Arian. This version of Christianity had enjoyed considerable imperial support in the fourth century before it was finally condemned at the Council of Constantinople in 381. But there were still separate Arian churches in Constantinople. Most barbarian peoples who converted in the fourth century (e.g., the Goths) were also Arians.

numbers, much land in all parts of the world, and every kind of wealth one can imagine that actually exists and has a name among all of mankind. This was because not one of the emperors who reigned in the past had yet disturbed their property. [19] In fact, a large number of people, including many who were orthodox, derived their entire livelihood by working for these sects, and justified it by saying that they were only doing their job. [20] So, to begin with, by confiscating the assets of these churches the emperor Justinian deprived them suddenly of all their money, with the result that many people were henceforth cut off from their livelihood. [21] Many men soon began to visit every region of the empire and to force everyone whom they met to abandon his ancestral faith.[80] [22] But this struck peasants in particular as irreligious and they unanimously decided to resist the men who were preaching these orders. [23] Consequently many of them were killed by the soldiers while many others actually killed themselves, stupidly thinking this was a religious act. But the majority abandoned their ancestral lands and fled. The Montanists, however, who lived in Phrygia, shut themselves in their own churches, which they then set on fire, perishing along with them for no good reason. These policies, then, filled the Roman Empire with murders and refugees.

[24] A similar law was immediately enacted regarding the Samaritans too, and it threw Palestine into turmoil and confusion.[81] [25] All of them who lived in my home town of Kaisareia as well as in the other cities deemed it foolish to suffer harm on behalf of a stupid doctrine, and so they simply replaced their present name with that of the Christians, managing to evade the punishment threatened by the new law through dissimulation.[82] [26] Those of them

80. One such "internal missionary" is known: Yuhannan of Amida (whom modern historians call John of Ephesos) was sent by Justinian in 542 to the region around Ephesos, where he preached against Jews, Montanists, and pagans.

81. The Samaritans were (and are) a parallel track of Judaism, claiming to preserve the original form of worship of the ancient Israelites (i.e., before the First Temple). Their holy site of worship is on Mount Gerizim (by Nablus). The Samaritans had revolted as recently as 484, seizing the area, though they were then suppressed and their temple on Mount Gerizim was destroyed; there were disturbances also under Anastasios (see *Buildings* 5.7). For Justinian's legislation regarding Samaritans, which often assimilated them to pagans and heretics and called for their conversion, see *Codex Iustinianus* 1.5.12–13, 1.5.17–19, 1.5.21; *Novellae* 45, 129, 144.1. See also 18.34, 27.7–10, and 27.26–27 below.

82. Insincere conversions are attested as soon as it became socially advantageous to be thought a Christian, i.e., already under Constantine the Great. The sixth century abounds with references to religious dissimulation, motivated either by

who were sensible and prudent did not refuse to also embrace their new faith, but the majority seemed to be resentful that they had been forced to renounce their ancestral faith not by their own free will but because of the law, and they instantly defected to the Manicheans and the so-called polytheists.[83] [27] As for the Samaritans who tilled the fields, all of them assembled together and decided to take up arms against the emperor, setting up a rival emperor for themselves from among the bandits, a man named Ioulianos, the son of Sabaros. [28] When they joined battle with the soldiers they held their ground for a while, but then they were routed and destroyed along with their leader. [29] It is said that ten times ten thousand men were lost in that fight and that this land, which is the most fertile in the entire earth, became destitute of farmers as a result.[84] [30] This, moreover, had disastrous consequences for the owners of the land who were Christians. For even though they derived no revenues from their lands, they were still required to pay in perpetuity the crushing annual tax to the emperor, for no leniency was shown in the collection of these dues.

[31] Moving on, he turned the persecution against those who are called "Greeks," torturing their bodies and plundering their money.[85] [32] But in this case too, many of these Greeks who decided to accept Christianity did so in name only, as a ward against the difficulties that they now found themselves in, and most of them were caught soon afterward performing their libations and sacrifices

---

fear or ambition (see also 26.27 and 27.7 below, and *Buildings* 5.7.9 on the Samaritans under Zenon and Anastasios). Justinian complained in an edict that some were pretending to be Christians in order to hold high office (*Codex Iustinianus* 1.5.18.5)—it was formally required.

83. The religion of the Persian prophet Mani (third century) spread from the Roman Empire to China. It advocated a dualist view of the world and was persecuted severely by both pagan and Christian emperors. For Justinian's measures against it, see *Codex Iustinianus* 1.5.12.3, 1.5.15–16, 1.5.18–19, 1.5.21.

84. The Samaritan revolt occurred in 529. Ioulianos was actually proclaimed emperor: he took Neapolis (Nablus) and presided over chariot races there. His head was sent to Justinian.

85. Those who adhered to the traditional cults of the Graeco-Roman world were called *pagani* by Latin Christians and *Hellenes* (i.e., Greeks) by the eastern Church. There were still many adherents in the countryside and among the upper classes and intellectuals. Justinian periodically attempted to purge his administration of pagans. For his legal measures against them, see *Codex Iustinianus* 1.5.18.4–5 and the edicts collected in 1.11.

and other unholy rites. [33] As for what was done regarding the Christians, that will be recounted by me in a later book.[86]

[34] After that he issued a law prohibiting male homosexual acts,[87] but instead of investigating any incidents that may have been committed *after* the passage of the law he turned on those who had been caught performing this sick act at some point in the past. [35] Moreover, the prosecution of these men was most irregular in that punishment was imposed in the absence of a formal accuser, for example on the word of a single man or a boy, and a slave at that, if no one else happened to be available, even if he had been forced against his will to testify against his master. This was considered irrefutable proof. [36] Those who were convicted in this way had their genitals cut off and were then paraded through the streets in disgrace.[88] At first, however, this atrocity was not inflicted on everyone but only on those who were believed to be Greens or rich or on those who happened to have offended the tyrants in some other way.[89] [37] Not only that, they turned viciously against the astrologers as well. That was why the authorities in charge of cases of theft took to maltreating them;[90] there was no other reason for it. After flogging many of them on the back, they paraded them on camels through the entire city in disgrace, though they were old men and otherwise completely respectable citizens, having nothing other to charge them with than that they wanted to be experts regarding the stars in a place such as this.

[38] As a result of all this, an unbroken stream of people was rushing into flight not only to the barbarians but also to Romans who lived in distant lands. In both the countryside as well as in every city it was always possible to see crowds of strangers. [39] For the sake

86. This may be a forward reference to the *Ecclesiastical History* that Prokopios was planning to write (see the Introduction, p. xxvii).

87. The term is *paiderastein*. For Justinian's measures and rhetoric, see *Novellae* 77 (blasphemies and the like cause earthquakes and famine); and 141 (male-on-male depravity is a form of atheism); *Institutes* 4.18.4 (on the *lex Iulia adulteriis coercendis*). For the punishment mentioned by Prokopios, see also 16.18–21 below.

88. According to a later source, when Justinian was asked why he imposed *that* penalty on "the corrupters of men," he answered "had they committed sacrilege, would I not have cut their hands off?"

89. According to the *Chronicle* of Ioannes Malalas (18.18), the most prominent victims of the 528/529 purge were two bishops.

90. This magistrate was the "*praetor* of the people" instituted in 535 (see 20.9 below).

of evading these authorities, each person thought little of exchanging his ancestral abode for a foreign one, just as if his native land had been captured in war by the enemy.[91] [40] It was through means such I have just described, then, that Justinian and Theodora managed to plunder the wealth of those reputed to be prosperous and were beneath the rank of senator, both in Byzantion and every other city. [41] How they prevailed in seizing all the money of the senators as well I will now explain.

Senators Whose Property Was Seized

12. There was a man named Zenon in Byzantion, a grandson of that Anthemios who had formerly been emperor in the West.[92] In furtherance of their plans, they appointed him prefect of Egypt and dispatched him there.[93] [2] He filled a ship with his most valuable possessions and prepared to sail. For he owned an immeasurable quantity of silver and gold plate adorned with pearls, emeralds, and other such precious stones. But they bribed some of those who seemed to be most loyal to them to unload the money from the ship as soon as possible and then throw firebrands into the hold. They were instructed to tell Zenon at this point that the fire had ignited spontaneously in the ship and that all the money had been destroyed. [3] At a later time it happened that Zenon died suddenly and they became the owners of his property, as his heirs. [4] For they produced a will of sorts, which was widely rumored not, in fact, to have been composed by him.

[5] Through similar methods they made themselves the heirs of Tatianos, Demosthenes, and Hilara, who in rank and other respects were leading members of the Senate of the Romans.[94] But in some cases they seized properties not by fabricating wills but rather

91. The most famous refugees who fled from Justinian's oppression to the barbarians were the seven philosophers, including Damaskios and Simplikios, who traveled from Athens to Persia after their schools were closed; they returned in 532 when the Persian king Chosroes intervened on their behalf. Their story is told by Prokopios' continuator Agathias, *Histories* 2.30–31. For the workers in silk who also fled to Persia, see 25.25 below.

92. Anthemios (r. 467–472) was a native of Constantinople. He failed to obtain the throne there in 457 upon the death of his father-in-law, the emperor Markianos. He was appointed to the throne in the West by Leon I (r. 457–474).

93. Sometime between 527 and 548.

94. Tatianos was *magister officiorum* in 520 and 527. Flavius Theodoros Petros Demosthenes was praetorian prefect of the East in 521–522 and 529; he died in 532. Hilara is otherwise unknown.

letters.[95] [6] This was how they became the heirs of Dionysios, who lived in Lebanon, and Ioannes, the son of Basileios, who was the most notable among all the citizens of Edessa but was forcibly handed over as a hostage to the Persians by Belisarios, as I recounted in an earlier book.[96] [7] Chosroes then refused to release this Ioannes, charging the Romans with having violated all the terms upon which Belisarios had handed the man over to him in the first place. He was, however, willing to release him in exchange for a ransom, as he considered him now a prisoner of war. [8] The man's grandmother, who happened to still be alive, paid the ransom, no fewer than two thousand pounds of silver, trusting that she would thereby buy back her grandson. [9] But by the time this ransom reached Daras, the emperor had learned about it and forbade the agreement from being concluded in order to prevent the barbarians, he claimed, from gaining Roman wealth.[97] [10] Not long afterward it happened that Ioannes became ill and departed from this world. The magistrate in charge of the city forged a letter of some sort that Ioannes had allegedly written to him as a friend not long before, expressing his will that the emperor inherit his property. [11] I could not, however, enumerate the names of all the others whose "spontaneous" heirs they became.[98]

[12] At any rate, until the so-called Nika riots they were content to pick off the properties of the wealthy one by one, but after that event occurred, as was explained by me in an earlier book, they confiscated the property of just about all members of the Senate in, so

95. For the law of codicils, see *Digest* 29.7.

96. In the negotiations over the withdrawal of Persian forces from Roman territory in 542, Ioannes was given against his will by Belisarios to Chosroes as a hostage (*Wars* 2.21.27). Dionysios is not otherwise known.

97. But compare Justinian's subsidies to the Huns: see note 25 above. The chronicler Ioannes Malalas, who often echoes Justinian's propaganda, notes that in 529 the emperor paid ten thousand coins to the Huns in exchange for the captured general Konstantiolos (*Chronicle* 18.21). Daras was the last Roman fortress before the Persian border.

98. In many of his edicts Justinian presented himself as a champion of the validity of wills, and the chronicler Ioannes Malalas, a propagandist for the regime, reported an anecdote in which Justinian himself provided the funds for the inheritance of three orphan girls (*Chronicle* 18.23, in 528). Prokopios is trying to undermine this image. It was traditional, from the early days of the empire, for leading men to remember the emperor in their will, in part as an assurance that the rest of their bequests would be upheld. But the forgery of documents was a persistent problem in the later Roman Empire (see the story of Priskos at 28.1–15 below). Justinian created the office of *quaesitor* to deal with it (and other matters); *Novella* 80.7 (of 539) discussed by Prokopios at 20.9 below.

to speak, one fell swoop.[99] With one hand they reached out and seized all the furniture that they fancied and all the best lands, while with the other they discarded those properties that were burdened by harsh and oppressive taxes and gave them back to their previous owners under the guise of "generosity." [13] As a result, these senators were strangled by the tax collectors and worn down by the ever-flowing interest on their debts, longing for death in the miserable life that they unwillingly endured.

The Demonic Nature of Justinian and Theodora

[14] Therefore, both to me and also to many of us these two never seemed to be human beings at all but rather murderous demons of some kind, or as the poets would say, "a baneful pair they were for all mortal men,"[100] who conspired together for the purpose of destroying all the nations and the works of men as efficiently and quickly as possible. They put on a human form, thereby becoming man-demons, and in this way demolished the entire world. [15] One could cite many things as proof of this but especially the potency unveiled in their actions. Now it happens that demonic creatures may be distinguished from human beings by one important criterion. [16] In all of history there have of course been many people who have, whether by chance or by their nature, inspired terror to the utmost degree, and who have ruined cities or countries or whatever else lay within their power; but to have devastated all of mankind and visited disaster upon the entire inhabited world, no one has been able to accomplish this except for these two people.[101] To be sure, Chance assisted their plans by effecting the ruin of mankind at their side. [17] For in these times, much damage has been caused by earthquakes, plagues, and the flooding of rivers, as I am about to recount.[102] Thus they worked this evil through a power that was not human, for it had a different source.

99. Prokopios' account of the Nika riots of 532 (*Wars* 1.24) is translated in related text 2. After the slaughter, Justinian confiscated the property of many members of the Senate who had sided against him (*Wars* 1.24.57–58).

100. Prokopios is probably not quoting a specific verse here but drawing on poetic vocabulary, e.g., from Homer, *Iliad* 5.31; Aischylos, *Suppliants* 665.

101. Prokopios still calls them people (*anthropoi*) even while he is (rhetorically) arguing that they were not.

102. See especially 18.36–45 below.

[18] It is said that even his own mother told some of her friends that he was not the son of Sabbatios, her husband, nor indeed of any mortal man; [19] and that, right before she conceived him, she was visited by a demonic creature that was invisible but that made its presence known to her through the kind of sensation that a man makes on a woman when he lies with her. It then vanished as though in a dream.[103] [20] And some of those who were present in discussions with him late at night,[104] obviously in the palace, men whose souls were pure, believed that they had witnessed some kind of apparition, a strange demonic being that had taken his place. [21] One of them said that Justinian would suddenly rise up from the imperial throne and roam about the hall; for he was not in the habit of staying seated still for long. It seemed then that his head suddenly disappeared, while the rest of his body continued its perambulations. He who witnessed this sight supposed that there was something wrong with his eyes, so he just stood there for a long while in distress and confusion. [22] But later the head returned to the body, and he thought that what was previously missing was now, disturbingly, all filled out again. [23] Another man was once standing by while Justinian was seated and said that his face suddenly became like shapeless flesh: there were neither eyebrows nor eyes in the places where those things should have been, nor did his face show any other feature at all. In time, however, he saw the shape of his face return. I write these things not as a firsthand witness but based on the testimony of those who insisted that they did see them happen at the time.

[24] It is also said that a certain monk, whom God loved exceedingly, was persuaded by those who lived in the desert with him to journey to Byzantion on behalf of some nearby communities that were being unbearably oppressed with violence and injustice, and that on his arrival he was immediately granted an audience with the

103. Throughout ancient history the mothers of extraordinary men (whether good or evil) were said to have conceived them after the visitation of a supernatural being. A similar tale was told about the mother of Justinian's nemesis, Chosroes (pseudo-Zacharias, *Chronicle* 9.6).

104. Justinian was notorious for working and studying theology at night (see also 13.28–30, 15.11, and 18.29 below as well as *Wars* 7.32.9, translated in related text 10: "A Plot to Kill Justinian"), and the emperor himself drew attention to his nocturnal labors in the preface to *Novella* 8 (translated in related text 5: "An Attempt to Curb Corruption in the Provinces"). He was known in Constantinople as the "emperor who doesn't sleep."

emperor.[105] [25] But just as he was about to enter his presence and had just placed one foot across the threshold, he suddenly withdrew it and pulled back. [26] The eunuch in charge of audiences and all those present begged the man urgently to go forward but he made no reply and, like a man deranged, ran away from there back to the room where he was staying. When his acolytes asked him why he had done this, his answer, they say, was that he had seen the Lord of Demons himself facing him,[106] seated on the throne right there in the palace. Such a being he would never approach, nor would he ask anything of him. [27] How, indeed, could this man not have been a loathsome demon when he never drank, ate, or slept enough to satisfy the needs of a human being? He would but occasionally taste a bit of what was set before him and then stalk the palace halls at odd hours of the night. And yet, despite all this, he was infernally addicted to the pleasures of sex.[107]

[28] It is likewise said by some of Theodora's lovers—this was in the days of her stage career—that some kind of evil spirit materialized among them and drove them from the room where they were planning to spend the night with her. And then there was the case of a certain dancing girl named Makedonia who belonged to the Blues in Antioch and had acquired much power for herself. [29] By writing letters to Justinian—this was when he was still governing the imperial power for Justin—she effortlessly destroyed whomever she wished among the prominent men in the East and caused their money to be confiscated by the public treasury. [30] They say that this Makedonia made Theodora most welcome when she was making her way back from Egypt and North Africa, and noticed that she was furious and offended by the insulting treatment she had received at the hands of Hekebolios and by the money she had lost during the trip.[108] She tried hard to console the woman and cheer

105. Justinian was accessible to petitioners: see 13.1 and 15.11 below. Monks were often chosen by provincial communities to represent them before the imperial authorities and even to travel to the capital on their behalf. Their moral standing strengthened their case.

106. For the Lord of the Demons, see Matthew 12.24; Mark 3.22; Luke 11.15.

107. For Justinian's ascetic habits, see also 13.28–30 and 15.11 below (and *Buildings* 1.7.7). We have no information regarding his addiction to sex other than his infatuation with Theodora (on which see 9.30–32 above). Yet in his *Novella* 74.4 (of 538 on the legitimacy of children), Justinian declared that "we know, though we are lovers of chastity . . . that nothing is more vehement than erotic mania."

108. For Theodora and Hekebolos/Hekebolios, see 9.27 above. The story of Makedonia is awkwardly inserted into this part of the text.

her up, explaining that Chance was quite capable of again becoming her patron and endowing her with great wealth. [31] It is said that Theodora then declared that a dream-vision had appeared to her that past night telling her not to worry about money anymore. [32] For she would go to Byzantion, slip into bed with the Lord of Demons, and that every method would be used to make her as his wife. As a result, she would be the mistress of *all* the money in the world.

Justinian's Lifestyle and His Corruption of the Laws

13. That, at any rate, is how it seemed to most people. Now Justinian's character was generally as I have described it, except that he made himself easily accessible and was gentle with those who approached him. No one at all was barred from gaining an audience with him and he never showed impatience even with those who failed to follow protocol in the way that they stood or spoke before him.[109] [2] But he did not, for all that, ever blush when speaking with those whom he was about to destroy. He never let slip so much as a hint of anger or irritation even when he was in the presence of those who had offended him. With a gentle visage, a calm brow, and a soft voice he would give orders for the destruction of tens of thousands of people who had done no wrong, for the razing of cities and the confiscation of all their property to the treasury. [3] One might have deduced from these manners of his that the man was as gentle as a lamb. But if anyone tried to conciliate him and, through humble supplication, obtain reprieve for those who had fallen out of favor, then "baring his teeth and snarling in anger"[110] he would seem to be at the point of exploding. This was to drive all hope out of his supposed "associates" that any such favors would be granted in the future.

[4] He seemed to have firm faith as regards Christ, but this also worked to the ruin of his subjects. He allowed priests to use violence against their neighbors with impunity and congratulated them when they had plundered the property of adjacent estates, thinking that he was being pious toward God by doing this. [5] In judging such cases he believed that he was acting in holy manner if a priest managed to grab something that did not belong to him and walk away with a verdict in his favor. He thought that justice was when

109. For Justinian's accessibility, see also 15.11 below. Protocol was perhaps more strict when Theodora was present: see 30.21–26 below.

110. An allusion to Aristophanes, *Peace* 620; the same at 1.13 above.

priests prevailed over their opponents. [6] Moreover, when he took possession through irregular means of property belonging to the living or the dead and immediately dedicated it to a church, he would pride himself on this pious pretext, but his real purpose was to ensure that the ownership of it would not ever revert back to the victims from whom it had been taken. [7] Not only that, in pursuit of his goals in this regard he committed a countless number of murders as well. To squeeze everyone into a single faith regarding Christ, which was what he wanted, he killed all the rest for no good reason at all, doing all this under the cover of "piety." It did not seem to him to be murder if the victim belonged to a different faith than his own. [8] Thus he was earnestly devoted to the constant destruction of mankind and, along with his wife, never ceased devising whatever schemes would promote this end. [9] For the desires of these two people resembled each other, for the most part, like sisters, and even when they employed different means still they were both up to no good. But they did put on a show of being opposites in order to destroy their subjects.[111] [10] As for him, his will was lighter than dust and was blown this way or that by those who would take advantage of him[112]—at least so long as the matter did not involve compassion or loss of profit; he was, moreover, continuously driven about by gusts of flattery. [11] Toadies could easily persuade him that he would "rise to the heavens and walk on air."[113] [12] One time, for example, Tribonianos, who was in attendance, stated that he was extremely fearful lest Justinian be suddenly snatched up to heaven because of his piety without anyone noticing. Such praise, or rather such jokes, he took quite seriously.[114]

111. For this feigned discordance, see also 10.15 above and 14.8 and 27.13 below.

112. This image is used again at 22.30 below.

113. A mocking allusion to the caricature of Sokrates in Aristophanes, *Clouds* 225–228 (see also 18.29 and 20.22 below). It suggests that Justinian had his head in the clouds, especially because of his religious preoccupations, and not on governing properly. Prokopios himself provides an example of how the emperor's piety could be manipulated by flattery. When he praises Justinian for Hagia Sophia in the *Buildings*, he includes another allusion to this very Aristophanic line about "walking on the air" (1.1.61).

114. Tribonianos was first a member and then director of the commission that codified Roman law in 528–534, producing the *Corpus iuris civilis*. He served Justinian as *quaestor* from 529 to 532, when he was dismissed during the Nika riots (*Wars* 1.24.16, translated in related text 2). He served as *magister officiorum* from 533 to 535, at which point he was reappointed *quaestor* (possibly until the early 540s: *Wars* 1.25.1, translated in related text 7); he appears also at 20.16–17

[13] Anyone whose virtue he happened to praise one day he would revile as a scoundrel on the next. And if he vilified one of his subjects he would, soon afterward, praise him, having changed his opinion for no apparent reason. [14] For his thoughts opposed his own words and the impression he wanted to make. [15] What his character was with regard to friendship and enmity I have already indicated, citing as evidence the man's tendencies in his actual deeds. [16] As an enemy one could depend on him to be unrelenting, but his friends found him most unreliable, so that he actually ruined many whom he favored, but he never befriended anyone whom he had once hated. [17] Those in fact who seemed to be his closest and most intimate associates he betrayed before long to their death by making a gift of them to his wife or someone else, even though he knew well that they would die precisely because of their loyalty to him, and of that alone. [18] It was obvious that he could be counted on in nothing except cruelty and greed. It proved impossible for anyone to break his addiction to the latter. [19] Even when his wife could not persuade him in some matter, by injecting into him the hope that much money would come from it she could induce the man to do whatever she wished, even if he was otherwise unwilling. [20] For the sake of ill-gotten gain he had no compunction against laying down laws and then revoking them.

[21] He would judge legal cases not according to the laws that he himself had issued but rather was led to whatever decision promised a greater and more magnificent bounty of money for himself. [22] He believed that it did not bring any disgrace upon himself to nibble away at the property of his subjects if he did it through piecemeal thefts, in cases, that is, where it was not possible for him to grab the whole lot at once on some pretext, either by leveling a criminal charge out of the blue or by invoking some nonexistent will. [23] While he was ruler of the Romans, there was no faith or doctrine regarding God that remained stable, no law that was firm, no business reliable, no contract that could be trusted. [24] When he dispatched some of his own men to deal with a certain matter, if they happened to kill many of those whom they encountered and plunder

---

below. Tribonianos was one of the greatest jurists of Roman law of all time and, like many intellectuals of this period, possibly not a Christian. In this instance he may have been alluding to Cicero's ambiguous quip about Octavian (later Augustus): "let him be praised and lifted up," i.e., "done away with" (*Letters to his Friends* 11.20.1). For other courtiers who flattered Justinian, see 14.16–17 and 22.29 below.

a great sum of money, they instantly seemed to be esteemed gentlemen in the emperor's eyes and worthy of being so named, because they had carried out all their instructions to the letter. But if they returned to him after having treated people with a certain leniency, he henceforth resented them and became their enemy. [25] He gave up on them as if the characters of these men were simply too old-fashioned for his needs, and never called them to service again. As a result, many would try hard to show him that they were in fact immoral, even though they were not, at least in their own private lives. [26] Often, when he had made a promise to someone he would strengthen it with an oath or a written guarantee but would then willingly forget all about it very quickly, believing that such acts made him all the more glorious in some way. [27] And these things Justinian did not only to his subjects but also to many of his foreign enemies, as I have already related.[115]

[28] He did not sleep, at least for the most part, and never took his fill of food or drink; rather, he tasted it with hardly more than his fingertip, and then was done with it. [29] Such things seemed to him like a distraction imposed on him by Nature, and he regularly went without food for two days and nights, especially when it was required during the period leading up to the feast called Easter. [30] At that time, as I said, he would habitually go for two days without food, surviving on sips of water and some wild herbs. He would sleep for only one hour, if that, and spent the rest of the time continuously making his rounds.[116] [31] Yet if he had desired to devote that same brief time each day to good deeds, public affairs would have reached a high point of prosperity. [32] As it was, he set all the power within him to undermine the Romans and managed to tear their state to their ground. All his constant vigilance, pains, and labors were undertaken for no other purpose than to devise ever more elaborate disasters for each day of his subjects' lives. [33] He was, as I have said, exceedingly eager to devise and swift to implement unholy deeds,[117] so that even the good aspects of his nature were turned by him to the mistreatment of his subjects.

14. Those were dark times for public affairs, and no traditional practices remained in use. I will mention a few examples, passing by

115. See 11.12 above and *Wars* 8.25.7–10 for a later example.

116. For Justinian's ascetic habits, see also 12.27 above (and *Buildings* 1.7.7); for his nocturnal labors, see 12.20 above and 15.11 below.

117. An allusion to Thucydides, *History* 1.70.3; see also 8.26 above and *Wars* 3.9.25.

the rest in silence lest this book become endless. [2] First of all, neither did he himself possess any of the qualities appropriate to the imperial office nor would he deign that others guard its dignity for him; rather, he acted like a barbarian in his manner of speech, dress, and thinking. [3] When he wished to issue a rescript in his own name, he did not delegate the matter to the man who held the office of *quaestor*, as was customary, but saw fit for the most part to dictate them himself, even though his level of style was not up to the task and a large crowd of bystanders [. . .];[118] his goal thereby was to ensure that those who were wronged by his rescript could not speak out against it.[119] [4] As for the officials known as *asecretis*,[120] they were not assigned the prerogative of drafting the emperor's confidential correspondence—the function for which they had originally been created—but, rather, he wrote almost everything out himself. For example, whenever it was necessary for him to send instructions to those arbitrating disputes in the city, he would tell them what direction their decisions should follow. [5] For he would not allow anyone in the Roman Empire to render verdicts based on his own autonomous judgment, but stubbornly and irrationally meddled in pending cases and delivered his own decisions based on hearsay evidence that he took from one of the disputants. He would also, without investigating the evidence, reverse the outcome of cases that had already been adjudicated, led not by any consideration of law or justice but blatantly being driven by a disgraceful desire for gain. [6] The emperor was not ashamed to take bribes either, as his lust for profit had smothered any sense of shame.

[7] Often matters that had already been reviewed by both the Senate and the emperor would have to be settled by a second, more definitive, decision. [8] For the Senate sat as though it were in a painting, having the power neither of its own vote nor of doing any good, assembling for the sake of appearances only and because of

118. A verb is missing here. Dewing suggests "listened," "attended," or "gave servile applause." Prokopios is not expressing here the contempt of a learned Greek for Latin but specifically for Justinian's prose, which one scholar who has studied the legal texts of the period characterizes as "pretentious and vulgar" (T. Honoré). Prokopios knew these texts firsthand, as is shown by Part III of *The Secret History* (Chapters 19–30). Yet Justinian often delegated the composition of his edicts to his *quaestor*, for example Tribonianos (for whom see 13.12 above and 20.16–17 below).

119. Imperial decisions could not be appealed.

120. These were confidential imperial secretaries (from Latin *a secretis*, Greek *asekretis*); see *Wars* 2.7.15 for Justinian's *asecretis* Ioulianos.

ancient custom, as it was altogether impossible for any member of that assembly to so much as raise his voice and speak. What really happened was that the emperor and his consort would typically pretend to take different sides in the debate, but the side would always prevail that was chosen by them in advance on any matter.[121] [9] If someone who had broken the law was uncertain as to whether he would win, all such a person had to do was offer more gold to this emperor to instantly obtain for himself a law that directly contradicted all existing laws. [10] And if someone else subsequently invoked that other law, I mean the one that had been abrogated, the emperor had no compunction against immediately reenacting it and replacing the new one with it again. Law was drained of power and stability, and the scales of justice oscillated wildly and unpredictably depending on which side was weighed down with the more gold. They were now set up in the public places of the market, where before they had been in the palace itself. Wares for sale now included not only justice but also the enactment of laws.

[11] As for the officials called *referendarii*, they no longer restricted themselves to introducing the petitions of suppliants to the emperor and then, as was customary, merely to report to the relevant magistrate what his decision had been regarding each suppliant. Instead, they mustered all the unjust arguments[122] that they heard from every person and would deceive Justinian with sophistries and various verbal tricks,[123] for he was susceptible by nature to those who were skilled in such things. [12] Then they would leave the council chamber and order the imprisonment of their clients' opponents, extorting as much money as they needed, given that no one could defend himself against them or question their tactics.[124] [13] As for the soldiers who were on duty in the palace guard, they would stand by the arbitrators in the imperial portico and bring cases before them using violence.[125] [14] In sum, just about every-

121. For this feigned discordance, see also 10.15, 13.9, and 27.13.

122. An allusion to the character of Unjust Argument in Aristophanes, *Clouds* 889 ff.

123. An allusion to Aristophanes, *Knights* 632.

124. Prokopios is complaining that the *referendarii* exceeded their authority both in influencing the emperor's decisions and by taking sides in their enforcement. Justinian himself tried to curb some of these abuses with *Novellae* 113 (of 541) and 124 (of 544–545: "the *referendarii* will do what they are ordered without interfering with the judgments rendered," etc.).

125. It is not clear who is doing what to whom here. For the trials held at the imperial portico, see *Buildings* 1.11.12; *Novella* 82.3. It was a vast courtyard lo-

one had abandoned his proper post and all were wandering on whatever paths enabled them to abuse their power, paths that had previously been closed to them and so not trodden. Public affairs were now entirely in a wretched state and names did not even retain their proper meaning.[126] The state resembled a kingdom of children at play.[127] [15] I will pass by all the rest, as I said I would at the beginning of this section.[128] I will, however, declare who it was who first persuaded this emperor to take a bribe while he was hearing a case.

[16] There was a certain Leon, a Kilikian by origin, who was diabolically devoted to the pursuit of money. This Leon became the most powerful of all the flatterers and was capable of insinuating his views into the minds of those who lacked education.[129] [17] His skill at persuasion played on the tyrant's stupidity for the destruction of other people. This man was the first to persuade Justinian to sell his legal decisions for money. [18] And once *he* had decided to steal in that way, he never let up. This evil grew larger with every step that it took. Whoever wanted to bring an honest man to an unjust trial would first go straight to Leon and, by pledging that a portion of the disputed property would go to the tyrant and to Leon, he would leave the palace having already won his case, unjustly. [19] From this Leon managed to pile up great riches for himself, acquired extensive lands, and was most responsible for bringing the Roman state to its knees. [20] There was no guarantee of last resort for those who had entered into a contract, no law, no oath, no written document, no reliable penalty, nor any other kind of security except through the giving of money to Leon and the emperor. [21] Yet not even this could ensure the solidity of Leon's support, for he was prepared to hire himself out to the opposing side as well. [22] As he was always stealing from both sides, it never entered his mind that it was

---

cated just to the west of Hagia Sophia. Prokopios' successor Agathias complained that, as a lawyer, he had to spend too much time in the imperial portico trying cases rather than reading and writing history books (*Histories* 3.1.4).

126. An allusion to the discussion in Thucydides, *History* 3.82–83, of how civil strife changes the meanings of words.

127. An allusion to the game of "king" played by the future king of Persia Kyros, when he was a child, with his friends, in Herodotos, *Histories* 1.114; see the Introduction, p. xxxvii.

128. At 14.1 above.

129. He was a *referendarius;* for more information regarding him, see also 17.31–32 and 29.28–36 below.

shameful on his part to neglect to promote the cases of those who had placed their hopes in him, or even to actively work against them. [23] He thought that there was nothing shameful in playing both sides, so long as he made a profit.

The Lifestyle and Crimes of Theodora

15. So much, then, for Justinian; that's what sort of a person he was. Theodora, for her part, had rooted her mind solidly and irrevocably in inhumanity. [2] She never did anything because she had been persuaded or forced by another person; rather, she herself stubbornly executed her own plans with all the power at her command and no one dared even to intercede on behalf of those who had angered her. [3] Nothing could mollify her wrath in the slightest, not the passage of time, nor punishment indulgently imposed, nor any means of supplication, nor the threat of death that looms in heaven above the entire human race. [4] In sum, no one ever saw Theodora reconciled with someone who had angered her, not even if that person had died; in fact, the son of the deceased inherited the empress' hatred along with everything else belonging to his father, and then passed it on to the third generation. [5] For her sense of indignation was most eager to be stirred up for the destruction of other people, and it was impossible to placate.

[6] She paid more attention to the care of her body than was necessary but still less than she would have liked. [7] She would rush to her bath first thing in the morning but would tarry there for a long while. Having bathed so sumptuously, she went to breakfast. [8] After breakfast she rested. At lunch and dinner she liked to taste every variety of food and drink. Sleep always took hold of her for long stretches, her daytime naps lasting until night set on and she slept again at night until the sun rose. [9] Yet even while she had lapsed into such an indulgent and luxurious lifestyle, wasting away the greater part of the day, still she insisted on governing the entire empire of the Romans. [10] Were the emperor to delegate a certain matter to a person without first asking her opinion, the fortunes of that person would soon afterward know such a reversal that his position of honor would be removed in a most insulting way and he would die a most disgraceful death.[130]

130. Even the powerful prefect Ioannes the Kappadokian eventually succumbed to her hostility. Prokopios' account of his downfall (*Wars* 1.25) is translated in related text 7.

[11] Now Justinian found it easy to handle everything himself, not only because of his mental agility but also because he slept so little, as I explained above, and was so accessible to everyone.[131] [12] For people were easily given permission not only to present themselves before this tyrant but, even if they were complete nobodies with no prestige, to have casual discussions with him and confer about confidential matters.[132] [13] But with the empress not even a magistrate could gain an audience without going to a great deal of trouble and waste of time, as all of them were always made to wait for her hour upon hour in a small room with no ventilation, like slaves in attendance, for it was too risky for any magistrate to be absent. [14] They had to stand, always on the tips of their toes, each trying to keep his face higher than the others to catch the attention of the eunuchs coming out from within. [15] Having gone to all this trouble, a few of them were summoned inside after many days of waiting. They entered into her presence fearfully anxious to leave as soon as possible after doing nothing more than prostrating themselves and briefly brushing the sole of each of her feet with their lips.[133] [16] For to speak or to request anything unbidden by her was absolutely forbidden. The state was thereby reduced to a slave-pen and she was our teacher in servility. [17] It was in this way, then, that the fortunes of the Romans collapsed, as the tyrant was believed to be excessively good-natured while Theodora had a reputation for being nasty and harsh. [18] But behind his good nature there was instability, while her nastiness inhibited every initiative.

[19] While the differences in their mentality and lifestyle were apparent, they had in common avarice and lust for murder along with never speaking the truth. [20] Both were extremely adept liars. If a man who had angered Theodora was said to have committed some wrong, no matter how minor or insignificant, she would immediately fabricate charges that were utterly incommensurate with the man's actual guilt and magnified the case into a major crime. [21] A swarm of accusations was always in motion and there was a special court [. . .][134] devoted to the subversion of established institutions. The judges who sat on it were chosen by her and it was inevitable that they would compete with each other to see who of

131. For Justinian's sleeping habits, see 12.20 and 13.28 above.

132. For Justinian's accessibility, see also 13.1 above.

133. This protocol is discussed more extensively at 30.21–26 below (see also 15.27 below).

134. The text is corrupt at this point.

them was most capable of satisfying the empress' desire through the inhumanity of his verdicts. [22] In this way, she had the property of anyone who angered her confiscated to the treasury and, after having him most cruelly tortured, even if he were the scion of an ancient and noble family, she would not hesitate to impose a penalty of exile or death. [23] But if one of her cronies happened to be arrested on the charge of murder, or another of the major crimes, she mocked and traduced the prosecutors' efforts and forced them to keep quiet against their will about the facts of the case.

[24] When it suited her interests, she converted even the most important matters into a farce, treating them like one of those stage skits they put on in the theater. [25] There was once a patrician, who was very old and had spent many years in office. I know his name but will not under any circumstances divulge it lest I perpetuate the dishonor that was done to him. He was owed a large sum of money by one of her servants and so approached her because he was unable to collect it from him, accusing the other party to the contract and imploring her for assistance in finding some measure of justice. [26] Theodora had learned of this in advance and sent out her eunuchs to meet the patrician upon his arrival. They were all to form a circle around him listening carefully to what she would say, and she instructed them what to chant in response to her words.[135] [27] When the patrician entered the women's quarters, he prostrated himself according to the manner of prostration that was customary in her presence,[136] and, with a face as though he had been crying, said the following. "My Lady, it is a hard thing for a man of patrician rank to lack money.[137] [28] What generates pity and compassion for others brings only dishonor upon a man of my standing. [29] For any other person who finds himself financially ruined can just inform his creditors of that fact and thereby he immediately evades the troubles that would come to him from there; but if a man of patrician rank lacks the means by which to repay the debts he owes to his creditors, it is most likely that he would be too ashamed to mention it. And if he were to mention it, he would not be believed, for

135. The farce that Theodora was about to stage was, in part, a parody of the Christian liturgy. This type of "antiphonal" chanting was used by the fan-clubs in the hippodrome too (see 7.13 above). Contemporaries had noted the similarity.

136. For the required form of prostration, see 30.21–26 below (and 15.15 above).

137. The patrician insists on his rank throughout his speech, perhaps because Theodora had held the same since her engagement to Justinian (see 9.30 above).

poverty does not dwell in a house of such rank. [30] But if, on the other hand, he were to be believed, the most disgraceful and painful things would then happen to him. [31] Well then, my Lady, in my dealings some people have lent me their money while others have borrowed my own. [32] And those who have lent me money are continuously pressing me for its return and I am not able, on account of the prestige of my rank, to put them off; but those who owe me, who happen not to be patricians, resort to various inhuman excuses. [33] I therefore entreat you and beg and beseech you to help me assert my rights and escape from these pressing evils." [34] That is what he said. The woman replied to him by singing out the words, "O patrician so-and-so," at which point the chorus of eunuchs intoned a refrain in response, "That's a big hernia that you have!" [35] The man pleaded again, making another speech similar to the one above, and again the woman responded in the same way with the chorus chanting its response. This went on until the poor man gave up, prostrated himself in the prescribed manner, and went home.

[36] She spent most of the year in the suburbs by the coast, mostly in the palace known as Herion.[138] This imposed considerable hardship on her army of attendants, [37] for necessities were in short supply and they incurred dangers from the sea too, especially if a winter storm happened to pick up or the whale made a surprise appearance.[139] [38] But they[140] believed that the evils that afflict all of mankind were as nothing, at least so long as it was possible for them to live in luxury. [39] Next I will explain how Theodora treated those who offended her, selecting only a few cases lest I seem to be belaboring the point ad nauseam.

More Victims of Theodora

16. When Amalasountha had decided to take her leave of the Goths and change the direction of her life altogether, and was thinking of

138. Or Hieron, on the Asiatic side of the Bosporus by the entrance to the Black Sea, where Justinian had built a palace (*Buildings* 1.11.16–17 and 1.3.10 for a church in the vicinity). For the toll station there, see 25.2 below.

139. For Porphyrios the whale, see Prokopios' account (*Wars* 7.29.9–16) translated in related text 9. The chronicler Ioannes Malalas reports that, on one occasion, Theodora was accompanied by over four thousand people (*Chronicle* 18.25).

140. I.e., Justinian and Theodora.

moving to Byzantion—as I stated in an earlier book[141]—Theodora considered that the woman was of noble ancestry and a queen, very impressive to look upon, and swift at devising plans to get what she wanted; also, she felt threatened by the woman's magnificence and exceptionally manly bearing, and had little trust in her husband's fickleness. No, her jealously of the woman was no small thing, and so she schemed to bring her within her grasp and kill her. [2] She persuaded her husband to send Petros alone as his ambassador to Italy. [3] When the emperor dispatched him, he gave him the directives that I described in the relevant section of my narrative, though it was impossible for me there, because of fear of the empress, to reveal the truth about what happened.[142] [4] *She* gave him this one directive only, namely that he remove that woman from this world as soon as possible, and she filled the man with heady hopes of the huge rewards he would receive if he carried out her instructions.[143] [5] When he arrived in Italy—for the nature of man is such that we rush to commit unjust murders if we hope for some high office or large sums of money—he persuaded Theodahad (by what arguments I do not know) to kill Amalasountha.[144] This deed pro-

141. *Wars* 5.2.22–29 and 5.3.28. Amalasountha was the daughter of Theodoric the Great, Gothic king of Italy (r. 489–526). She governed Italy as regent for her son Athalaric, who died in 534, whereupon she ruled as queen. Due to opposition from elements in the Gothic nobility, she thought of fleeing to the eastern empire. Prokopios greatly admired her (*Wars* 5.2.3–7).

142. To secure her failing rule, Amalasountha elevated her learned but corrupt cousin Theodahad to the throne in late 534, thinking that she would continue to rule in fact. Petros was a lawyer and eloquent advocate in Constantinople (*Wars* 5.3.30) who was sent to Italy by Justinian in late 534 in the hope of securing the peaceful surrender of Italy to the empire (for Justinian's instructions, see *Wars* 5.4.17). Along the way he learned of the death of Athalaric and the elevation of Theodahad and, then, of Amalasountha's imprisonment. Thereupon Justinian instructed him to make known to the Goths his support of Amalasountha (*Wars* 5.4.22). Apparently, as Prokopios is about to relate, Petros had received different instructions from Theodora.

143. An allusion to Aristophanes, *Knights* 1244.

144. At *Wars* 5.4.25, Prokopios states merely (and ambiguously) that "when Petros arrived in Italy, it happened that Amalasountha had been removed from among men." *The Secret History* places the murder *after* his arrival. In a letter to Theodora (of 535), Theodahad implies that it was she who had sent Petros, while an accompanying letter by his queen Gudeliva to Theodora refers cryptically to a matter that had brought them closer together (in Cassiodorus, *Variae* 10.20–21).

pelled him to the honor of the *magister*. Much power now came to him and he earned more hatred than had any other man.[145]

[6] That, then, was how the business with Amalasountha ended. [7] Now, Justinian had a secretary to handle his correspondence named Priskos, who was quite devious and a Paphlagonian,[146] and his character was such as to be pleasing to his patron. He was very favorably disposed toward Justinian and believed that the feeling was mutual. Hence he quickly acquired great wealth, though not by legal means. [8] But Theodora slandered this man to her husband, claiming that he was arrogant and always trying to block her plans. [9] She had no success at first, but not long after she had the man placed on board a ship in the middle of winter and sent to a place of her choosing. There she had his head shaved and, completely against his will, forced him to become a priest.[147] [10] Justinian, for his part, put on an act that he knew nothing of what had happened: he made no inquiry to find out where on earth Priskos was, and put the matter out of mind, sitting in silence as if he had suffered a memory loss. He did, however, plunder the little bit of money that Priskos had left behind.

[11] She also came under the suspicion of being madly in love with one of her servants, a certain Areobindos, who was of barbarian origin, a handsome lad, and whom, it so happened, she had appointed her steward. Wishing to refute the charge—even though, they say, she was infatuated with the man to an unnatural degree—she decided to torture him horribly for the time being without accusing

145. Theodahad at first considered surrendering Italy to Justinian but changed his mind. Petros had been sent to Italy in 535 and then again in 536 to secure this arrangement, and he was there when the Roman invasion began. He was arrested by the Goths (*Wars* 5.7.11–25) and not released until the summer of 539 (6.22.23–24). Petros was then promoted to *magister officiorum*, a position that he held for an unprecedented twenty-six years (until 565). He authored various works of history and ceremonial protocol. For his thefts in office, see 24.22–23 below.

146. Ever since Aristophanes' attack on the Athenian politician Kleon ("the Paphlagonian") in the *Knights* and the satirical works of Lucian, Paphlagonians were perceived as vulgar, ignorant, and superstitious. The joke was probably inspired by the similarity with the Greek verb *paphlazô* ("to bluster, seethe"). Priskos was honorary consul in 529 and *comes* of the palace guard of the *excubitores* when he fell.

147. The chronicler Ioannes Malalas says that Justinian banished him to Kyzikos for insulting the empress Theodora, from where he escaped, so he was forced to become a deacon and ordered to live in Nikaia (*Chronicle* 18.43 and *De insidiis* 3.45).

him of anything in particular. After this we learned nothing about his fate and no one has seen him to this day. [12] For when she wanted to cast a veil of secrecy over something that had been done, it became classified and unmentionable by everyone; henceforth, he who knew it was forbidden from telling even his closest friend about it, nor could anyone who wanted to know about it make an inquiry, no matter how curious he was. [13] No tyrant has inspired such fear for as long as human beings have existed, given that it was impossible for dissidents to escape detection.[148] [14] An army of spies informed her of everything that was both said and done in public and within private households. [15] When she did not want the punishment that she had imposed on a certain offender to be widely known, she proceeded as follows. [16] She summoned the man, if he happened to be of high standing, and she herself, with no witnesses present, handed him over to one of her servants with the directive to convey him to the farthest limits of the Roman Empire. [17] And in the middle of the night this servant of hers would place him bound and hooded on a ship and escort him to the place she had indicated, where he would, before departing and with the utmost secrecy, turn him over to someone there who specialized in this service. The latter was instructed to guard him as safely as possible but without revealing his presence to anyone, until such a time as the empress took pity on the poor wretch or until he wasted away and suffered a lingering death on account of the hardships of the place.[149]

[18] She was also furious against a certain Basianos, a young Green of high social status, because he was slandering her everywhere. Basianos took refuge in the church of the archangel, for he did not long remain unaware of her rage.[150] [19] She immediately set loose on him the magistrate in charge of the populace but specified that Basianos was not to be accused of slandering her, but rather of sodomy.[151] [20] The officials pulled the man from the sanctuary and

148. Prokopios expresses similar fears in the Preface, 1.2 above.

149. For a possible instance of this "disappearing" method, see 17.20–23 below (her son Ioannes).

150. Several churches were dedicated to the archangel Michael at this time. Justinian required magistrates to swear by God, the Virgin, the Gospels, and the archangels Michael and Gabriel upon taking office (*Novella* 8, translated in related text 5: "An Attempt to Curb Corruption in the Provinces").

151. For *paiderastia*, see 11.34 above and 16.23 below. For Justinian's new magistracies for dealing with crime and disturbances, see 20.9 below.

began to torture him with a vicious form of punishment, but when the entire populace saw such misfortune being inflicted on a body that was noble and raised in luxury all his life, they could not bear the sight of it and groaned their lament up to heaven, demanding that the young man be pardoned. [21] But she made his punishment even worse: he lost his genitals and then his life, though without a trial, and his property was confiscated to the treasury. [22] And so it went every time this bitch got worked up: no sanctuary was safe, no law could offer any protection, and it seemed that not even an entreaty by the entire city was sufficient to shield anyone who had given her offense. There was nothing, anywhere, that could stand up to her.

[23] A certain Diogenes also stirred her rage because he was a Green. He was a charming man and dear to everyone, including the emperor himself, but this made her no less eager to slanderously accuse him of sex with men. [24] She persuaded two of his slaves to testify in court as witnesses against their owner. [25] But he was not tried in secret and under a veil of silence, as had become customary, but in public, and the judges appointed to his case were many and distinguished, on account of Diogenes' high social standing. They scrutinized the slaves' testimony and found it to be insufficient for a verdict against the man, for they were but slave-boys. So she imprisoned Theodoros, one of Diogenes' closest friends, in one of her usual cells.[152] [26] Here she worked on the man, now with smooth words, now with long sessions of torture. As she was getting nowhere, she had a strip of ox leather tied around his head, at the height of his ears, and then increasingly twisted and tightened it. [27] It reached the point where Theodoros felt that his eyes had popped out of their sockets, but he resolutely refused to testify to events that had never happened. [28] Hence the judges acquitted Diogenes for lack of evidence against him, and the entire city, as one, celebrated the event.[153]

17. That, then, was how that story ended. I have already recounted in the first part of this book all that she did against Belisarios, Photios, and Bouzes. [2] And there was this also. Two militants of the Blues, of Kilikian origin, lay violent hands on Kallinikos, the governor of the province of Second Kilikia, in a riotous disturbance. They killed his groom, who was standing nearby trying to defend

152. For Theodora's cells, see 4.7 above.

153. This story reveals that some independent justice still existed.

his master, in plain view of the governor and the entire populace. [3] So the governor had the militants arrested, legally tried, and executed for this and many other murders. But when *she* learned of this, making a show of her support for the Blues she had him impaled over the murderers' grave, while he was still in office and without charging him with anything. [4] The emperor, for his part, pretended to cry and lament over the murdered man, sitting there and sounding like a grunting pig.[154] He made many threats against those who had done the deed, but followed through on none of them. And, of course, he did not neglect to plunder the dead man's money.

[5] But Theodora also made a point of devising punishments for sins of the flesh. For instance, she rounded up more than five hundred whores who sold themselves in the middle of the marketplace, the "three obol girls"[155] (though one can barely live off this). She sent them to the opposite shore and locked them up in the monastery named Repentance, forcing them to put on and wear a different life and habit. [6] But, during the night, some of them would throw themselves off the walls, escaping their involuntary conversion in that way.[156]

[7] There were two maidens, sisters, in Byzantion who were descended from a consular father and grandfather and, before them, their entire line back to its very origins could be traced to the Senate. [8] They both married but their husbands died, so they became widows. Thereupon Theodora took it upon herself to pair them up with two commoners, revolting men really, whom she had selected, alleging as a pretext that the girls were not living chastely. [9]

154. A possible allusion to Aristophanes, *Acharnians* 746. This episode is recorded independently by the late-sixth-century historian Euagrios (*Ecclesiastical History* 4.32), who names the two militants Paulos and Phaustinos; Kallinikos "was impaled and paid this penalty for a correct interpretation of the laws." Euagrios blames Justinian, however, though Prokopios was closer in time and to the court. The capital of the province was Tarsos.

155. An obol was a type of ancient coin; "three obols" was a proverbial wage for prostitutes. Though the ancient coin itself was long obsolete, the term was still in use; see 25.11–12 below.

156. At *Buildings* 1.9.1–10 (translated in related text 4: "The Covenant of Repentance"), Prokopios would later provide a positive account of this action, based presumably on the imperial couple's propaganda. The monastery was a converted palace on the Asian side of the Bosporus, by the entrance to the Black Sea. For a modern parallel to *The Secret History* from Thailand, see the Introduction, p. li.

Terrified lest this actually happen, they fled to the church of Hagia Sophia and, entering the holy baptistery, clasped the font there tightly. [10] But the empress inflicted such privation and hardship on them there that they eventually came around. In order to escape the evil that they were enduring there they were willing to exchange it with the evil of the proposed marriages. Thus, where she was concerned, no asylum remained inviolable or undefiled.[157] [11] So the girls were unwillingly married to men who were poor and far beneath them in rank, though they did not lack for suitors among the nobility. [12] Their mother, likewise a widow, attended the betrothal though without daring to lament or cry out in protest of her disgrace. [13] Theodora later wanted to purify herself of this obscenity and decided to give them a consolation prize, albeit one that harmed the public interest: [14] she made each of these men a magistrate. This did not, however, make the girls feel any better and, moreover, it turned out that these men inflicted ruinous and unbearable miseries on almost all their subjects, which I will recount later.[158] [15] But Theodora had no regard for the dignity of office or the rights of the state, nor did she care about anything else at all so long as she got her way.

[16] It so happened, during the days when she was still on the stage, that she became pregnant by one of her lovers and realized her misfortune late in the term.[159] As usual, she did everything in her power to induce an abortion, but none of her methods rid her of the infant while it was still an embryo, given that it was now close to developing full human form. [17] So, as nothing was working, she stopped trying and was forced to give birth. When the father of the newborn baby saw that she was on the verge of poverty and distressed—for now that she was a mother she could no longer exploit her body for work—and, also, he rightly suspected that she would resort to infanticide, he lifted the baby with his hands, acknowledging it as his own, and named it Ioannes (for it was a boy). He then departed for Arabia, which was his destination. [18] When he was about to die, and Ioannes was a teenager, he revealed to his son everything regarding his mother. [19] Ioannes performed all the customary rites upon the departure of his father from this world.

157. See also 3.25 above for the same accusation.

158. Prokopios apparently never wrote this account, nor does he give the men's names here. He may have intended to tell more about these men in his *Ecclesiastical History* (see the Introduction, p. xxvii).

159. For Theodora's pregnancies and abortions, see 9.19 above.

Some time later he came to Byzantion and announced himself to those who had constant access to his mother. [20] They did not suspect that her reaction would be different from that of the rest of humanity and so they announced to his mother that her son, Ioannes, had arrived. [21] But the woman feared lest news of this reach her husband. She bid them bring him into her sight [22] and, when she saw that he had entered, she turned him over to one of her servants, a man to whom she always delegated such cases. [23] By what means this poor lad was made to disappear from this world I am not able to say, but no one has seen him again to this very day, not even after the empress died.[160]

[24] It was during this time that the morals of almost all women too were corrupted. For they were given full license to cheat on their husbands and no risk or harm could come to them because of their behavior. Even those convicted of adultery remained unpunished, because they would go straight to the empress and turn the tables by hauling their husbands into court through a countersuit, despite the fact that the men had been charged with no crime. [25] All the men could do, even though they had not been convicted of anything, was to pay back to their wives the dowries that they had received, only twofold, to be whipped and then, for most of them, led off to prison. After this, they had to look on again as these adultresses preened and lusted after their seducers, only more flagrantly this time. Many of these seducers even received ranks and honors for performing this service. [26] From then on most men were only too happy to endure without protest the unholy deeds of their wives. So long as they were not being whipped, they gave their wives the freedom to do whatever they wished by pretending not to know what was going on.

[27] She insisted on presiding over every branch of state and on always having her way. She appointed both magistrates and priests, scrutinizing the candidates in every case to prevent one thing alone, namely that any good or virtuous man happen to occupy an office, and to screen out those who would be unable to execute her commands. [28] She also arranged marriages as if she held some kind of divine authority, and so people stopped entering into voluntary engagements before marrying. [29] All of a sudden each man would find that he had a wife, not because this pleased him, which is how these things are done even among the barbarians, but because it had

160. For the way in which Theodora made people disappear, see 16.12–17 above.

been decided by Theodora.[161] [30] Conversely, the women suffered the same thing, for they were forced to live with these men against their will. [31] Often she would even snatch the bride away from the bridal chamber, arbitrarily and before the groom had a chance to consummate the union, stating in a fit of anger[162] only that the woman did not please her. [32] She did this to many people, among them Leontios, who held the office of *referendarius*,[163] and Satorninos, the son of Hermogenes (who had attained the position of *magister*). This Satorninos was betrothed to his cousin's daughter, a virgin of good birth and proper manners whose hand her own father Kyrillos had given to him directly, as Hermogenes had already departed from this life.[164] [33] The doors of the bridal chamber had already been shut when Theodora detained the groom and led him into a different room where she married him off, wailing and lamenting, to the daughter of "Goldilocks." [34] This Goldilocks had formerly been a dancer and was later a call girl, but at this time she was living in the palace with another Goldilocks and a certain Indaro. [35] Yes, this was how they were now running public affairs instead of being concerned with the penis and with life on the stage. [36] When Satorninos slept with this wife of his and found that she had already been deflowered, he told one of his friends that he had married one who was "not unperforated." [37] When this comment reached Theodora, she ordered her servants to lift him up the way one does schoolchildren and give his back a good long whacking for showing off and boasting about things to which he had no right. She then told him not to run his mouth off again.

[38] What she did to Ioannes the Kappadokian was explained in an earlier book.[165] Her grievance, the reason for which she did all that against the man, was not of course related to his crimes against

161. For a similar incident of this kind, see the story of Artabanes in *Wars* 7.31.13–14, translated in related text 10: "A Plot to Kill Justinian."

162. A possible allusion to Aristophanes, *Knights* 41.

163. This was probably the same man as the Leon in 14.16 above and the Leontios in 28.29 below.

164. Satorninos' father Hermogenes was a high official (*magister officiorum*), diplomat, and general active on the eastern front, 529–535 (he died in 535–536); he appears often in Book 1 of the *Wars*. Kyrillos was a cavalry commander serving under Belisarios in the East and North Africa, where he was murdered in the summer of 536. The marriage, therefore, was probably set to take place in 535–536.

165. For the downfall of Ioannes (in 541), see Prokopios' account (*Wars* 1.25) translated in related text 7.

the state—the proof of this is that she did nothing against those who later behaved even worse toward their subjects—but because he dared to oppose that woman in various matters and especially because he slandered her to the emperor, bringing her almost to the point of having to wage war with her own husband. [39] As I said above, it is necessary for me here to give the truest account of the causes of that incident.[166] [40] When she had confined him to Egypt,[167] after he had suffered all that I described, she was still not satisfied that she had punished him enough and so never relented in the search for false witnesses to bring against him. [41] Four years later she managed to find two Greens of the militants at Kyzikos who were said to have participated in the revolt against the bishop.[168] [42] After she had worked on them with flattery, arguments, and threats, one of them, alternately terrified and elated by the hopes she dangled before him, blamed Ioannes for that loathsome murder. [43] The other one, however, adamantly refused to speak anything but the truth, even though he was subjected to such brutal tortures that he became certain of his own imminent death. [44] Because of him, however, she was unable to make any progress in her machinations against Ioannes; this pretext, at any rate, would not work. Still, she cut off the right hands of the two young men, the one because he would not give false witness and the other so that her plot would not be revealed to everyone. [45] And while all these things transpired in the public places of the marketplace, Justinian made as though he did not know anything of what was going on.[169]

The Destruction of the World by the Demon Justinian

18. That he was no man but rather some kind of anthropomorphic demon, as was stated,[170] could be proven by the sheer magnitude of the evils that he inflicted on humanity. [2] For it is in the enormity

166. See 1.3 above.

167. In August 541.

168. The bishop Eusebios of Kyzikos (the first place of Ioannes' exile) was murdered after Ioannes' arrival. See the account translated in related text 7.

169. Ioannes Malalas, a propagandist for the regime, says that in 547 Andreas and Ioannes Dandax had their right hands cut off for being implicated in the murder of the bishop of Kyzikos. He says nothing about Justinian or Theodora in this connection, at least not in the abbreviated version of his chronicle that survives (*Chronicle* 18.101).

170. At 12.14 above.

of the deeds that the power of the doer is revealed. [3] To specify exactly how many people were destroyed by him would not, it seems to me, ever be possible for any man, or even for God. [4] It would be easier to number all the grains of sand than those whom this emperor killed. Making a rough estimate of the lands that are now devoid of inhabitants, I would say that ten thousand times ten thousand times ten thousand died. [5] For example, North Africa has been so devastated that, despite its size,[171] it would be difficult and noteworthy to find anyone else there even if one were to traverse miles of road. [6] Yet the Vandals who took up arms at the beginning of the war there numbered 80,000,[172] and who could estimate the number of their women, children, and slaves? [7] As for the North Africans who previously lived in the cities, tilled the land, and worked at sea—most of this bustle I chanced to witness myself[173]—how could anyone be in a position to enumerate the vast extent of their multitude? Even more numerous than them in that region were the Moors, who are now all destroyed along with their women and offspring. [8] Moreover, the earth there lies upon a host of Roman soldiers and those who followed them from Byzantion. So that if one were to claim that five hundred times ten thousand human beings were lost in North Africa, he would not, I believe, even be coming close to the truth of the matter.

[9] The reason for this is that as soon as the Vandals were defeated, he made no provision to establish and consolidate his governance of the land nor thought ahead about how to secure control over its resources by winning over the goodwill of its inhabitants, but rather he immediately ordered Belisarios to return with no delay, accusing him of plotting against the throne, a charge that was utterly baseless.[174] His purpose, of course, was to have a free hand in the administration of North Africa so as to swallow it all up through plunder. [10] And indeed the first thing that he did was to send out

171. The Roman provinces of North Africa, which Prokopios calls "Libya," included roughly the territory of modern Tunisia and coastal Algeria and Libya.

172. At *Wars* 3.5.18, Prokopios gives the same number for the army of the Vandal king Gaiseric (r. 428–477).

173. Prokopios had accompanied Belisarios to North Africa in 533 and so had seen the state of the land and its people before the war.

174. In 534, some officers slandered Belisarios to the emperor, saying that he intended to revolt. Justinian gave him a choice between returning and staying there; Belisarios returned posthaste (*Wars* 4.8.2–5). Prokopios here quotes the very language he uses in the *Wars* to call this charge "utterly baseless."

assessors of the land and impose the harshest taxes, the likes of which were previously unknown in those parts.[175] He appropriated for himself the best fields and prohibited the Arians from celebrating their own mysteries. [11] He was always late in paying his soldiers and, generally, treated them in a heavy-handed way. This caused many revolts that resulted in widespread devastation.[176] [12] For it was never his intention to abide by established customs; it was, rather, in his nature to stir up everything and throw it into confusion.

[13] As for Italy, on the other hand, which is no less than three times the size of North Africa, it has in all places been denuded of human habitation to an even greater degree, so that an estimate of the numbers killed there too will lie close at hand.[177] [14] I have already explained the cause of the disasters that befell Italy.[178] Everything that Justinian did wrong in North Africa he did here as well. [15] And by sending, in addition to all the other officials, those called *logothetai*, he reversed his gains and immediately wrecked everything.[179] [16] Before this war, Gothic rule extended from the land of the Gauls to the borders of Dacia, where the city of Sirmium stands. [17] When the Roman army arrived in Italy,[180] the Germans held

175. The assessors were named Tryphon and Eustratios, "and they seemed neither moderate nor bearable to the Libyans" (*Wars* 4.8.25). For the taxes imposed by Justinian, see 23 below.

176. The stability of the North African provinces was rocked by military revolts. Discontent was caused by Justinian's decision to confiscate the land and not grant it to his soldiers, even those who had taken Vandal wives (*Wars* 4.14.8–10); by arrears in military pay (e.g., *Wars* 5.15.55, and see 24 below); and the prohibition of Arian worship (*Wars* 4.14.11–15). Those who believed that the Son (Christ) was not of the same substance (*ousia*) as God the Father could be labeled Arians. The Vandals, like the Goths, had converted to this version of Christianity, which had enjoyed imperial support in the fourth century. In moving against Arianism in North Africa (*Novella* 37 of 535), Justinian was thinking primarily of the Vandal hierarchy, but it happened that there were about one thousand Arian soldiers in his own army, who were put off by this measure and joined the mutineers. On the devastation of North Africa, see also the grim last sentence of the *Vandal War* (4.28.52) and of the supplementary Book 8 of the *Wars* (especially 8.17.22).

177. Prokopios does not actually estimate the number of dead in Italy (as he does for the Balkans at 18.21 below and has already for North Africa).

178. See especially *Wars* 6.20.15–33, 7.1.28–33, 7.9.1–6 on various abuses by Justinian's administration and the devastation of war.

179. The *logothetai* were agents of the treasury; see also *Wars* 7.1.28–33 and 7.9.13 for the *logothetes* Alexandros in Italy, and 24.2 below (24.9–11 and 26.29–30 for Italy specifically).

180. In 536.

sway over most of Gaul and the land of the Veneti.[181] [18] Sirmium and its surrounding territory were held by the Gepids,[182] but this entire region, to put it bluntly, was entirely depopulated. [19] Some people had died in war and others of disease and famine, which follow closely on the heels of war. [20] As for the Illyrians and all of Thrace, that is, the territory from the Adriatic[183] to the suburbs of Byzantion, including Greece and the Chersonnese, it was being raided almost every year by Huns, Slavs, and Antai from the moment that Justinian came to power among the Romans. The inhabitants of this region suffered ruinous devastation at their hands. [21] I believe that in each of their raids more than twenty times ten thousand of the Romans who lived there were either killed or enslaved, so that this entire territory came to resemble the proverbial Skythian wilderness.[184]

[22] Such were the consequences of this war for Africa and Europe. As for the Romans of the East, Saracens were constantly conducting raids against them throughout this entire period, ranging from Egypt to the borders of Persia. These attacks were so thorough that the regions in question became thinly populated; it would not ever be possible, I fear, for anyone to know exactly how many people were lost in this way, even if he should make a careful inquiry. [23] Chosroes and the Persians four times invaded the rest of Roman territory and razed the cities.[185] Of the people whom they seized, either in the cities that they captured or in their hinterlands, some they killed while others they marched away with them, leaving the land destitute of residents wherever they happened to attack. [24] And

181. Prokopios' "Germans" are the Franks. When Belisarios took Sicily, the Gothic king Theodahad gave to the Franks the areas of (Transalpine) Gaul (i.e., southern France) under Gothic rule and parts of northern Italy in exchange for their neutrality in the war (and covert assistance against their allies, the Romans). Vitigis confirmed this agreement in 537 (*Wars* 5.13.14–29, 7.33.2–6). The geographical digression in this section of *The Secret History* summarizes that in *Wars* 7.33, describing the state of affairs in 549.

182. A Germanic tribe settled north of the Danube (see especially *Wars* 7.33–35, 8.25–27).

183. Prokopios and other ancient and Byzantine writers called this the "Ionian Gulf."

184. An allusion to Aristophanes, *Acharnians* 704 (the proverb was common). Prokopios describes the raids of the Slavs and Antai into the Balkans mostly in Book 7 of the *Wars*.

185. In 540, 541 (Lazike; see 2.26–37 above), 542 (called the third invasion at 3.30 above), and 544 (or 543; there is dispute about this). Prokopios gives the same number of invasions at *Wars* 2.26.1.

from the time that they also invaded the land of Kolchis, the Kolchians, Lazoi, and the Romans have known nothing but destruction to this day.[186]

[25] Nor, for that matter, did the Persians, Saracens, Huns, the clans of the Slavs, or any other barbarians depart unscathed from Roman territory. [26] In their raids and still more in sieges and battles they encountered much opposition and were themselves likewise destroyed to a no lesser degree. [27] For it was not only the Romans but virtually all the barbarians as well who fell victim to Justinian's bloodlust. [28] Both he and Chosroes were malicious in character and, as I have explained in the proper place, our emperor provided theirs with all the pretexts that he needed for this war.[187] [29] He did not bother to adapt his policies to the circumstances but did everything at the wrong moment. During peace or a truce he was constantly fabricating causes of war with treacherous intentions against his neighbors, while in wartime he would sit back for no reason and be sluggish in directing operations because he hated the expense involved. Instead of taking direct charge of these matters, he would "ponder the heavens" and meddle into the question of God's nature.[188] So, on the one hand, he would not let go of the war because he was bloodthirsty and murderous, but, on the other hand, he was not able to prevail over his enemies because his stinginess prevented him from doing what had to be done. [30] Thus, during his reign, the entire earth was drenched with human blood, a constant stream that was being poured out by almost all the Romans and the barbarians.

[31] That, in sum, was what befell all the lands of the Romans during these times because of war. [32] And by calculating the number of victims claimed by the riots that occurred both in Byzantion and in every other city, I have come to the conclusion that the people who were slaughtered in those events were no fewer than in the

186. Chosroes invaded Kolchis/Lazike in 541 and held it until 547–548, when the Romans returned; the war there lasted until 556.

187. See 11.12 above.

188. A mocking allusion to the caricature of Sokrates in Aristophanes, *Clouds* 225–228 (see also 13.11 above and 20.22 below). Prokopios believed that the theological effort to ascertain the precise nature of God was idiotic (*Wars* 5.3.5–9). For Justinian's theological preoccupations, see *Wars* 7.32.9, translated in related text 10: "A Plot to Kill Justinian." He sometimes lost interest in the wars he was waging: *Wars* 7.36.6 ("perhaps because some other concern come up") and 8.26.7 (Justinian was negligent in prosecuting the war in Italy).

wars.[189] [33] As justice and appropriate retribution were hardly exacted for the crimes committed, and as the emperor excessively favored the one of the two fan-clubs, neither side kept quiet: the one was oppressed, the other emboldened, and so both were always desperate and out of control. Sometimes whole crowds of them went at each other, sometimes they battled in small groups, or, if it came to it, they even set ambushes for solitary targets. For thirty-two years they never relented for a single moment from doing horrible things to each other even while many of them were being executed by the authorities in charge of the populace.[190] [34] Of course, retribution for these crimes was largely imposed on the Greens. In addition, the punishment of the Samaritans and the so-called heretics filled the Roman Empire with more killings. [35] But I mention these things here only in summary, as I have adequately described them a little earlier.[191]

[36] That, then, was what befell the whole of humanity while this demon held human form, and he caused all of it, as he was emperor. I will now relate all the evils that he inflicted on mankind through his occult power and demonic nature. [37] For when he was governing Roman affairs, it happened that many other disasters also occurred, which some attribute to the presence of this malicious demon and his contrivances, while others believe that the deity so hated what he was doing that it turned its back on the Roman Empire, giving it over to avenging demons to ruin in this way. [38] For the Skirtos River flooded Edessa, creating a myriad of calamities for its inhabitants, as I will recount in a later book.[192] [39] Then, the Nile rose in its usual way but did not subside at the right time, with terrible consequences for those who dwelled by it, as I described earlier.[193] [40] The Kydnos River swamped almost all of Tarsos,

189. Especially the Nika riots of 532. Prokopios' account (*Wars* 1.24) is translated in related text 2.

190. For Justinian's new magistracies for dealing with crime and disturbances, see 20.9 below.

191. See 11.14–30 above.

192. The manuscript says "that will have been written by me in an earlier book"—a contradiction. Haury changed "earlier" to "later," because Prokopios describes this event (of 525) at *Buildings* 2.7.2–16. But Prokopios was not referring to the *Buildings* at this point. The Edessa flood occurred in the midst of a religious persecution, which is precisely the kind of material that he planned to include in his *Ecclesiastical History*.

193. At *Wars* 7.29.6–8, translated in related text 9: "Porphyrios the Whale and Other Natural Disasters"; this happened in 547–548.

keeping it under water for many days, and did not retreat before doing irreversible damage.[194] [41] Also, earthquakes leveled Antioch, the first city of the East, as well as Seleukeia, its neighbor city, and Anazarbos, the most notable city of Kilikia. [42] Who could estimate the number of people lost in these cities? One could add to them the losses in Ibora, Amaseia (which happens to be the first city in Pontos), Polybotos in Phrygia, the city that the Pisidians call Philomede, Lychnidion in Epeiros, and Corinth, which used to be very populous since antiquity. [43] But in these times all of them have been toppled by earthquakes and have lost virtually all of their inhabitants.[195] [44] And then the plague broke out as well, which I described earlier, and carried away half the survivors.[196] [45] That was the extent of the destruction of human life that occurred first while Justinian was governing the state[197] and later when he held sole imperial authority.

194. Prokopios would later describe this event (of 550) at *Buildings* 5.5.14–20.

195. Major earthquakes struck the region of Antioch in 526 (followed by extensive fires) and 528; Anazarbos, Epeiros (including Dyrrachion and, presumably Lychnidion, modern Ochrid), Corinth, and Anazarbos in 525; the Pontos (including Amaseia and Ibora) in 529. We know about many of these events from the notices in the *Chronicle* of Ioannes Malalas.

196. For the Justinianic plague, which struck Constantinople in 542, see Prokopios' account (*Wars* 2.22–23) translated in related text 8.

197. I.e., while his uncle Justin was still reigning (518–527).

Part III

The Corruption of Law, Administration, and Policy

Justinian's Greed and Profligacy

19. I turn now to explain how he soaked up all the money in the world. I will first relate a vision that was seen in a dream toward the beginning of Justin's reign by one of the notables. [2] He said that it appeared to him in the dream that he was standing somewhere in Byzantion by the shore of the sea, at a point across from Chalcedon, and that he saw Justinian standing in the very middle of the channel. [3] And first he drank up all the water in the sea, so that it seemed to him from now on that Justinian was standing upon dry land, as the current of the channel was no longer there. But then other water poured in, all filth and muck, from the sewer outlets on either side. He drank this up too, drying up the channel basin again.

[4] That is what the dream-vision announced. This Justinian fellow, then, when his uncle Justin was raised to the throne, found the state well endowed with public money. [5] For Anastasios had been the most diligent and fiscally prudent of all emperors.[1] His fear was—which indeed came to pass—that if his successor on the throne fell short of cash he might perhaps resort to plundering his subjects. So he glutted all the public treasuries with gold before the end of his allotted life span. [6] Justinian, however, squandered them all as soon as he could, some on pointless constructions by the coast and some in his generous bribes to the barbarians.[2] Yet one might have thought that these sums would have sufficed for a hundred years, even for an extremely wasteful emperor. [7] Those who are in charge

1. Anastasios (r. 491–518).

2. For the coastal constructions, see especially 8.7–8 above; for the bribes to the barbarians, see 8.5–6 and 11.5–11 above and 19.13–17 below.

of the treasuries, funds, and other aspects of imperial finance claim that Anastasios, who ruled the Romans for more than twenty-seven years, left behind him three thousand two hundred *kentenaria* of gold in the public treasury.[3] [8] In fact, during Justin's nine-year reign, this Justinian stirred up so much confusion and disorder in the state that he managed to rake in four thousand *kentenaria* to the imperial coffers—illegally, of course.[4] Yet by the end of that reign, not one bit of this money was left; this person managed to spend it all, even while Justin still lived, in the way that I mentioned earlier.[5] [9] And as for what he improperly swindled and managed to consume during the whole of his lifetime, there is no document, no calculation, no method of accounting that would tell us what that sum was. [10] Persistent like an ever-flowing river, he washed away his subjects' wealth and ravaged their lives, yet the current carried everything down into the hands of the barbarians.

[11] No sooner had he thus "exported" the public wealth than he turned his gaze on his subjects, separating most of them from their property by snatching it up through unjustified violence and by accusing those reputed to be prosperous in Byzantion and in every city of crimes that had not even taken place. Some were accused of polytheism or, if they were Christian, of belief in an unorthodox heresy;[6] others of sodomy,[7] or of having sex with holy women,[8] or of some other kind of unnatural intercourse; or inciting a riot; siding with the Green fan-club; of insolence toward him;[9] or any other crime. He would become the default heir of the deceased and even, if need be, of the living, on the pretext that he had been adopted by them.[10] [12] Such were his most statesman-

3. I.e., 23,040,000 coins (see the Glossary). Ioannes Lydos puts Anastasios' reserves at countless tens of thousands of gold pounds (*On the Magistracies of the Roman State* 3.51). Prokopios praised Anastasios for his careful administration (*Wars* 1.10.11) and fostering peace and prosperity (*Wars* 7.21.23).

4. I.e., 28,800,000 coins (see the Glossary). Obviously, not all of this revenue, if the figure is correct, could have been acquired illegally.

5. Either in the passage immediately above or at 8.4–11 above.

6. See primarily 11.14–33 above.

7. See primarily 11.34–36 above; also 16.19.

8. This is not mentioned elsewhere in *The Secret History*. Justinian punished relations with nuns in *Codex Iustinianus* 1.3.53 and 9.13.2 (of 533); *Novella* 123.43 (of 546).

9. Probos, a relative of Emperor Anastasios, was tried for insulting Justinian (and forgiven by him) in 528 (Ioannes Malalas, *Chronicle* 18.22).

10. See 12.3–11 above.

like actions, indeed. A short while earlier I also recounted how he took advantage of the riots named "Nika" that were directed against him in order to become, at a stroke, the heir of all the Senators and how, even before the riots, he had privately seized the property of not a few, one at a time.[11]

[13] There was no time at which he ceased giving huge gifts of money to all the barbarians, to both easterners and westerners as well as out toward the North and to the South, as far as the inhabitants of Britain and to all the peoples of the inhabited portions of the earth whom we had not even heard of formerly. Now, however, we learned their names at the same time that we first set eyes on them.[12] [14] For when they found out what kind of man he was, they poured into Byzantion from every corner of the world in order to reach him.[13] [15] This, of course, hardly troubled him, for he was overjoyed at this state of affairs, believing it to be a lucky opportunity to exhaust the wealth of the Romans and throw it out to the barbarians, as good as throwing it into the churning waves of the sea. Every day he would constantly send them back to their homes, each one of them loaded with cash. [16] In this way, then, all the barbarians together became the masters of any form of wealth the Romans had left, either through the emperor's cash subsidies, or by ransoming captives, or charging a fee for peace. This was how the dream-vision, which I just mentioned, was fulfilled, at least according to the man who saw it. [17] Justinian even managed to devise additional ways to rob his subjects, which I will promptly divulge, insofar as I am able. By these means he was continually plundering everyone's property, yet not all at once, but in small bits.

Corrupting the Highest Offices

20. First, he tended to appoint prefects over the populace in Byzantion who, in expectation of a share in the annual profits, gave to shopkeepers permission to sell their goods at whatever price they

11. See 12.12 above. Prokopios' account of the Nika riots of 532 (*Wars* 1.24) is translated in related text 2.

12. It was a commonplace of imperial rhetoric that the names of distant barbarian peoples were learned when the emperors conquered them; Prokopios is here subverting that motif, as it is the barbarians who are mastering Justinian.

13. A similar statement at 8.5–6 above. For criticism of Justinian's payments to the barbarians, see also 11.5–11 above.

wanted.[14] [2] The effect of this on people here was that they had to buy their necessities for triple the previous price and that there was no one to whom they could protest about it. [3] This policy had grave repercussions. Given that the imperial treasury had a stake in this source of income, the official in charge of such matters wished to enrich himself from it. [4] Also, this official's subordinates, appointed to oversee the shameful business, as well as the shopkeepers themselves, eagerly seized the opportunity to break the law and gouge consumers to their ruin, not merely, as I said, by charging many times the multiple of the price but by devising unspeakable ways of lowering the quality of their goods. [5] Second, he established many of these so-called monopolies, vending the welfare of his subjects to those who dared to exploit this loathsome trade.[15] And while he walked away in return with a cut of the profits, he gave his subcontractors the license to run their business however they pleased. [6] He openly committed the same outrage in dealing with all other government offices and bureaus. For as the emperor would always skim off a small share of the loot for himself, the magistrates as well as those placed in charge of each transaction proceeded to rob their victims with even greater confidence.

[7] And as if the existing magistracies that had long been established were not sufficient for his purposes, he devised two more to add to the state, even though the magistracy in charge of the city populace had previously handled all criminal accusations.[16] [8] But he decided to invent these two offices to ensure that the number of professional informers was always increasing and in order to expedite the process of bodily torture for people who had done no wrong. [9] One of the two was supposedly given jurisdiction over thieves and received the name "the *praetor* of the people." The other was appointed to punish those who habitually practiced sodomy with other men, or who had illicit sex with women, along with any whose

14. Prokopios is discussing the urban prefecture. The emperors Leon I and Zenon had forbidden private monopolies and the fixing of prices by cartels of merchants and artisans (*Codex Iustinianus* 4.59). Monopolies were formed when the state sold the exclusive right to deal in a certain good. Prokopios implies that Justinian ignored his predecessors' legislation.

15. For the monopolies, see also 25.13, 26.19, and 26.36 below. But in 544, soon after the first outbreak of the plague, Justinian addressed *Novella* 122 to the urban prefect ordering him to cap prices, blaming merchants and artisans for charging too much. It seems that he was trying to check the abuses that Prokopios is decrying here.

16. That is, the urban prefect.

religion was deviant, and he named this office *quaesitor*.[17] [10] If, then, the *praetor* happened to find amidst all the stolen articles that he confiscated any of great value, he would hand them over to the emperor, alleging that their owners were nowhere to be found. [11] This was a perpetual source of priceless goods for the emperor. The one called *quaesitor*, after finishing with those who were hauled before his court, would hand over to the emperor as much of the take as he saw fit, though his own personal profit, obtained illegally and at the expense of other people, was no less than his master's cut. [12] And the subordinates of these officials brought forth neither accusers nor witnesses for the crimes that were alleged. No, throughout this period a long procession of victims, who remained both unindicted and unconvicted, were being murdered secretly and parted from their property. [13] Later this Agent of Destruction decreed that the jurisdiction of both of these officials, in addition to that of the urban prefect, was to include any and all cases of criminal conduct, instructing them that they were to compete with each other to see who could destroy more people in the shortest time.[18] [14] It is said that one of them immediately asked him who was to have jurisdiction if someone were to be denounced to all three of them simultaneously. His answer was, "whichever one of you gets the jump on the others."

[15] He also introduced disorder into the office that is called the *quaestor*, whereas just about every previous emperor had taken extreme care to ensure that its holders were experienced in many things but were especially learned in the law, and also that they were manifestly incorruptible when it came to money on the grounds that the state would incur a terrible risk if the men who held this office were impeded by inexperience or driven by greed. [16] But the first man whom this emperor appointed to it was Tribonianos, whose dealings were adequately described in a previous book.[19] [17] When

17. For the institution of the *praetor* of the people (Greek *praitor* of the *demos*), see *Novella* 13 (of 535). This official was to prosecute pimps according to *Novella* 14 (of 535) and apparently also astrologers (based on 11.37 above). For the institution of the *quaesitor* (Greek *koiaisitor*), see *Novella* 80 (of 539), which is concerned with the surveillance of provincials who come to the capital for business; for the *quaesitor's* jurisdiction over the charge of sodomy, see 16.19 above. Justinian claimed that these two offices were instituted to handle the increase in crime caused by the influx of destitute people into the capital.

18. This enactment has not survived.

19. Tribonianos was first a member and then director of the commission that codified Roman law in 528–534, producing the *Corpus iuris civilis*. He served Jus-

Tribonianos departed from among men, Justinian seized a portion of his property even though the man left behind him a son and many grandchildren on the last day of his life. He then appointed Junillus, from North Africa, to this position, a man who had never even heard of "law" as a concept, given that he was not trained in formal rhetoric.[20] To be sure, he did know his Latin, but when it came to Greek he had not so much as studied under a grammarian. His tongue could not quite make the right sounds. In fact, he often volunteered phrases in Greek, but all this accomplished was to make his subordinates laugh. He was, however, extremely eager to make money through shameful means. He had no compunction whatever against auctioning imperial decrees and decisions in public. [18] With no shame he would spread his hand open for any passer-by, to be bribed even by the tiny sum of one gold coin. [19] For a period of no less than seven years he made the state into a laughingstock.

[20] When Junillus had reached the term of his life, Justinian appointed Konstantinos to the position. This one was not altogether ignorant of the law but was ridiculously young and had no actual experience of legal disputes in the courts.[21] He was, however, the biggest thief and braggart that humanity had to show. [21] This man became most appealing to Justinian, in fact one of his closest friends, since this emperor did not hesitate to use him also for his constant thefts and prosecutions. [22] As a result, Konstantinos amassed much money in no time and affected a superbly boastful manner, "walking on the air and looking down on" everyone.[22] Anyone who was prepared to hand over a large sum of money to him had to deposit it with certain of his trusted associates; he was then free to put his

tinian as *quaestor* from 529 to 532, at which point he was dismissed (during the Nika riots) because of the popular outcry against his venality (*Wars* 1.24.16, translated in related text 2; *Wars* 1.25.2 translated in related text 7), and again from 535–542. He has appeared at 13.12 above as a member of the court. Tribonianos was one of the greatest jurists of Roman law of all time and, like many intellectuals of this period, possibly not a Christian.

20. Junillus served as *quaestor* from 542 to 548/549; he also wrote a popular introduction to the Bible (the *Instituta regularia divinae legis*), a translation of a Greek work by Paulos of Nisibis. Formal rhetoric, both its theory and practice, were very much part of the legal profession at this time, in fact a qualification for it. Prokopios had that very training.

21. Konstantinos served as *quaestor* from 548–549 to 562 (and possibly later).

22. A mocking allusion to the caricature of Sokrates in Aristophanes, *Clouds* 225–228 (see also 13.11 and 18.29 above).

plans into effect.[23] [23] But to meet with him personally or contact him at all him was impossible for anyone, except when he was going to the emperor or coming from him. Even then it was never at a walking pace, but with urgency and great speed lest anyone approach him and waste his time with unprofitable matters.

21. Those, then, were the policies of the emperor in these spheres. As for the praetorian prefect, every year he collected more than thirty *kentenaria* above and beyond the public taxes.[24] [2] These he named "the air tax,"[25] by which, I think, he meant that this was not a regular or established tax but that it always seemed to fall by chance into his hands, as though out of thin air. More correctly, these were the fruits of his viciousness. [3] In the name of this tax, the holders of this office began to plunder their subjects with ever greater impunity. [4] They claimed, of course, that they were delivering the proceeds over to the emperor, but with no difficulty they acquired royal riches for themselves.[26] [5] Justinian made no move to press his rights and punish this behavior but bided his time: as soon as they had acquired great wealth, he accused them of some inexcusable crime or other; then, he could separate them from their property in one swoop. He did this even to Ioannes the Kappadokian.[27] [6] At any rate, all who held this position during this time suddenly became rich beyond measure, except, that is, for two of them: Phokas, who was mentioned earlier as a staunch guardian of the laws[28]—no profit stained this man while he was in office—and Bassos, who was

23. I.e., they had prepaid legal cover for the illegal activities that they had planned.

24. I.e., 216,000 coins in extra taxes (see the Glossary).

25. It is still unclear what kind of tax (or fine) the *aerikon* was. Its name appears to be derived from the Greek for "air," whence Prokopios' sarcasm, but it may be from Latin *aes* (gen. *aeris*), a type of coin.

26. The text is ambiguous: either they acquired riches worthy of an emperor or they more literally pocketed imperial money.

27. Ioannes served as praetorian prefect from 531 to 541, except for a few months after January 532 (he was dismissed during the Nika riots by popular demand; see *Wars* 1.24.12–15, translated in related text 2). Hatred for him was expressed by many during the reign, and he was powerful enough to occasionally counter Theodora. Prokopios' account of his downfall in 541 (*Wars* 1.25) is translated in related text 7.

28. Phokas served as praetorian prefect during 532 for a few months after the dismissal of Ioannes the Kappadokian. He was twice suspected of being a pagan and committed suicide in the purge of 545–546. He was admired by Prokopios (*Wars* 1.24.18) and Ioannes Lydos (*On the Magistracies of the Roman State* 3.72, 3.74).

appointed to this position at a later time.[29] [7] Of these two men, neither held this office for a full year, as they were removed from it after a few months on account of their being useless types, altogether out of touch with the times. [8] But if I were to go into the details of each case it would take forever, so I will say only that the emperor handled the other magistracies in Byzantion in the same way.

[9] In fact, Justinian implemented the following policies everywhere in the Roman Empire. He picked out the most villainous characters and sold to them, at a high price, the offices that they were to corrupt.[30] [10] For no man who was decent or who had a trace of good sense would ever dream of handing over his own money for the privilege of plundering those who had done no wrong.[31] [11] So pocketing the gold from his contractors, he would elevate them to positions of absolute power over his subjects. [12] The inevitable consequence of this was that they ruined all the lands under their jurisdiction, including the people in them, so as to spend the rest of their own life rich. [13] They would purchase offices that governed the cities by borrowing from the bank at hefty rates of interest and then paying it over to the one selling the position; and when they arrived in their cities they would invariably put every form of evil governance on display having no other concern than how to pay back their creditors and gain for themselves entry into the ranks of the superrich. These tactics carried for them no risk of danger or ill repute; quite the contrary, they stood to gain glory proportional to the number of people who fell into their hands and whom they managed to rob and kill for no good reason. [14] The labels of "murderer" and "thief" were translated for them into a reputation for brisk efficiency. [15] Of course, when he perceived that any of his officeholders was growing wealthy, he would immediately snare him with some charge or another and separate him from his money all at once.

[16] He then issued a law by which those seeking office had to swear an oath that they would keep themselves pure of all theft and would neither give nor receive anything in connection with their

29. Flavius Komitas Theodoros Bassos served as praetorian prefect during 548.

30. This sentence is corrupt in the manuscript tradition.

31. By selling offices the state made money while the officeholders recouped their investment by exploiting its legal (and illegal) opportunities for gain. This was practiced not only by the emperor but also by lower officials (selling the offices of their subordinates). The practice was limited to provincial administration, not "cabinet" positions.

duties. [17] And upon any who would deviate from these instructions he laid down all the curses that have been known since the most ancient times.[32] [18] Yet not a year had passed since this law was enacted before he himself violated his own curse-protected instructions and disregarded the shame in so doing. He began to bargain over the price of offices with even less hesitation than before and not behind closed doors either but in full public view. [19] And these "magistrates under oath" who had bought their offices now plundered everything even more than before.[33]

[20] Later he devised an additional scheme, shocking beyond belief. He decided that he would no longer, as before, sell those offices which he thought were highest in rank in Byzantion and all the other cities but would appoint to them some hirelings that he had sought out, bidding them, in return for some salary or another, to hand over *all* the loot to him. [21] Pocketing their wages, with even greater impunity they stacked up and carried away everything from all the width and breadth of the land. And so these mercenary officials would go around plundering their subjects in the name of lawful authority.[34] [22] Thus the emperor carefully scrutinized each man's credentials so as to always place in charge of affairs the most abominable men in the world—to call things by their proper names—and he could always sniff out the most loathsome man for the job. [23] In fact, when the first such scoundrels were appointed to positions of authority and the exercise of power brought their evil characters into the light, we were astonished that human nature could accommodate such wickedness. [24] But when those who, in time, succeeded them in these offices managed to far outstrip them, people wondered among themselves how such a great paradox had come to pass, namely that their predecessors, who had then seemed to be so villainous, were now so outdone by their successors that they were regarded in retrospect as perfect gentlemen in the performance

32. With *Novella* 8 (of 535), translated in related text 5, Justinian abolished the sale of provincial governorships on the grounds that it promoted corruption and extortion. Prokopios echoes the emperor's language in this passage. *Novella* 17 (of the same year) contained specific instructions for provincial administration, reiterating many of the provisions of *Novella* 8.

33. For the sale of offices by the praetorian prefect Petros Barsymes in the mid-540s, see 22.7–9 below.

34. The only realistic alternative to the sale of offices was salaried officials instructed to convey all taxes to the imperial government rather than skim off the top or extort in order to recoup their investment. The following passage is suspiciously vague and rhetorical compared to the rest of *The Secret History*.

of their official duties. And the third batch, in turn, set the bar even lower than the second for all-around malfeasance while, after *them*, the next group invented such bizarre grounds on which to put people on trial that they imparted on their predecessors a reputation for virtue. [25] As this evil state of affairs dragged on, everyone finally learned through hard experience that the wickedness of human nature has no limits, especially when it is nourished by the example set by predecessors and when the license granted by absolute power incites it to injure and punish anyone who crosses its path. Then this evil seems always to attain such proportions that the minds of its victims can scarcely comprehend it.

[26] That, then, was what the Romans had to cope with when it came to their officials. Often it happened that an army of enemy Huns was plundering Roman territory and enslaving the population. The generals of Thrace and Illyria were determined to set out and attack them but had to turn back upon receipt of written orders from the emperor Justinian forbidding them from attacking the barbarians on the grounds that they would be necessary allies for the Romans in the war against the Goths, perhaps, or against some other enemy.[35] [27] As a result, these barbarians would plunder those regions and enslave the Romans there as enemies, but when they returned home, driving before them not only their loot but captives as well, they did so as "friends and allies of the Romans." [28] Often some of the farmers of those regions, driven by longing for their own wives and children who had been enslaved, would band together and kill many of the departing enemies, even managing to seize their horses in addition to all the loot. But because of this they landed into difficulties indeed. [29] For certain men were sent out from Byzantion with instructions to torture them, mutilate their bodies, and impose fines on them, and not to relent until they had returned all the horses that they had seized from the barbarians.

Petros Barsymes and the Praetorian Prefecture

22. When the emperor and Theodora had rid themselves of Ioannes the Kappadokian and wanted to replace him with a successor in that office,[36] they made a joint effort to find someone more villainous than him. They were looking around basically for an instrument of

35. This passage seems out of place in this section of *The Secret History*.

36. For the downfall of Ioannes (in 541), see Prokopios' account (*Wars* 1.25) translated in related text 7.

their own tyranny and so scrutinized the mentality of all candidates to see who would help them destroy their subjects even more quickly than before. [2] For the time being, they replaced him with Theodotos in that magistracy, not exactly a good man but not such as to please them immensely.[37] [3] Then they made a most thorough search in all directions, landing upon an unexpected choice, a certain money changer named Petros, of Syrian origin, who was surnamed Barsymes. In past years he had sat at a table changing bronze coins, making an unseemly profit through this occupation. He was especially skilled at stealing money, his light fingers always cheating those with whom he did business. [4] He was handy when it came to casually stealing the property of those who came his way; when caught, he would swear as to his innocence and so cover up the sin of his hands by the unscrupulousness of his tongue. [5] When he was enrolled in the prefect's bureau, his conduct was so outrageous that Theodora was absolutely delighted with him, and he was eager to help her implement the most unlikely of her criminal schemes. [6] Therefore Theodotos, whom they had appointed after the Kappadokian, was relieved of his office and Petros was put in his place, who did everything exactly as they liked it.[38] [7] He was never seen to express any shame or fear when he deprived soldiers of all their pay.[39] Not only that, he put offices up for sale even more pervasively than before, cheapening their dignity by granting them to people who did not scruple to engage in this sordid business. He gave those who purchased offices explicit permission to treat the lives and property of their subjects however they pleased. [8] For it was immediately understood between him and the man who paid the price for the district in question that the latter would have the authority to strip it bare and otherwise pillage at will. This selling of people's lives, then, proceeded from the very apex of the state, [9] as Petros bargained over the contract for the destruction of the cities. A legalized bandit, he prowled the highest courts and public spaces of the marketplace, defining his job as the collection of the sums paid in advance for high office, and there was no hope that these crimes

37. Theodotos served as praetorian prefect from 541 to the end of 542 (and again from 546 to 547, but Prokopios does not mention this second tenure).

38. Petros' first term as praetorian prefect lasted from 543 (at least) to 546 (the second from 555 to 562).

39. The *Wars*, especially the *Gothic War*, offers many examples of soldiers not being paid on time (or at all); see also 24.12 below.

would be punished.[40] [10] Of all the men serving in this bureau, who were many and distinguished, he invariably attracted the most villainous to himself. [11] And he was certainly not the only one to follow this evil course; so did all who held this office both before and after him.

[12] The position of *magister*, as that official is called, was similarly corrupted,[41] as were the palatine officials whose established responsibility was fiscal (to oversee both the so-called *privata* and the *patrimonium*);[42] the same was true, to sum it up, regarding all the other magistracies in Byzantion and the cities. [13] For from the moment that this tyrant took over the management of affairs,[43] the revenues that belonged to subordinate officials were arbitrarily seized either by him or by the magistrate heading up each department, so that those who served under them, being extremely poor, were forced to perform their duties always as if they were slaves.[44]

[14] A large supply of grain had been shipped to Byzantion but most of it had already rotted.[45] Yet he himself required that it be consigned to each of the cities of the East, even though it was no longer fit for human consumption, and he required additionally that it be purchased not at the price of the best-quality grain, but much more dearly than even that.[46] So it was necessary for the buyers to fork over huge sums to meet these oppressive prices, and then they

40. For the sale of offices under Justinian, see 21.9–25 above.

41. See 16.5 above for Petros "the Patrician" and 17.32 for Hermogenes.

42. The *res privata* and *patrimonium* were imperially owned estates and assets, each managed by a *comes*.

43. At 18.45 above this phrase refers specifically to Justinian's power during the reign of his uncle Justin.

44. Presumably, a greater proportion of the regional assets of these departments were to be passed on to Constantinople rather than spent locally (see *Edict* 13 for Egypt). This paragraph on the *magister* is awkwardly placed in this part of the text.

45. Constantinople, the largest city in the empire, was dependent on Egyptian grain. It was the responsibility of the governor at Alexandria, working with officials in the prefect's staff, to ensure these shipments on the Egyptian end (see *Edict* 13), and it was the praetorian prefect's job to oversee their distribution in the capital. Contrary winds could interfere with timely delivery; see *Buildings* 5.1.7–16.

46. This is again the praetorian prefect Petros Barsymes (following on 22.3–11 above), so we are in 543–546. Cities near Constantinople were apparently required to purchase surplus grain from the capital at a price set by Petros and regardless of quality.

had to toss the grain into the sea or into some drain. [15] Conversely, when he had a large surplus there of quality grain that had not yet rotted, he decided to sell this also to the many cities whose supplies were running low. [16] Thus he raked in twice the amount of money that the public treasury had previously taxed its subjects for the grain.[47] [17] But the following year the harvest was not as abundant and the grain fleet arrived at Byzantion with a smaller cargo than was necessary.[48] Petros was at a loss how to deal with this situation, and resolved to purchase a large supply of grain from the farms of Bithynia, Phrygia, and Thrace. [18] The inhabitants of these lands were accordingly saddled with the heavy burden of transporting these cargoes down to the sea and, from there, of conveying them to Byzantion at their own risk. They received pitiful reimbursements from him for this, indeed purely nominal. In fact, their loss was so great that they would have preferred it had they been allowed to hand over the grain at a public warehouse as a gift, and even be allowed to pay for the privilege. [19] This is the imposition commonly called a "requisition."[49] As even then there was still not enough grain in Byzantion, many complained about this to the emperor. [20] At this time the soldiers also, almost all of them, were stirring up trouble in the city and causing a commotion because they had not received their regular pay.[50]

[21] The emperor now gave the impression of being displeased with him and wanted to depose him from his position, both because of these events and also because he had heard that Petros had secreted away a huge sum of money that he had embezzled from the public treasury. [22] And indeed it was so. But Theodora would not allow her husband to do this, for she was deeply attached to Barsymes, it seems to me, because of his evil mind and his extraordinary ability to ruin those under his power. [23] She was cruel, overflowing with inhumanity, and preferred her subordinates to be like her in character. [24] They also say that he had placed a spell on her to favor him against her will. [25] For this Barsymes was obsessed with magicians and spirits and deeply admired the cult known as the Manicheans. He did not even hesitate to defend them

47. The state paid a nominal rate for Egyptian grain; Petros apparently sold the surplus at a higher rate to cities in need.

48. This was probably in 545–546.

49. See 23.11–14 below.

50. For Petros cheating the soldiers out of their pay, see 22.7 above.

publicly.[51] [26] Yet even when the empress had heard about these things, still she did not lift her favor from the man but decided to embrace his cause all the more, precisely because of all this, and show him even more affection. [27] For she too had consorted with magicians and poisoners since childhood, as her way of life had led her directly to it, so throughout her life she believed firmly in the occult and always placed her trust in it. [28] It is said, moreover, that she had managed to subdue Justinian to her will not by fawning on him but by the coercive power of demons. [29] For he was not sufficiently well-meaning or just or so steadfast in virtue as to resist such an attempt to subdue him; to the contrary, it was apparent that his love of murder and money got the better of him, and he easily succumbed to deceit and flattery. [30] Even in matters of great concern to him he could change his position for no apparent reason and become as light as dust that is carried on the wind.[52] [31] As a result, not one of his relatives or other associates could ever rely on him as his intentions and plans were constantly vacillating. [32] Thus, given that he was so vulnerable to witchcraft, as I just said, Theodora easily put him under her thumb. And for this reason she simply adored Petros, as he was very proficient in those very arts. [33] So the emperor was with great difficulty able to remove him from the position that he had previously held. Not long afterward, and at Theodora's insistence, he appointed him director of the treasuries and removed Ioannes from that position, which the latter had received only months earlier.[53]

[34] That man was originally from Palestine, and he was gentle and very kind. He simply did not know how to generate revenue from unjust sources, nor had he ever harmed a single person. [35] Not surprisingly, the entire populace loved him exceedingly, but for the same reason he displeased Justinian and his wife. Whenever they saw, to their surprise, that one of their subordinates was a kind and virtuous man, they became dizzy and dreadfully dismayed, and made it their top priority to get rid of him as soon as possible by any means necessary. [36] It was in this way that Petros replaced Ioannes and was

51. The religion of the Persian prophet Mani (third century) spread from the Roman Empire to China. It advocated a dualist view of the world and was persecuted severely by both pagan and Christian emperors. For Justinian's measures against it, see *Codex Iustinianus* 1.5.12.3, 1.5.15–16, 1.5.18–19, 1.5.21.

52. This image occurs also at 13.10 above; for this renewed discussion of the character of Justinian and Theodora, see the Introduction, p. xxxv.

53. In 547 or 548, Petros was made count of the sacred largesses (*comes sacrarum largitionum*).

made director of the imperial treasuries, where he again became the man chiefly responsible for great misfortunes that affected everyone. [37] He cut back most of the money that, by an ancient convention, the emperor doled out every year to many people by way of "consolation."[54] He, however, enriched himself improperly at public expense, giving only a portion of it to the emperor. [38] Those whose subsidies had been cut crumpled in anguish and despair, especially given that he did not continue to issue the gold coin as before, but made it smaller, a thing that had never occurred in the past.[55]

Impoverishing the Landowners

[39] Those were the emperor's policies regarding officeholders. I turn now to explain how he ruined landowners in every region. [40] When a short while earlier we made reference to the governors who were sent out to all the cities,[56] there was no need to relate also the sufferings of the locals themselves. For the first victims of these governors' greed were the landowners. This, then, and all else too, will now be revealed.

23. First of all, it was an established custom since ancient times for each ruler of the Romans to remit to all his subjects the arrears of what they owed in taxes to the public treasury, and not just once, at that, but often. This was so as not to continuously suffocate those who were financially spent and had no means by which to pay off the remainder, and also to provide no pretexts for the tax collectors to bring cases against subjects who were liable to be taxed but who currently owed nothing. Yet for thirty-two years this emperor did no such thing for his subjects.[57] [2] As a result, those who could not pay had no choice but to flee and never again return.[58] [3] And

54. Little is known about how these salary supplements worked.

55. Lighter gold coins may have been minted to cover budget shortfalls or to reduce the cost of diplomatic gifts, barbarian subsidies, or foreign trade. The rate of seventy-two coins to the Roman pound had been set by Constantine the Great.

56. At 21.20–25 and 22.7–9 above.

57. Prokopios is here referring to general cancelations of arrears. In the preface of *Novella* 147 (of 553, so after *The Secret History* was finished), Justinian stated that he had granted some specific cancelations (which are, anyway, attested in other sources; and see 23.6 below) but admitted that he not yet granted a general one.

58. In the preface to *Novella* 80 (of 539), Justinian stated that many farmers were abandoning their lands and drifting to the capital, a development that, in his

informers harassed those who were better off by threatening to accuse them of paying less in tax than their district really owed, and of having done so for many years. [4] These unfortunate people, then, were terrified not only at the new rates of taxation but also at the prospect of being saddled with the burden of so many years' worth of unjust back taxes. [5] In fact, many simply handed their property over to the informers or to the state just to be rid of the trouble.

[6] Added to this, the Medes and the Saracens were plundering most of the Asian provinces while the Huns, Slavs, and Antai were plundering all those on the European side. They razed some of the cities to the ground and stripped others bare of every last bit of wealth. Their citizens they carried off into slavery along with all their money, leaving each province denuded of its inhabitants by these daily raids. And yet he did not remit taxes for anyone at all, except in the case of captured cities, and then for only a year. [7] Even if, like the emperor Anastasios, he had remitted the taxes of captured cities for seven years, that, in my opinion, would still not have been enough, considering that Kavades hardly damaged the cities' infrastructure before he departed whereas Chosroes burned everything to the ground and inflicted greater misfortune on those who fell into his hands.[59] [8] And to those who received this laughable tax exemption and to all the others—given that they often had to endure the army of the Medes, that the Huns and Saracens were continually plundering the eastern lands, and that the barbarians of Europe were causing no less damage on the European side to the Romans there, all the time and every day—to those same people this emperor quickly became an even greater enemy than all the barbarians.[60] [9] No sooner had the foreign enemies departed than the landowners were utterly ruined by the "requisitions," the so-called impositions, and the levies. [10] What these terms are and what they mean, I will now explain.

---

mind, required the institution of the *quaesitor* to strengthen law enforcement (see 20.9 above). In discussing the abandonment of lands in this chapter, Prokopios is echoing the language of that *Novella* (as was Ioannes Lydos, *On the Magistracies of the Roman State* 3.70).

59. Emperor Anastasios (r. 491–518) remitted seven years of annual taxes for the city of Amida, which was captured by King Kavades of Persia in 502–503 and held for one year (*Wars* 1.7.35). Chosroes was Kavades' son.

60. In *Novella* 32 (of 535), Justinian proclaimed that some types of creditors were worse calamities for farmers than were barbarian invasions. Prokopios seems to be using the emperor's language against him here.

[11] They compel landowners to supply the Roman army according to the measure of the tax that is due from each, and the goods are handed over not according to the needs of the present moment but according to convenience and the chain of command, while the officials make no inquiry to determine whether each landowner actually has the necessary goods on his land. [12] It therefore fell upon these sorry wretches to transport supplies to both soldiers and horses that they had bought at great cost, far more than they were worth, in some cases from districts that were far away from wherever the camps happened to be. Then they had to measure the supplies out to the camp quartermasters, not, however, on the terms that are used by people everywhere but rather according to the wishes of the quartermasters themselves. [13] This is what they call a "requisition,"[61] due to which all landowners have been economically hamstrung [14] for it forces them to pay no less than ten times the annual tax; not only, as was said, do they have to supply the army, but the burden often falls on them to transport the grain to Byzantion. The one called Barsymes was not alone in daring to require this unjust source of grief; the Kappadokian had earlier done it too as did later those who succeeded Barsymes in this office.[62]

[15] So much, in general, for the "requisition." As for the "imposition," its very name denotes an unforeseen calamity that suddenly assails landowners and rips up from the root any hopes that they may have left in life. [16] For it is a tax on lands that are abandoned or lie unused, whose owners and farmers have either all passed away or have abandoned their ancestral lands, in short those who lie buried under the evils that oppress them on account of this. And they do not hesitate to impose this burden on any landowners who are not yet completely destroyed.[63]

61. For the *synônê* (Latin *coemptio*), a compulsory purchase for military needs, see *Codex Iustinianus* 10.27.2; and *Novella* 130 (of 545), which calls for much fairer practices than Prokopios describes. The system was no doubt abused (for another example from later in the reign, see Agathias, *Histories* 4.22).

62. For the grain requisition imposed by Petros Barsymes, see 22.17–19 above. He was succeeded as prefect by Theodotos (who was also his immediate predecessor; see 22.2 above) and Bassos (who also briefly replaced Ioannes the Kappadokian in 532 and is said to have been an honest man; see 21.6–7 above).

63. Lands that were abandoned were assigned to be cultivated by the owners of neighboring lands or to heirs, who henceforth paid their taxes. For the *epibolê*, see *Novellae* 17.14 (of 536) and 128.7–8 (of 545); for the abandonment of lands, see 23.20–21 below and note 58 above.

[17] Such was the meaning of "imposition," a term that understandably gained much currency during these times. As for the "levies," we may dispose of them briefly as follows. [18] That the cities suffered from many harmful demands was inevitable, both at other times generally but especially during this period. I will not at present explain their causes and forms, lest my account go on without end. [19] These demands were met by the landowners, each paying in proportion to his tax assessment. [20] But their hardship did not end there. When the plague broke out, no less in the Roman Empire than it did in the entirety of the inhabited world, and wiped out the majority of the farmers, this caused many estates to be deserted, as you can imagine.[64] Yet *he* showed no leniency toward their owners. [21] He never once waived the annual tax, demanding not only the sum that was assessed on each of them but also, from them too, that which was due from their deceased neighbors.[65] [22] In addition to this they had to endure all the rest that I mentioned just above, which was imposed on those who had the misfortune of owning estates. And as if all that were not enough, they also had to host soldiers in their most spacious and furnished rooms and wait on them there like servants, while they themselves had to live all this time in the most miserable and unfinished hovels that were left over.[66] [23] It happened, moreover, that all these hardships afflicted people continuously during the reign of Justinian and Theodora, given that throughout this period there was no interruption in war or in any other terrible calamity. [24] Having just mentioned the occupation of rooms, I should not neglect to add this, that homeowners in Byzantion had to put up barbarian soldiers numbering some seventy thousand. So not only did they not enjoy the use of their own property, they were worn down by these other difficulties.

64. For the Justinianic plague, which struck Constantinople in 542, see Prokopios' account (*Wars* 2.22–23) translated in related text 8.

65. In other words, taxes owed on abandoned lands were imposed on the tax district generally; see *Novella* 128 (of 545).

66. Regarding the billeting of soldiers, Prokopios seems to be inverting *Novella* 130.9 (of 545), which stipulates that soldiers should not be billeted in homeowners' primary residence.

Shortchanging the Troops

24. Nor should I bury in silence his treatment of the soldiers, over whom he put the most devious types that there are,[67] bidding them to squeeze as much money as possible from this source too on the explicit understanding that they would keep one twelfth of what they raked in. [2] He called these officials *logothetai*,[68] and they devised the following mischief for the annual budget. By law, military pay is not given equally to all, for those who are still young and have only recently enlisted are paid less. After they have served for a while and climbed to the middle of the muster rolls, their pay increases. [3] And when they have advanced in years and are about to be discharged, their salary is even more hefty so that they may live well as private citizens thereafter and be in a position, when they have measured out the term of their life, to leave a surplus of their funds to their families by way of consolation. [4] Time, then, continually raises lower-ranked soldiers to take the place of those who die or who are discharged from the service, allocating military pay to each based on his seniority. [5] But these so-called *logothetai* would not allow the names of those who died to be removed from the rolls, even when a majority of them were killed in battle together, largely because of the constant wars. Nor would they bring the rolls up to strength, not even after long stretches of time. [6] As a result, the state is always falling short in military manpower while the soldiers who remain are prevented by comrades who died long ago from rising up to the ranks that they have earned. And they are paid less than they ought to be, based, that is, on the rank that they *ought* to have, and all has been done so that the *logothetai* could, throughout this period, turn over a share of the military payroll to Justinian.

[7] They devised many other forms of harassment by which to grind down the soldiers, as if to reward them in this way for the dangers they faced in war. For example, they would derisively label some of them "Greeklings," as if it were altogether impossible for anyone brave to have come from Greece.[69] Others they accused of

67. For the same accusation, see *Wars* 2.15.9 (regarding the administration of Lazike).

68. The *logothetai* were agents of the treasury; see also 18.15 above, 24.9–11 and 26.29–30 below.

69. This insult reflected the negative ancient Roman view of the Greeks, especially when it came to war. It was occasionally applied by barbarians to Justinian's armies: *Wars* 4.27.38, 5.18.40, 5.29.11, 7.9.12, 7.21.4, 7.21.12–14, 8.23.25. These Greeks (*Graikoi*, from Latin *Graeci*, whose diminutive form *Graeculi* was

being in the service without an imperial appointment, and when the soldiers produced an imperial order on this very point, the *logothetai*, without hesitation, dared to cast doubt on its authenticity. And still others they accused of taking leave from their comrades for a few days.[70] [8] Later, too, some palatine guards were dispatched all around the Roman Empire on the pretext of ferreting out from the military rolls men who were least fit for service, and some of them went so far as to strip these men of their insignia on the grounds that they were useless or too old. Those discharged in this way could do nothing from then on but beg publicly for food from compassionate passers-by in the marketplace, and they became a constant source of tears and lamentation for all who chanced upon them. From the other soldiers they extorted large sums in exchange for not suffering the same fate. Thus it came to pass that soldiers were demoralized in so many ways, became poorer than all other classes in society, and no longer cared for fighting in war. [9] That is exactly how Roman interests in Italy too fell apart. When the *logothetes* Alexandros was dispatched there he had the gall, and was unscrupulous enough, to accuse the soldiers of these things. He extorted money from the Italians, claiming that he was punishing them for having participated as citizens in the state set up by Theodoric and the Goths.[71] [10] But it was not only the soldiers who were oppressed with poverty and desperation by the *logothetai*. All officers too serving under the generals, of whom there were a great many and all of them used to a high status, were reduced to hunger and dire poverty. [11] They had no means now by which to maintain their former standard of living.

[12] I will add one other thing to all this, seeing as I am on the topic of the soldiery. Emperors of the Romans in past times stationed a vast host of soldiers all around the most remote territories of the state to guard the boundaries of the Roman Empire, particularly in the East, where they repelled the incursions of the Persians and the Saracens; they used to call these soldiers *limitanei*. [13] But the emperor Justinian treated them at first with such indifference and stinginess that their paymasters were always four or five years behind

---

even more insulting) were different from the *Hellenes* (pagans) of 11.31 above; these two versions of the ethnonym had different senses. But for Prokopios, *Hellenes* could also simply signify people from Greece (*Hellas*); see 26.30 below and *Wars* 2.4.11, 5.15.24.

70. For soldiers who hired themselves out to private interests and left their camps, see *Novella* 116 (of 542).

with their pay, and when peace was established between the Romans and the Persians these poor wretches were forced to waive their rights to the salaries owed to them for a set number of years, which reverted to the treasury, on the pretext that they too would share in the blessings of peace. And later he stripped them of their commission altogether for no reason. [14] From then on the boundaries of the Roman Empire remained ungarrisoned while the soldiers suddenly developed a keen interest in the hands that doled out pious charities.[72]

[15] A different unit of soldiers, numbering no fewer than three thousand five hundred, had been instituted originally to guard the palace, and they were called the *scholae*.[73] [16] It was established that they would always receive higher pay from the treasury than all others. Earlier emperors had originally manned this unit with Armenians selected by merit and promoted to this honor. [17] But from the time that Zenon rose to the throne it became possible for anyone at all, even for unmanly and wholly unwarlike types, to claim this rank and disgrace it with their presence. [18] As time passed, even slaves could pay the entry fee and purchase the commission.[74] When Justin rose to the throne, this Justinian fellow elevated many to this honor, raking in huge sums of money for himself. [19] But when he saw that there was no more room on the rolls for any others, he added two thousand more to them, whom they then called "supernumeraries." [20] Yet when *he* became emperor, he instantly dismissed these supernumeraries, without returning any of their money to them.[75]

71. For Alexandros in Italy, see 26.29–30 below and *Wars* 7.1.28–33, 7.9.13. Theodoric the Great (r. 489–526) had brought peace, prosperity, and justice to Italy. Justinian's Italian war strained the loyalties of the local populations.

72. Since the fourth century, the Roman army was divided, broadly speaking, into mobile field armies (these are the armies that appear in the *Wars* for the most part) and border guards (the *limitanei*). Justinian certainly degraded these units in some way along the lines suggested here, though it is unlikely that he abolished them altogether (and he instituted them in North Africa after the conquest). It is not clear whether Prokopios is reporting on the fate of all such units or only of those in specific areas.

73. These elite palace guards (*scholae palatinae*) were instituted by Diocletian (r. 284–305) and Constantine the Great (r. 306–337).

74. By Zenon's time (474–475, 476–491), the *scholae* had become ceremonial (the real guard were the *excubitores*). At this time, *scholarii* would purchase their commission and recoup their investment from the salary and perks (legal and fiscal) associated with the position. See Agathias, *Histories* 5.15.1–6.

75. In other words, they lost their investment. Justinian ensured that the state made more money from them than it paid out to them.

[21] As for those who were enrolled in the regular number of the *scholae*, he devised the following. When an expeditionary force was about to be sent out to North Africa, Italy, or against the Persians, he announced that they too should prepare to march out with them, knowing full well that they were entirely unfit for active service. In terror lest this might actually happen, they waived their pay for a set period of time. And somehow this kept happening to the *scholarii* over and over again. [22] And Petros, for as long as he held the position of *magister*, as it is called, would constantly and every day wear them down with countless thefts. [23] True, he was a gentle man with no arrogance in him at all, but he was also more addicted to stealing money than anyone else alive and he simply stank of this filthy practice. This Petros was mentioned earlier as the one who plotted the murder of Amalasountha, the daughter of Theodoric.[76]

[24] But there are, in addition, others serving in the palatine units who are much higher ranked, given that the treasury traditionally pays them more, which is because they have to pay an even higher fee to obtain their commission. These are known as the *domestici* and *protectores* and they never have anything to do with actual warfare. [25] They are enrolled in the palace corps for the sake of rank and ceremonial appearances.[77] And from ancient times some of them are stationed in Byzantion, others in Galatia, and still others in different places. [26] But Justinian constantly terrorized them too in the way I just explained, forcing them to waive the salaries that they were due. I will give a summary account of how he did this. [27] There was a custom according to which every five years the emperor donated a set amount of gold to each soldier. [28] Every five years, then, they would distribute, everywhere in the Roman Empire, five gold coins to every soldier as a gift.[78] [29] There was no way that this could be left undone, no matter what happened. But from the moment that this man began to govern the state, he has neither done this nor given any sign of intending to do it, even though thirty-two years have already passed, so that some people have even quite forgotten all about this custom.

[30] I turn now to explain yet another means by which he stole from his subjects. All who serve the emperor and the magistrates in

76. See 16.1–5 above. The *magister officiorum* commanded the palatine guards.

77. The *protectores et domestici* were the officers of the *scholae*.

78. Donatives were distributed upon the accession of an emperor and every five years thereafter.

Byzantion personally either as guards or by handling their correspondence or in any other way are at first placed at the bottom ranks of the rolls, but as time passes they steadily rise to take the place of those who die or retire, and each advances in his respective hierarchy until he reaches the highest level and attains the pinnacle of honor. [31] And it was long ago decreed that those who reach this rank should receive such a large sum of money that their annual salary exceeds one hundred *kentenaria* of gold.[79] In this way they were able to care for themselves in old age and, as a rule, support many others as well from this income. This state of affairs contributed greatly to the efficiency of state business. [32] But this emperor deprived them of virtually all these benefits, harming not only them but all other people as well. For poverty came to them first and then worked its way through the ranks of all whom they had previously supported in some way. [33] And if someone were to add up the damage done to them by this over the course of thirty-two years, he would know the exact measure of their loss.

Squeezing the Merchants

25. That was how this tyrant treated men in the service. I turn now to state what he did to merchants, sailors, laborers, and ordinary craftsmen, and through them to all others. [2] There are straits on either side of Byzantion, one in the Hellespont between Sestos and Abydos, another at the mouth of the Black Sea, at a place called Hieron.[80] [3] In the Hellespont straits one could hardly say that there was a public customs station; rather, an official was sent out by the emperor and stationed at Abydos who inquired whether any ships were bringing weapons to Byzantion without imperial authorization, and also whether anyone was sailing out from Byzantion without the proper documents bearing the seals of the men charged with that function (for it was not permitted for anyone to depart from Byzantion without the permission of those men, who worked for the office of the *magister*, as he was called). He also extracted a fee from

79. I.e., 720,000 coins, a vast sum (see the Glossary). Justinian was probably trying to reduce the expense of a bloated and not altogether functional bureaucracy.

80. The Hellespont connects the Sea of Marmara to the Aegean (to the south of Constantinople) and the Bosporus connects it to the Black Sea (to the north). Abydos and Sestos face each other across the Hellespont; Hieron was on the Asiatic side of the Bosporus (for the palace built there by Justinian, see 15.36 above).

the owners of the ships, not anything that they would really feel but merely a form of compensation that was demanded by the holder of the office in exchange for providing this service.[81] [4] The one who was sent to the opposite straits, however, had always received his salary from the emperor and his job was to inquire carefully into the matters that I just mentioned as well as to ensure that nothing was being exported to the barbarians settled around the Black Sea, nothing, that is, of those articles whose export from Roman territory to foreign enemies was prohibited. And, in fact, this man was forbidden from accepting payment from those sailing in this direction. [5] But when Justinian became emperor, he established a customs station in both straits to which he regularly sent out two salaried officials.[82] While he did provide them with their own salaries, he also bid them to use any means at their disposal to bring in as much revenue as they could for him from this source. [6] And they, wanting nothing more than to prove their devotion to him, stole from merchants sailing by the full cash value of their entire cargo.

[7] That is what he did in the two straits. For Byzantion itself he devised the following scheme. He commissioned one of his associates, a Syrian by origin named Addaios, to make some profit for him from the ships that put in there.[83] [8] This person would not allow any ship that put in to the harbor at Byzantion to depart in peace, but rather he charged the shipmasters a fee proportional to the value of their ships or else forced them to report for service in North Africa and Italy. [9] As a result, some of them no longer wanted to take on a return cargo or work the seas anymore; rather, they burned their own ships and were glad to be rid of the whole business. [10] But for others this line of work was essential to their livelihood. They asked for triple the price from the local merchants and continued to take on cargos. The merchants, in turn, could recoup this

81. These fees are specified in an edict that Anastasios (r. 491–518) placed at Abydos, instructing that it be visible to all in order to eliminate the possibility for abuse.

82. Each custom station (*commercium*, Greek *kommerkion*) was now under the command of a *comes*, the one at Hierion being the *comes* of the Straits of the Pontic Sea. They survived into Byzantine times. According to Ioannes Malalas, a certain Ioannes was posted there in 528 with a naval unit of Goths to guard against Hunnic raids (*Chronicle* 18.14).

83. Flavius Marianos Iakobos Markellos Aninas Addaios was at this time in the financial office of the praetorian prefect (he would become prefect himself in 551). This reform probably dates to the 540s.

loss only by passing it on to the consumer. Thus every method was being used to kill the Romans through starvation.

[11] That is how things were regarding the management of the state. I think that I should not omit what the imperial couple did regarding small coins either. [12] The money changers were formerly prepared to exchange, on behalf of their clients, two hundred and ten obols (which they call *folles*) for one gold coin. But they devised a way to make a profit for themselves, by decreeing that only one hundred and eighty obols was now the proper exchange rate for a gold coin. In this way they shaved one seventh off the value of each gold coin[84] [. . .][85] of all men.

[13] When the imperial couple had corralled most trades into the so-called monopolies,[86] choking consumers off a little bit more every day, and the only trade that remained untouched by them were the garment-sellers, they contrived the following against them too. [14] Beirut and Tyre, the cities in Phoenicia, had an old tradition of manufacturing silk fabrics. [15] The merchants who dealt in this as well as the craftsmen and artisans employed in its production had always lived there, and from there their wares were exported to every part of the earth. [16] But in the reign of Justinian dealers in Byzantion and the other cities began to charge more for such garments, justifying their action by saying that they had to pay more to Persian middlemen than before and that there were now more customs stations within Roman territory. The emperor made it clear to everyone that he was displeased at this development and issued a law forbidding anyone from selling such garments at more than eight gold coins per liter.[87] [17] The fine that he decreed for those

84. The previous exchange rate had been set by Emperor Anastasios (r. 491–518), who had overhauled the coinage system. This change would presumably have benefited the lower classes who tended to use lower denomination coins (though there are too many unknown variables for us to be sure about its motives and effects, such as the amount of available bullion at the time that the change was made; the proportion of gold to bronze coins being minted; the proportion of each type of coin actually used in private and state transactions; the date of the reform and the weight of the *folles* at the time of the reform; etc.). The point is that it benefited Justinian and Theodora, though Prokopios does not specify how.

85. There is a gap in the text here.

86. For the monopolies, see 20.1–6 above (also 26.19 and 26.36 below).

87. Silk was imported overland from China via the Silk Road. It was purchased by imperial agents (*commerciarii*) who then sold whatever the state did not need to private traders (*metaxarii*). After 532, the Persians began to increase their prices (and for some of the new internal customs stations that also added to the

who violated this law was the loss of all their property. These measures were unanimously regarded as impractical and pointless. For it was not possible for merchants to sell their goods to their clients at a lower price than that for which they had bought them originally. [18] Therefore they gave up on this trade as unprofitable, secretly selling off their remaining stock in small batches to some of their old customers, men who liked to spend their money in order to prance around in such finery, or for whom it was necessary to do so for one reason or another.[88] [19] When the empress was informed by some of her whisperers that this was going on, even though she did not carefully inquire into those rumors she immediately confiscated the merchants' entire stocks and fined them one *kentenarion* of gold. [. . .][89]

Among the Romans this trade is supervised by the official in charge of the imperial treasuries. [20] It was not long after they had appointed Petros (the one named Barsymes) to this dignity that they allowed him to resume his unholy deeds.[90] [21] While he, then, demanded that all others scrupulously conform to the law, he required the craftsmen of this particular trade to work for his own benefit and his alone. No longer disguising the arrangement, he sold dyes publicly in the market, the common sort at no fewer than six gold per ounce while the imperial dye, which is generally known as *holoverum*,[91] at more than twenty-four gold per ounce. [22] And from this source he made a large profit for the emperor as well, though he also managed to get away with embezzling an even greater sum for himself. This practice, having begun from that, then became permanent. [23] For he openly remains the sole merchant

final price, see 25.1–10 above). Justinian's law stipulating eight *solidi* per liter (of raw silk or woven?) no longer survives. An undated *Novella* (*App*. 5), either by Justinian or one of his successors, requires the *commerciarii* to sell silk to the *metaxarii* at the same price that they bought it from the barbarians, namely fifteen *solidi* per liter of raw silk; presumably this came after the law mentioned by Prokopios.

88. Some high officials were required to wear silk garments on ceremonial occasions.

89. I.e., 7,200 coins (see the Glossary). There is a gap in the text here.

90. For Petros' second appointment as *comes sacrarum largitionum* (which began in 547/548), see 22.33 above. He had served as *comes* previously as well (before 543), but Prokopios implies here that he was resuming the wicked ways he had practiced as praetorian prefect (in 543–546).

91. A hybrid Greek-Latin word, meaning "all-pure."

and retailer of these goods to this very day. [24] All the merchants who had formerly dealt in this trade, in Byzantion and the other cities, whether by sea or by land, understandably now had to endure the harmful effects of this practice. [25] In the cities I mentioned, virtually the entire populace suddenly found themselves beggars. Craftsmen and manual workers, as you can imagine, had to struggle against hunger, and because of this many of them fled, expatriated themselves, and took up with the Persians. [26] Through all this, the director of the treasury remained the sole dealer in these wares, and while he deigned to give a portion of the proceeds to the emperor, as I said, he kept most of it for himself, enriching himself at public loss. That, then, is how this matter turned out.[92]

Degrading All Classes of Society, Especially the Poor

26. We turn now to the means by which he managed to destroy everything that created order and adornment in the cities, including Byzantion and all the others. [2] First he decided to abolish the profession of the advocates. He immediately deprived them of all the rewards that had previously enabled them to live in comfort and which they were accustomed to take pride in after completing their duty in the courts. He decreed that disputants should settle their differences by swearing oaths among themselves. Contemptuously discarded in this way, the lawyers were simply despondent.[93] [3] And after he had parted the members of the Senate, as well as all who were reputed to be prosperous both in Byzantion and throughout the Roman Empire, of their entire properties, as was said above, the profession was reduced to idleness. [4] For people did not own anything of value over which they could go to court with each other. In no time, then, they became few who had once been many, and from prestige they went to obscurity everywhere on earth, being oppressed by extreme poverty, as happens in such conditions, and earning only contempt from the practice of their profession.

92. Not long afterward, some monks managed to smuggle silkworm eggs from China into the empire, enabling local production (*Wars* 8.17.1–8, translated in related text 11). The silk trade remained a strictly regulated imperial monopoly in Byzantine times, its products enhancing the empire's prestige and greasing its diplomacy.

93. Prokopios is claiming that Justinian's edicts favored arbitration over litigation. For the two parties swearing oaths (on the Gospels), see *Codex Iustinianus* 3.1.14.4 (of 530).

[5] Doctors too and the teachers of those subjects that free the mind he caused to be without the necessities for life. For this emperor entirely abolished the assistance from public funds that his predecessors had assigned to these professions.[94] [6] Not only that, but whatever revenues the residents of all the cities collected at home for their own political or cultural events he likewise dared to divert away and mix in with the imperial income.[95] [7] From then on, there was no concern for doctors and teachers nor was anyone in a position to make plans for public works. Lamps no longer illuminated public spaces in the cities at night, and there was nothing left to make their citizens' lives more pleasant. [8] For the theaters, hippodromes, and wild beast shows had all mostly been closed down, those places, in other words, where his wife happened to have been born, raised, and instructed in the ways of life.[96] [9] Later he ordered that these shows be shut down in Byzantion in order to spare the treasury from the expense associated with these customary subsidies from which many people drew their livelihood, so many people in fact that they were almost innumerable. [10] Thus depression and misery overcame both private and public life, as if yet another calamity had struck from above, and life was without joy or laughter for anyone. [11] People had nothing else to talk about, whether they were at home, in the market, or even speaking to their priests, than the sheer magnitude of these disasters, their suffering, and all the new forms of misfortune that had found them.

[12] That was the state of affairs in the cities. And what remains to be said is actually quite interesting. In the past, there were two consuls of the Romans each year, one in Rome, the other in Byzantion.

94. Teachers: Prokopios may be alluding to the prohibition of pagans from the profession (*Codex Iustinianus* 1.5.18.4, 1.11.10) and the closing of the schools of Athens (Ioannes Malalas, *Chronicle* 18.47; Agathias, *Histories* 2.30–31). Doctors: according to one view, Justinian transferred many of them from civic employment to the hospitals that were just then being established.

95. Since the fourth century, the imperial government had been appropriating the funds and functions of the city councils, often to the detriment of cultural life and civic amenities. Many of Justinian's edicts regulated imperial officials' management of those responsibilities (see *Edict* 13 for Egypt).

96. It was not uncommon for emperors to suspend the games and theater performances after riots. Anastasios, who was admired by Prokopios (see 19.5–7 above), probably did so more regularly than Justinian. We lack specific information about Justinian's measures. In 529, the theater of Antioch was temporarily closed (Ioannes Malalas, *Chronicle* 18.41). There were no games for a long time after the Nika riots (possibly for two years, when the capital celebrated Belisarios' defeat of the Vandals).

[13] Whoever was called to this honor was expected to spend more than twenty *kentenaria* of gold for the public benefit, some of it from his own money but most was provided by the emperor.[97] [14] This money was given to those others whom I have mentioned and, for the most part, to those who were most destitute, especially to those who worked on the stage, thereby providing constant support for civic events and activities. [15] But from the time that Justinian came to the throne, these things were no longer done at the proper time. At first, consuls were appointed for the Romans only at long intervals but, in the end, such appointments were not even seen in our dreams.[98] Because of this many people's lives were squeezed continuously by poverty, as, on the one hand, the customary subsidies no longer flowed from the emperor to his subjects while, on the other, he stripped them everywhere of the little that they did own through all the means at his disposal.

[16] I believe that I have offered adequate proof for my assertion that this enemy of humanity swallowed up the entirety of the public funds and separated every member of the Senate individually, and the entire body collectively, from the whole of their property. [17] I think that I have also sufficiently demonstrated that he separated all those who were reputed to be prosperous from their money by leveling false accusations against them; and not only them but soldiers too and magistrates' subordinate officials, palace guards, farmers, landowners and estate masters, professional advocates, and more still: merchants, shipowners, sailors, craftsmen, manual laborers, shopkeepers, and all those whose livelihood derived from stage performances, in addition to everyone else *indirectly* affected by the damage that he could do.

[18] We can now recount what sorts of things he did against beggars, the common folk, the poor, and those with any kind of disability (for what he did in relation to priests will be discussed in a later book).[99] [19] First of all, as was said, he took possession of all

97. It was customary in the later empire for the consuls to distribute money to the people and the various guilds that provided entertainment. The sum mentioned here corresponded to 144,000 coins (see the Glossary).

98. In *Novella* 105 (of 537), Justinian limited the expenses associated with the consulship, claiming that his intention was to make the office "immortal." It was then abolished in 541. Ioannes Lydos saw this as the abolition of the last vestige of Roman freedom (*On the Magistracies of the Roman State* 2.8).

99. This is probably a forward reference to the *Ecclesiastical History* of this period that Prokopios planned but apparently never wrote (see the Introduction, p. xxvii)

the shops and established the so-called monopolies over the most necessary goods, requiring all people to pay more than three times the usual price.[100] [20] Given that the other things that he did in this regard seem to me, at least, to be beyond number, I would not be so ambitious as to enumerate them all, even if my account were to be infinite in length. During this entire time he was mercilessly stealing from those who buy bread, namely manual laborers, the poor, and those with any kind of disability, people for whom it was simply impossible *not* to buy bread. [21] It was his goal to squeeze up to three *kentenaria* every year from this source,[101] and so the loaves were made more expensive and baked with ash—for this emperor did not hesitate to allow his shameful avarice to sink to such a despicable level.[102] [22] Those officials appointed to the "honor" of overseeing this business used it handily as a pretext to devise means by which to enrich themselves, creating, in the process, a man-made famine for the poor in a period of abundance, which was a strange thing to observe. This was because it was no longer permitted for anyone to import grain from anywhere else, making it necessary for everyone to eat those loaves that were on sale.

[23] Though they saw that the city's aqueduct was broken and was bringing in only a small fraction of the water to the city, they nevertheless utterly neglected the matter and did not wish to spend any money on it, despite the fact that crowds were congesting in asphyxiating numbers at the fountains and all the baths had been closed.[103] And yet he sank huge sums, for no good reason, into his building projects by the sea and in other stupid constructions, sprawling out into the suburbs, as though the imperial palace could not fit the two of them, a palace where all previous emperors had wanted to spend every day of their entire lives. [24] The reason why

100. For the monopolies, see 20.1–6 above (also 25.13 above and 26.36 below).

101. I.e., 21,600 coins (see the Glossary).

102. Heavily subsidized bread was sold by the state to hundreds of thousands in Constantinople. The grain was brought mostly from Egypt (see 22.14–19 above). We know little about the public bakeries. Justinian apparently required them to raise their prices and lower their quality. In 533, to economize on firewood, the prefect Ioannes the Kappadokian undercooked the bread for the expedition against North Africa, with the result that many soldiers fell sick and five hundred of them died (*Wars* 3.13.12–20).

103. This accusation was probably meant to refute the emperor's own propaganda (reflected in Ioannes Malalas, *Chronicle* 18.17) that he had repaired the aqueduct in 528 (it is known today as the aqueduct of Valens and was about fifteen kilometers long).

he decided to neglect the repair of the aqueduct was not stinginess as much as it was his desire to destroy even more people. In all of history there has never been any person more willing than this Justinian to appropriate money in evil ways and then to spend it immediately in even worse ways. [25] So when it came to food and drink, people who were reduced to extreme poverty and want had only two options left, namely bread and water, yet this emperor managed to use both of these for harmful purposes, by making the first much more expensive for such people and the second altogether scarce.

[26] He did these things not only against the beggars in Byzantion but also against others who lived elsewhere, as I will now explain. [27] When Theodoric conquered Italy,[104] he allowed the armed guards of the palace at Rome to remain at their posts because he wanted to preserve some trace of the ancient constitution of the place, and he continued to pay each a small daily stipend. [28] These men were extremely numerous. For those called *silentiarii*, *domestici*, and *scholarii* were included among them, though they were military units in name only and also with respect to this stipend, which barely enabled them to get by.[105] Theodoric decreed that the stipend should be passed on to their children and descendants. [29] He also arranged for the public treasury to provide three thousand *medimnoi* of grain every year to the beggars who lived in the vicinity of the church of Peter the Apostle.[106] All of them received these subsidies until the arrival in Italy of Alexandros the Scissors.[107] [30] Without a second thought, this man immediately decided to cancel all these benefits. When Justinian, the emperor of the Romans, learned about this decision, he not only ratified it but began to hold Alexandros in even higher esteem than before. During his journey, Alexandros had done the following to the Greeks as well.

104. Theodoric the Great ruled Italy from 489 to 526. Prokopios praised him as a ruler (see *Wars* 5.1.24–39).

105. The *silentiarii* were part of the emperor's immediate staff (*Wars* 2.21.2). For the late Roman *scholarii*, see 24.15–23 above; for the *domestici*, 24.24–26.

106. This church built by Constantine the Great was replaced by the current St. Peter's. A Greek *medimnos* was equivalent to about fifty-two liters (or six Roman *modii*).

107. Alexandros was one of the *logothetai*, agents of the treasury; see also *Wars* 7.1.28–33 and 7.9.13 as well as 18.15, 24.2, and 24.9–11 above. He was sent to Italy in 540 and was called "the Scissors" because he could trim gold coins to save (or make) money.

[31] The garrison of Thermopylai had long been entrusted to the farmers of the lands around the pass. They guarded the wall there in turns whenever an incursion into the Peloponnese by this or that barbarian tribe was imminent. [32] But when Alexandros arrived there, alleging a concern for the Peloponnesians, he declared that the garrison there should not be entrusted to farmers. [33] So he established some two thousand soldiers there, but decreed that their salaries not be paid by the public treasury. Instead, he used this as a pretext to transfer to the treasury all the money that was being raised by every city in Greece for political and cultural events, which fund would now be used to supply the soldiers there. As a result, both in the rest of Greece and no less in Athens itself no building was restored at public expense nor could any other beneficial project be undertaken. [34] And Justinian did not hesitate to ratify the Scissors' arrangements.[108]

[35] That, then, was how this matter turned out. We should also turn our attention to the poor in Alexandria. There was a certain Hephaistos among the local advocates who, when he was placed in charge of the Alexandrians, put an end to the rioting of the fan-clubs by terrifying the militants, but he also brought about the extreme forms of the worst evils imaginable for the city's inhabitants.[109] [36] The first thing that he did was to convert all the shops in the city into the so-called monopolies, allowing no other merchant to practice this trade.[110] Having, then, become the sole retailer in the city, he began to sell all goods himself, fixing their prices through the authority of his office. The city of the Alexandrians was now choked off by a scarcity of necessities, despite being a place where formerly even those who were utterly destitute could easily find sufficient means by which to live. He squeezed them especially in their bread supply. [37] For he alone purchased grain from the Egyptians and he did not allocate the right to sell even a single *medimnos* to anyone

108. In 540, some Huns, possibly Bulgars, found the mountain path around Thermopylai, even though the wall itself was "vigorously defended" by the garrison (*Wars* 2.4.9–11). This is why Alexandros stopped there on his way to Italy. At *Buildings* 4.2, Prokopios praises Justinian for strengthening the wall at Thermopylai and establishing the two thousand soldiers there.

109. Flavius Ioannes Theodoros Menas Narses Chnoubammon Horion Hephaistos was prefect of Alexandria starting in 545/546 (and went on to become praetorian prefect in 551/552). The duties of this office had been laid out by Justinian in *Edict* 13.

110. For the system of monopolies, see 20.1–6, 25.13, and 26.19 above.

else.[111] In this way, he controlled the supply of bread and set its price however he wished. [38] In a short time, therefore, he had amassed fabulous riches for himself and also satisfied the emperor's wishes in the matter. [39] On the one hand, then, the populace of Alexandria endured their present miseries quietly out of fear of Hephaistos while, on the other hand, the emperor was awed by the money that was continuously pouring in for him and so he came to simply adore the man.

[40] Considering how he might be able to worm his way even deeper into the emperor's affections, this Hephaistos contrived the following plan. [41] When Diocletian had become emperor of the Romans he decreed that a large supply of grain was to be offered every year at public expense to those Alexandrians who were in need.[112] [42] At the time, the populace had distributed it among themselves and they had passed this tradition down to their descendants of the present day. [43] But Hephaistos deducted from this source up to two hundred times ten thousand *medimnoi* every year,[113] taking them from those who needed these necessities the most and storing them in imperial facilities, and wrote to the emperor that it was neither just nor in the public interest that these men should have benefited from this measure until now. [44] As a result, the emperor, who ratified this action, held him in even higher esteem. As for the Alexandrians, whoever of them depended on this source for their livelihood enjoyed this inhumanity in the midst of their need.

Various Episodes Illustrating Justinian's Character

27. Justinian's crimes were so many that all of eternity would not suffice for an account that attempted to record them all. [2] It will be enough for me to select and write down only a few from among their multitude by which his character will be revealed to future generations clearly and in its entirety, namely that he was a dissembler; that he had no respect for God or for priests or for the laws, not even for the populace to which he seemed on the surface to be so devoted; that there was not a shred of decency in him and no con-

111. A Greek *medimnos* was equivalent to about fifty-two liters (or six Roman *modii*).

112. Diocletian (r. 284–305) was in Alexandria in 297–298 to suppress a rebellion and reform the administration.

113. A Greek *medimnos* was equivalent to about fifty-two liters (or six Roman *modii*).

cern for the interest of the state or for anything that might be to its advantage; that he did not care whether his actions were excused by some pretext or not;[114] and, finally, that nothing mattered to him other than how to seize all money that could be found everywhere in the world. I begin, then, with this.

[3] It was he who appointed as archpriest over the Alexandrians a man named Paulos. It happened at that time that a certain Rhodon, a Phoenician by origin, was governor of Alexandria. [4] Justinian bid this man to assist Paulos in all matters and with alacrity, and not to leave a single one of his orders unfulfilled. [5] For in this way he hoped to persuade the [. . .][115] of the Alexandrians to accept the Council of Chalcedon.[116] [6] Now there was a certain Arsenios, a Palestinian by origin, who had served the empress Theodora well in the most sensitive matters and because of this had acquired great power, fabulous riches, and a seat in the Senate, despite being a loathsome person. [7] Even though he was a Samaritan, he decided to take on the name of a Christian so as not to lose the power that he now held. [8] Emboldened by this man's power, however, his father and brother, who resided in Skythopolis and retained their ancestral faith, began to persecute all the Christians viciously, following his instructions in this. [9] The inhabitants, accordingly, rose up against them and killed them both in a most cruel manner, from which it came to pass that many misfortunes befell Palestine. [10] At the time, neither Justinian nor the empress made any move against him, though he was most responsible for all of these disturbances, but they did forbid him from ever entering the palace again, for the Christians were not giving them any rest in their protests against him.[117]

114. Yet elsewhere Prokopios records Justinian's pretext while uncovering his true motivation (e.g., 13.6, 13.22, 19.11 above and 29.25 below).

115. "The heretics," "the priests," or "the Christians" can be supplied to fill this gap. Prokopios is alluding to the major theological controversy of his time, namely between those who accepted and those who rejected the Council of Chalcedon (451), especially regarding the precise way in which the human and the divine natures came together in the person of Christ. The Alexandrians were mostly opposed to the council, and Justinian tried various ways to impose it on them. At *Wars* 5.3.5–9, Prokopios makes clear that he regarded these controversies as idiotic.

116. This was in late 537 or early 538.

117. The chronology is confusing here. Arsenios' father Silvanos had oppressed the Christians of Palestine in 518, when he held an unspecified imperial position. This was before Justinian even met Theodora. Silvanos was burned alive

[11] Hoping to ingratiate himself with the emperor, this Arsenios not long afterward volunteered to accompany Paulos to Alexandria in order to assist him in general, but more specifically to add all of his power to Paulos' effort to bring the Alexandrians around. [12] For he claimed that while he had been barred from the palace he had made a close study of all the different doctrines found among the Christians. [13] But this infuriated Theodora, for she was pretending to work against the emperor in this matter, as I explained above.[118] [14] At any rate, when they reached Alexandria, Paulos turned over to Rhodon a certain deacon named Psoes to be put to death, claiming that Psoes was the only obstacle blocking his effort to execute the emperor's instructions.[119] [15] Rhodon, heeding the emperor's missives, which arrived one after the other and were most intimidating, decided to torture the man. He was laid down on the rack, and died. [16] When news of this reached the palace, the empress put strong pressure on the emperor, who promptly began to move on all fronts against Paulos, Rhodon, and Arsenios, as though he had forgotten all the instructions that he himself had given these men. [17] He appointed Liberius, a patrician from Rome, to govern the Alexandrians and dispatched some of the leading priests to conduct an inquiry into the matter, including the archdeacon of Rome Pelagius, who was acting in place of Vigilius the archpriest, having been authorized to do so by Vigilius himself.[120] [18] When

---

by Christians in the aftermath of the Samaritan revolt of 529 (see 11.24–30 above). His son Arsenios lobbied Theodora against the Christians of Palestine, but the latter had lobbyists too, and as a result he had to flee the palace in fear for his life. It was at this time that he converted. Arsenios had actually entered the Senate under Justin (i.e., before 527), though it is just possible that this was through Theodora's influence (who married Justinian at an unknown date in the 520s).

118. See 10.15, 13.19, and 14.8 above. Theodora supported the Monophysite (anti-Chalcedonian) position.

119. Psoes had informed the (presumably Monophysite) general Elias that Paulos would relieve him of his command (Justinian had given Paulos the authority to dismiss any officers who stood in the way of enforcing Chalcedon in Egypt).

120. Petrus Marcellinus Felix Liberius was about seventy at this time, having served Odovacer and Theodoric the Great in Italy. He was sent on an embassy to Constantinople by Theodahad in 534 (see note 142 in Part II), and stayed there. He was made prefect of Alexandria in 538/539 (see also 29.1–11 below). Vigilius (537–555) had just been made pope (through the influence of Theodora) and had returned to Rome from Constantinople (see note 13 in Part I). Pelagius himself was later appointed pope by Justinian (556–561).

the murder was exposed, they immediately deposed Paulos from the priesthood.[121] Rhodon fled to Byzantion where the emperor parted him from his head as well as from his money, which he confiscated to the treasury—this despite the fact that the man brought forth thirteen letters that the emperor had written to him which instructed and impressed upon him the urgent importance of assisting Paulos in anything he bid him do and of not opposing him in anything for the purpose of enabling Paulos to carry out their plans regarding the faith. [19] As for Arsenios, he was impaled by Liberius on Theodora's instructions. The emperor decided to confiscate his money as well, even though he could accuse him formally with nothing other than that he associated with Paulos.

[20] It is not my intention to express an opinion as to whether he did these things rightly or not. The reason I have narrated them is instead the following. [21] Paulos showed up at Byzantion a short time afterward and offered this emperor seven *kentenaria* of gold in exchange for being restored to the priesthood, on the grounds that he had not been legally deposed from it.[122] [22] Justinian accepted the money graciously and held the man in honor, agreeing to appoint him archpriest over the Alexandrians immediately, even though someone else already held that honor and as if he did not know that he himself had executed and confiscated the property of those who had associated with Paulos and had dared to assist him. [23] This "revered Augustus," then, took up the cause earnestly, plotting and scheming to bring it about, and Paulos had every reason to think that, one way or another, he would get his priesthood back. [24] But Vigilius, who happened to be present at the time, decided that he would in no way yield to the emperor in this matter, should he command it. He claimed that he was not in a position to overturn his own verdict, meaning the decision by Pelagius.[123] [25] The point is that nothing else mattered to this emperor than the removal of money from the hands of others.[124] There follows yet another event to the same effect.

121. Paulos was deposed by an ecclesiastical council at Gaza, though the formal grounds may have been different. One source says that it was for commemorating his predecessor Dioskouros, who had been condemned for heresy.

122. I.e., 50,400 coins (see the Glossary). This took place after 547 (see 27.24 below).

123. Vigilius had returned to Constantinople in early 547, where he would stay for eight years, at loggerheads with Justinian regarding ecclesiastical policy.

124. In other words, in taking up Paulos' cause Justinian was violating his own edicts that banned the sale of ecclesiastical office; *Novellae* 6 (of 535), 123 (of 544), and 137 (of 565).

[26] There was one Phaoustinos from Palestine, a Samaritan by descent though he had accepted the label of a Christian through legal coercion.[125] [27] This Phaoustinos attained the rank of senator and became governor of the region. Not long afterward he was removed from this position and came to Byzantion, where some of the priests slandered him with the accusation that he adhered still to the beliefs of the Samaritans and had horribly mistreated the Christians who lived in Palestine. [28] Justinian seemed to be angry and indignant on account of this, namely that anyone should have insulted the name of Christ while he ruled the Romans. [29] The members of the Senate made an inquiry into this and imposed a penalty of exile on Phaoustinos; the emperor, after all, was putting pressure on them to do so. [30] But when the emperor had extracted from him all the money that he wanted, he immediately overturned the verdict. [31] Phaoustinos was restored to his former rank and was now on good terms with the emperor, who appointed him overseer of the imperial estates in Palestine and Phoenicia. Here he was able to do whatever he wanted with even greater impunity. [32] Regarding the manner, then, in which Justinian chose to defend the rights of Christians I have not said much, but what I have said, however brief, provides sufficient evidence. [33] A very brief story will now explain how he overturned the laws without any hesitation when money was at stake.

The Scandal at Emesa

28. There was a certain Priskos in the city of Emesa who was unusually good at forging other people's documents, making him an extremely skilled artist in this form of mischief.[126] [2] It happened that many years earlier the church of Emesa had been named the heir of one of the leading citizens there. [3] This man was of patrician rank and his name was Mammianos; he came from a noble family and had great wealth. [4] During the reign of Justinian, this Priskos investigated all the families of the city and, if he found any who were at the very pinnacle of good fortune and seemed able to withstand a great loss of money, he looked closely into their ancestors. When he came across any of their old papers, he would forge

125. For the Samaritans, their persecution by Justinian, and religious dissimulation, see 11.24–26 above.

126. The forgery of documents was a persistent problem in the later Roman Empire. Justinian created the office of *quaesitor* to deal with it (and other matters); see *Novella* 80.7 (of 539), discussed by Prokopios at 20.9 above.

many documents, allegedly written by them, in which they declared that they owed Mammianos great sums of money that they had received from him in order to make a down payment. [5] The amount of gold that was supposedly owed in all these thoroughly forged promissory notes amounted to no less than one hundred *kentenaria*.[127] [6] Priskos, with marvelous skill, forged the handwriting of a certain man who had a great reputation for honesty and the rest of virtue, and who used to sit in the marketplace during Mammianos' lifetime certifying all the official documents of his fellow citizens by sealing each one with his own signature; the Romans call such a man a *tabellio*.[128] Priskos, then, turned this dossier over to the administrators of the church of Emesa, receiving assurances from them that he would be awarded a portion of the money that was collected on its basis.

[7] But the law stood in the way of this plan as it imposed a thirty-year limitation for all cases except for a few, those involving so-called mortgages, for which it extended this period to forty years. So they contrived the following scheme. [8] Arriving at Byzantion, they gave this emperor a large sum of money and besought him to become their accomplice in damming their fellow citizens, men who, in fact, were debtors to no one. [9] He took the money and unscrupulously wrote a law by which churches were prevented from bringing forward their own claims not after the set period but only after a full one hundred years had elapsed, and he made this valid not only in Emesa but throughout the Roman Empire.[129] [10] He then appointed a certain Longinos to arbitrate this matter for the Emesenes, an energetic man with an amazingly strong physique, who later became the official in charge of the populace at Byzantion.[130] [11] The administrators of the church began by filing a suit against one of the citizens who, according to the dossier, owed two *kentenaria*,[131] and of course the verdict immediately went against him, as he could offer no argument in a case that was so old, nor could he have known what had transpired back then. [12] All the others fell into a deep mourning too who were likewise assailed by

127. I.e., 720,000 coins (see the Glossary).

128. Public notary.

129. This is *Codex Iustinianus* 1.2.23 (of 530) and *Novella* 9 (of 535). See note 132 below for its repeal.

130. Longinos was urban prefect of Constantinople from 537 to 541/542.

131. I.e., 14,400 coins (see the Glossary).

the false accusers, and especially the most notable among the Emesenes. [13] But when this evil had already spread to a majority of the citizens, some succor happened to arrive from God, and it took the following form. [14] Longinos ordered Priskos, who had fabricated this whole business, to bring him the entire dossier and, when he refused, Longinos struck him with all his strength. [15] Priskos could not withstand a blow by such a strong man and fell on his back. He was trembling and full of fear that Longinos knew about the whole matter and so confessed everything. And thus this fraud was brought fully into the light and all the false accusations ceased.[132]

[16] It was not only the laws of the Romans with which he was constantly and every day tampering in this way, but he exerted himself to abolish those that the Hebrews honor as well. [17] Whenever the cycle of the calendar happened to bring their Paschal feast before that of the Christians,[133] he would not permit the Jews to celebrate it at the proper time, not even to consecrate anything to God at it or to practice any of their customs. [18] And his officials charged many of them with violating state law in that they had eaten lamb meat during this period, and fined them heavily.[134]

[19] Even though I know countless other deeds on Justinian's part that are similar to these, I will not record them here, because at some point I must put an end to this narrative. Those I have set down should suffice to indicate clearly his character.

Justinian's Hypocrisy

29. I will now demonstrate that he was a dissembler and manifestly insincere. He removed this Liberius fellow, whom I just mentioned,[135] from the position that he held and replaced him with Ioannes, an Egyptian, who was surnamed Laxarion. [2] When Pelagius,[136] who was an intimate friend of Liberius, learned this he asked

132. With a vague appeal to things not working out the way they were intended, Justinian lamely repealed the earlier decrees in *Novella* 111 (of 541), reducing the hundred years to forty for religious institutions; see also *Novella* 131.6 (of 545).

133. I.e., Easter.

134. Justinian passed a number of other restrictions on Jews, but this one is known only from here.

135. See 27.17 above. The present story occurred probably in 542.

136. This was the future pope; see 27.17 above. At this time he was the representative in Constantinople of Pope Vigilius.

the emperor whether the rumor concerning Laxarion was true. [3] The emperor immediately denied it, rejecting the notion that he had done any such thing, and gave him a letter addressed to Liberius which instructed him to take charge of his office with the utmost confidence and not be moved from it by any circumstance. [4] For he had no desire at this time to remove him from it. Now Ioannes had an uncle in Byzantion named Eudaimon, who had attained the consular rank and was extremely wealthy; he was also a former overseer of the private imperial estates.[137] [5] When this Eudaimon heard all that I just recounted, he too asked the emperor if his nephew's office was secure. [6] The emperor denied all that he had written to Liberius and wrote a letter addressed to Ioannes instructing him to take back possession of his office by all means at his disposal. [7] For he had not in any way changed his mind about the matter. Trusting in this document, Ioannes ordered Liberius to vacate the headquarters of the office seeing as he had been deposed from it. [8] Liberius declared that he would in no way obey him, as he too was relying on a letter by the emperor. [9] Ioannes armed his followers and attacked Liberius, while the latter resisted with his own men. There was a battle in which many fell, among them Ioannes himself, who held the office. [10] Eudaimon now brought heavy pressure to bear on the matter. Liberius was immediately recalled to Byzantion where the Senate made an inquiry into the events and acquitted the man, since he had not been the aggressor; he was acting in self-defense when the bloodshed occurred. [11] The emperor, however, did not let the matter rest until he had secretly fined him a certain sum of money.

[12] This was Justinian's way of being truthful and a straight talker. For my part, I think that a digression following up on the previous story would not be irrelevant at this point. This Eudaimon died not long afterward leaving many relatives behind him but no will or other indication as to his wishes. [13] At that time, the master of the palace eunuchs, a certain Euphratas,[138] also happened to die, leaving behind a nephew but making no arrangements for the disposition of his estate, which was quite vast. [14] The emperor

137. His exact office is difficult to identify; either *comes rerum privatarum* or *curator domus divinae*.

138. Euphratas was an Abasgian eunuch who had been sent to the Abasgians when they converted to Christianity and Justinian banned the practice of castration among them (*Wars* 8.3.19; Abasgia is in the Caucasus, in the eastern Black Sea region).

seized both estates, automatically becoming their heir; not a half-drachma did he give to the legal heirs. [15] This was typical of the respect shown by this emperor to the laws and the relatives of his own associates. [16] It was in the same way that he had seized the property of Eirenaios, who had died long before these events, even though he had no legal right to it whatsoever.[139]

[17] I would also not remain silent about a closely related event that took place at that same time. There was a certain Anatolios whose name was inscribed at the very top of the roll of Askalon's city council. His daughter had married a man from Kaisareia named Mamilianos, whose family was highly distinguished. [18] Now the daughter was an heiress, as Anatolios had no other children. [19] According to an ancient law, whenever a city councilor departs from this world without leaving male offspring, one fourth of his estate goes to the city council while all the rest is given to the heirs of the deceased.[140] The emperor revealed his character here too. It happened that he had just issued a law reversing the way that such cases were handled: now, when a councilor died without male issue, one fourth of his estate went to the heirs while all the rest went to the imperial treasury and the city council.[141] [20] Yet there was no precedent in all of history for the treasury or an emperor taking a share of a councilor's property. [21] But this law was now in force, so when Anatolios reached the last day of his life his daughter dispersed portions of his estate to the treasury and the city council, in accordance with the law. Both the emperor himself and the roll members of Askalon's council wrote to her and released her from any counterclaim on this property on the grounds that they had properly received from her what was rightfully due to them. [22] Later Mamilianos passed away too, Anatolios' son-in-law, leaving behind only one child, a daughter, who, naturally, alone inherited her father's property. [23] After some time, and while her own mother was still alive, she too departed this life. She had been married to one of the notables, but had given birth to neither male nor female offspring. [24] Justinian immediately took possession of all

139. Possibly the general from Antioch who was sent to Lazike in 527 (*Wars* 1.12.14) and helped to suppress the Samaritan rebellion in 529 (on which see note 81 in Part II). For Justinian claiming the estates of deceased notables, see 12.1–11 above.

140. *Codex Iustinianus* 10.35.1 (of 428).

141. *Novella* 38.1 (of 536) may be this law, except that it does not assert the rights of the imperial treasury in the matter. Prokopios may be referring to a lost edict.

her money making the astonishing argument that Anatolios' daughter was now an old woman and that it would be quite improper for her to enjoy the riches of both her husband and her father. [25] Yet lest the woman now join the ranks of the beggars, he arranged that she be given one gold coin per day for as long as she lived. In the executive order by which he stole this money, he actually put down that this coin was allowed for the sake of piety: "for it has always been my custom," he said, "to do what is pious and righteous."

[26] What I have said suffices regarding this matter; I do not want my account to become tiresome since it is impossible for any person to remember everything. [27] Now I will demonstrate that when there was money at stake he had no regard for the Blues either, to whom he was ostensibly devoted. [28] A certain Malthanes, a Kilikian by origin, was the son-in-law of that Leon who, as I said earlier, held the position known as *referendarius*.[142] [29] This man he sent to stop the violence among the Kilikians.[143] Using this appointment as a pretext, Malthanes committed atrocious crimes against the majority of the Kilikians. He plundered their wealth and sent some of it to the emperor while claiming the rest for his own enrichment. [30] But while the others endured this silently, the Blues among the people of Tarsos, emboldened by the license granted to them by the emperor, publicly chanted abuse against Malthanes in the marketplace when he was absent. [31] When Malthanes learned of this he immediately led a force of soldiers to Tarsos, arriving at night, and, in the dim morning twilight, sent them to the houses all around, instructing them to billet themselves there. [32] Believing that this was a raid, the Blues improvised a defense. Many were harmed in the darkness, and Damianos, a councilman, fell to an arrow. [33] This Damianos was a patron of the local Blues. When news of his death reached Byzantion, the Blues were bitterly angry and caused disturbances all around the city. They sorely harassed the emperor about the matter and railed loudly against Leon and Malthanes, making the most dire threats against them. [34] And the emperor too made no less a show of being infuriated at what had happened. He immediately fired off instructions that Malthanes' official acts be investigated and punished. [35] But Leon gave him a pile of gold, at which point he set his anger aside along with his warm support for the Blues. The affair was still not examined when Malthanes came to the emperor in Byzantion, where

142. See 14.16 and 17.32 above.

143. This was in the late 540s. The man's name was probably Marthanes.

he was warmly welcomed and held in honor. [36] As he was leaving the emperor's presence, the Blues, who were waiting for him, landed some good blows on him in the palace and would have killed him had they not been hindered by some of their own number, who had been secretly bought off by Leon. [37] And so, who would not diagnose this polity as utterly pitiful in which an emperor is bribed to leave crimes unexamined and militants, while the emperor is in his own palace, dare without any hesitation to rise up against one of the magistrates and lay violent hands upon him? [38] In fact, no punishment was imposed on Malthanes on account of these events nor on those who rose up against him.[144] From all this, then, let anyone who wishes ascertain the character of Justinian.

Various Ill-Intentioned Reforms

30. Whether he took any account of state interests will be shown by what he did to the public post system and the spies. [2] The emperors of the Romans who lived in previous times planned in advance that everything should be reported to them swiftly and with no delay, namely information regarding enemy actions in every province, riots in the cities or other disasters that occurred unexpectedly, as well as the actions of magistrates and all other officials throughout the Roman empire. They also ensured that those who transported the annual tax revenues were safe from danger and untoward delay. For these purposes they instituted a swift form of the public post going in all directions, and did so in the following manner. [3] Along the distance that a lightly equipped man could be expected to cover in one day they built stations, sometimes eight of them, sometimes fewer than that, but at any rate no fewer than five. [4] Up to forty horses were stabled at each station and grooms appointed to the stations in proportion to the number of horses. [5] By constantly changing their horses—which were of the best breeds—those who were assigned to this service could possibly cover in a single day what otherwise would be a ten-day journey, and so performed all the functions I just mentioned. Moreover, landowners everywhere, especially those whose lands happened to be inland, benefited enormously from this system. [6] For every year they sold their surplus crops to the state to feed the horses and grooms, and so profited greatly. [7] The result of all this was, on the one hand,

144. Marthanes is again attested as a general in 559/560.

that the state always received the taxes that were due from each subject while, on the other, those who paid them immediately received them back in turn, and in all this there was the additional advantage that the needs of the state were thereby met.

[8] That is how things *used* to be. This emperor, by contrast, first shut down the post from Chalcedon to Dakibiza, forcing the couriers to sail against their will from Byzantion all the way to Helenopolis. [9] So they sail in the small boats that are commonly used to make the crossing there and, if a storm should fall upon them, they incur great danger. As it is necessary for them to hasten, the option of waiting for better weather and delaying in hope of calm seas is ruled out.[145] [10] After that, while he did allow the road leading to the Persians to remain in its former condition, all the other roads in the East as far as Egypt he decreed should have only a single-station-per-day journey and these, moreover, were not to have horses but only a few asses. [11] Therefore, whatever happened in each province was scarcely reported, and even then too late and long after the events, and so it was unlikely that there could be any effective response. And those who own the lands, now that their crops rot unsold, have permanently lost this source of profit.

[12] As for the spies, matters stood as follows. Many men had always been maintained at public expense who would infiltrate the enemy and enter the palace of the Persians on the pretext of trade or something else, and there they would carefully investigate everything. When they returned to Roman territory, they were in a position to reveal all the enemy's secrets to the magistrates. [13] The latter, being warned in advance, were on their guard, and therefore nothing unexpected befell them. This institution could be found among the Medes since ancient times as well. In fact, they say that Chosroes increased his spies' salary and so enjoyed better intelligence. [14] For nothing [that happened among the Romans escaped his attention. But Justinian spent nothing on his own and as a result][146] he blotted out the spies' very name from Roman territory, from which cause many things went wrong, including the loss of

145. In other words, Justinian eliminated about 40 km of the land route from Constantinople to Nikomedeia (Dakibiza is about at the halfway point) and replaced it with a slower and more dangerous sea route—a very small segment of the total Roman *cursus*. This reform is blamed by Ioannes Lydos on agents of the prefect Ioannes the Kappadokian (*On the Magistracies of the Roman State* 3.61).

146. Haury added these words to fill the gap.

Lazike to the enemy, given that the Romans had no idea where on earth the Persian king and his army were.[147] [15] Nor was that all. Another old custom was that the state maintained camels in large numbers, whose function was to follow Roman forces marching against the enemy and carry its supplies. [16] Thus it was not necessary in those times to press farmers into corvée services or for soldiers to lack basic necessities. But Justinian abolished these too, almost all of them, and as a result when Roman armies today march out against the enemy nothing can be done right.

[17] The most important state business, then, was being handled in this way. I see nothing wrong in recounting here one of his most ridiculous actions too. [18] There was a certain Euangelos among the advocates of Kaisareia, a very distinguished man. The winds of fortune had blown in his favor, bringing him many forms of wealth, not least of which was the ownership of much land. [19] Later he purchased a village by the coast called Porphyreon, for three *kentenaria* of gold.[148] When Justinian learned this, he immediately seized this land, reimbursing him for only a small portion of the price and saying only this, that it was unseemly for Euangelos, who was only an advocate, to be the owner of such a village.[149] [20] I will now stop speaking about these matters, having covered them more or less sufficiently.

[21] The following must also be included among Justinian and Theodora's many innovations in governance. In the past, whenever the Senate entered into the imperial presence it would do obeisance in this way. A man of patrician rank would salute him on his right breast. [22] The emperor would then kiss his head from above, and dismiss him. All others bent the right knee to the emperor, and withdrew. [23] There was no requirement whatever of doing obeisance before an empress. But with Justinian and Theodora, everyone, including those of patrician rank, had to make their entrance by falling straight on the ground, flat on their faces; then, stretching their arms and legs out as far as they would go, they had to

147. The Romans lost Lazike in 541 (*Wars* 2.15, 2.17). For the failure of the Roman spies in this instance, see *Wars* 2.16.3, but the accusation here seems exaggerated.

148. I.e., 21,600 coins (see the Glossary).

149. I.e., a village that had an "imperial" name (which referred to the production of the purple dye, porphyry, a color reserved for the emperor in some settings and items; private citizens could be arrested for owning certain purple items). The village may have been confiscated to establish an imperial monopoly over the dye.

touch, with their lips, one foot of each of the two. Only then could they stand up again. [24] Nor did Theodora waive this protocol for herself, she who demanded to receive ambassadors of the Persians and of other barbarians in her own right and give them gifts of money as if the Roman Empire lay under her command, a thing that had never yet happened in all of history. [25] And again, in the past those who spoke with the emperor called him "emperor" and his wife "empress" and they addressed each of the other magistrates by the office that he happened to be holding at the moment. [26] But if anyone spoke to either of them and referred to the "emperor" or "empress" rather than calling them "Master" or "Mistress," or if he attempted to refer to the magistrates as anything but "slaves," he would be regarded as ignorant and vulgar of tongue, and was thrown out as if he had committed a bitter offense and deeply insulted the persons who least deserved it.

[27] Furthermore, in the past few people would enter the palace, and even they with difficulty. But from the time that these two gained the throne, officials together with everyone else would be spending all their time in the palace. [28] The reason for this was that, in the past, it was permitted for magistrates to exercise their own independent judgment in making decisions about what was just and lawful. [29] Therefore, in executing their proper functions, magistrates resided in their own official headquarters while subjects, who neither heard nor saw any act of violence, troubled the emperor little. [30] But these two, who were always requiring, to the ruin of their subjects, that they be consulted on each and every matter, forced everyone to court them in a most servile way. Almost every day it was possible to see all the law courts virtually empty of people, but in the imperial court there was a vulgar mob, pushing, shoving, and always debasing itself into total servility. [31] It seemed, moreover, as though the assistants of the imperial couple had to stand continuously throughout the day and then during a long part of every night. Sleepless and famished at all the wrong times, they lost their health. This, then, is what all their alleged good fortune amounted to in the end. [32] And when they were finally released from all this, these people would quarrel among themselves over the question of where the money of the Romans really was. [33] Some asserted that the barbarians had got it all, others that the emperor had it stored away in many vaults. [34] So whenever Justinian departs from this life, in the case that he is human after all, or when, as Lord of Demons, he sets this life aside, whoever will be lucky enough to have survived that long will know the truth.

Related Texts

1. A Law for the Marriage of Justinian and Theodora

Codex Iustinianus 5.4.23[1]

Date: between 520 and 524. Prokopios discusses this edict and the circumstances under which it was issued at Secret History *9.47–54. It was probably composed by Justin's* quaestor *Proklos (who is mentioned at 6.13 and 9.41). The translation conveys the convoluted and pompous style of the legal Latin of late antiquity.*

The emperor Justin Augustus to Demosthenes, praetorian prefect:

Believing that it is a peculiar duty of Imperial beneficence at all times not only to consider the convenience of Our subjects but also to attempt to supply their needs, We have determined that the errors of women on account of which, through the weakness of their sex, they have chosen to be guilty of dishonorable conduct, should be corrected by a display of proper moderation, and that they should by no means be deprived of the hope of an improvement of status, so that, taking this into consideration, they may the more readily abandon the improvident and disgraceful choice of life which they have made. For We believe that the benevolence of God and His exceeding clemency toward the human race should be imitated by Us as far as Our nature will permit. God is always willing to pardon the sins daily committed by man, accept Our repentance, and bring us to a better condition. Hence, We should seem to be unworthy of pardon Ourselves were We to fail to act in this manner with reference to those subject to Our empire.

(1) Therefore, just as it would be unjust for slaves, to whom their liberty has been given, to be raised by Imperial indulgence to the status of men who are born free and, by the effect of an Imperial privilege of this kind, be placed in the same position as if they had

1. The translation is by S. P. Scott, *The Civil Law*, vol. 6 (Cincinnati: Central Trust Co., 1932), slightly modified.

never been slaves, but were freeborn;[2] but that women who had devoted themselves to theatrical performances and, afterward, having become disgusted with this degraded status, abandoned their infamous occupation and obtained better repute, should have no hope of obtaining any benefit from the Emperor, who had the power to place them in the condition in which they could have remained if they had never been guilty of dishonorable acts, We, by the present most merciful law, grant them this Imperial benefit under the condition that where, having deserted their evil and disgraceful condition, they embrace a more proper life and conduct themselves honorably, they shall be permitted to petition Us to grant them Our Divine permission to contract legal marriage when they are unquestionably worthy of it. Those who may be united with them need be under no apprehension, nor think that such marriages are void by the provisions of former laws;[3] but, rather, they shall remain valid and be considered just as if the women had never previously led dishonorable lives, whether their husbands are invested with office, or, for some other reason, are prohibited from marrying women of the stage,[4] provided, however, that the marriage can be proved by dotal contracts reduced to writing. For women of this kind having been purified from all blemishes and, as it were, restored to the condition in which they were born, We desire that no disgraceful epithet be applied to them and that no difference shall exist between them and those who have never committed a similar breach of morality.

(2) Children born of a marriage of this kind shall be legitimate and the proper heirs of their father, even though he may have other lawful heirs by a former marriage; so that such children may also, without any obstacle, be able to acquire the estates of their parents, either from an intestate or under the terms of a will.

(3) If, however, women of this description, after an Imperial Rescript has been granted them in accordance with their request, should defer contracting marriage, We order that their reputations shall, nevertheless, remain intact, as in the case of all others who may desire to transfer their property to anyone; and that they shall be competent to receive anything bequeathed to them, in accordance

2. The emperor is not saying that it is unjust to grant freedom to slaves but that it would be unjust to do so while not being likewise indulgent to fallen women who have changed their ways (the reader must continue with the rest of the long sentence in the text).

3. See note 60 at *Secret History* 9.51 for such previous laws.

4. This provision, perhaps, alludes to Justinian's special circumstances.

with law, or an estate which may descend to them on the ground of intestacy.

(4) We also decree that such of these women as have obtained a privilege from the Emperor shall occupy the same position as those who have obtained some other benefit which was not bestowed by the sovereign but was acquired by them as a voluntary donation before their marriage; for, by a concession of this kind, every other stigma on account of which women are forbidden to contract lawful marriage with certain men is absolutely removed.

(5) To this We add that when the daughters of women of this kind are born after the purification of their mother from the disgrace of her former life, they shall not be considered as the children of females belonging to the stage or be subject to the laws which forbid certain men to marry such women. Where, however, they were born before that time, they shall be permitted to petition the Utterly Unconquered Emperor for a Rescript, which should be granted without any opposition, by means of which they may be permitted to marry just as if they were not the daughters of actresses; and those men shall not be prohibited from marrying them who are forbidden to take as wives girls belonging to the stage, either on account of their own rank or for some other reason, provided, however, that in every instance dotal instruments in writing are executed by the parties concerned.

(6) If, however, a girl born of a theatrical mother who practiced her profession until the time of her death should, after her mother's decease, petition for Imperial indulgence and obtain it, she shall be freed from the blemish of her mother's reputation and herself be granted permission to marry; and she also can without the fear of former laws be united in matrimony with those who not long ago were prohibited from marrying the daughter of an actress.

(7) Moreover, We have thought that what was prescribed by former laws (although this was somewhat obscure) should be abolished, namely, that a marriage contracted between persons of unequal rank shall not be considered valid unless dotal instruments with reference to it were executed. When, however, this does not take place, such marriages shall still be absolutely valid, without any distinction of persons, provided the women are free and freeborn and that no suspicion of any criminal or incestuous union arises, for We, under all circumstances, sever criminal and incestuous unions as well as those which were especially prohibited by the provisions of former laws, with the exception, however, of such as We authorize by the present decree and direct shall be considered legal, in accordance with the rights of marriage.

(8) Therefore these matters having been settled in this manner, by this general law which must hereafter be observed, We order that any such unions which have subsequently been made shall be regulated in accordance with the aforesaid provisions; so that where anyone has married a wife of this kind during Our reign (as has already been stated) and has children by her, they shall be legitimate and be entitled to succeed to their father if the latter was intestate as well as under a will, and the wife, as well as any children hereafter born of her, shall also be considered legitimate.

2. The Nika Riots

Wars 1.24

Date: January 532. The Nika riots (see below for the name) was the most destructive and bloody social uprising of Justinian's reign, probably of the entire later Roman period. Prokopios refers to the event in The Secret History *on a number of occasions as it had serious repercussions for Justinian's relationship with the Senate, the fan-clubs, and the people of Constantinople (12.12, 18.32, 19.12). It temporarily halted the careers of two men whom he mentions often (the praetorian prefect Ioannes the Kappadokian and the* quaestor *Tribonianos) and caused the destruction of the original church of Hagia Sophia, enabling Justinian to rebuild it on a grander scale. The notes to the translation below summarize events that occurred during the riots that Prokopios did not include but that are known from other sources, mainly the* Chronicle *of Ioannes Malalas (18.71) and the* Paschal Chronicle *(s.a. 532).*

(1) At this same time the populace in Byzantion rose up without warning in a rebellion that, against all expectation, acquired huge dimensions and caused enormous harm both to the populace itself and the Senate. It happened in the following way. (2) The fan-clubs in each city had long been divided into Blues and Greens,[5] but it is a relatively recent development that, for the sake of these names and

5. Prokopios introduces the fan-clubs at *Secret History* 7.1, and they appear repeatedly after that. See note 17 in Part II of the text for an explanation of their nature.

the grandstands from which they watch the games,[6] they have been willing to spend money, offer their bodies up to be cruelly tortured, and do not even think it unworthy to die a shameful death. (3) They fight against the color that sits across from them without knowing why they are incurring such danger in the first place. What they do know well, however, is that even if they overcome their enemies in battle, the outcome for them will be that they will immediately be hauled off to jail, suffer extreme forms of torture, and then be killed. (4) So a hatred that has no cause grows up within them against their neighbors in the grandstands and it endures interminably for all of eternity, softening for no tie of marriage or kin relation or bond of friendship, even if those who are divided in their colors happen to be brothers or some other such thing. (5) They show no respect for sacred or human conventions in their zeal to win in these contests and simply do not care if some sacrilege is committed by anyone at all against God or whether the laws and the state are being violated by enemies within or without, even if they themselves are not particularly well-off and their homeland has been unjustly reduced to poverty. No, what matters is that it goes well for their "side," which is what they call those in the same fan-club. (6) Women too share with them in this accursed business, though they do not merely follow their men in it but even oppose them, if it should come to that, despite the fact they do not really attend the spectacles or have any other reason to become involved.[7] Thus, I do not know what else to call this if not a disease of the soul. That is how matters stand in the cities and among the populace in each.

(7) It was at this time, then, that the magistracy in charge of the populace in Byzantion led away some of the militants to be executed.[8] The two sides then came to an understanding with each other and made a truce; they seized those who had been arrested and

6. The Blues and Greens had designated grandstands in the hippodrome, right next to each other and facing the imperial box on the opposite side of the racetrack.

7. This comment foreshadows the involvement of Theodora in the imperial council at 33–38 below.

8. This magistracy was the urban prefecture, held in early 532 by Eudaimon (not the same man as in *Secret History* 29.4). Eudaimon sent three militants to be impaled and four to the gallows on 10 January, but two survived when the scaffold broke, one Blue and one Green. Some monks took them to a sanctuary, which Eudaimon had surrounded by soldiers. At the races three days later, on Tuesday 13 January, the fan-clubs clamored for the men's pardon. Justinian made no response, and a riot ensued when the fan-clubs joined forces.

broke into the jail, releasing all who were locked up there on charges of sedition or some other felony.[9] (8) And all the staff of the urban magistracy were killed for no reason, while all the law-abiding citizens were fleeing to the opposite continent.[10] The city was set to the torch as if it had been taken by enemies. (9) The temple of Sophia, the baths of Zeuxippos, and the imperial courtyard from the Propylaia all the way to the so-called House of Ares were burned up and destroyed, as were both of the great porticos that lead to the forum that is named after Constantine, the houses of prosperous people, and a great deal of other properties.[11] (10) The emperor, his consort, and some senators shut themselves up in the palace and kept quiet. The fan-clubs now fixed upon a watchword, *nika*, and this was the name that the uprising would bear until the present day.[12]

(11) The prefect of the court at that time was Ioannes the Kappadokian while Tribonianos, a Pamphylian by origin, was the emperor's counselor, which office the Romans call *quaestor*. (12) The first of these two men, Ioannes, had not even heard of liberal education or culture. He learned nothing at grammar school other than the letters themselves, and poorly at that. But through the strength of his natural ability he became the most powerful man of our times, (13) for he was the most capable at knowing what had to be done and at finding solutions to practical problems. However, he also became the most wicked of all men and bent all the force of his nature to it. No divine commandment or shame before his fellow man ever entered into him; rather, to destroy the lives of many people for the sake of profit and to pull down entire cities were his concerns. (14) In a short time he acquired a vast fortune and threw himself into a lifestyle of unrestrained drunken debauchery. Up to lunchtime each day he would plunder the property of his subjects

9. The rioters attacked the *praetorium* on the evening of Tuesday 13 January and set fire to it. It was located on the south side of the main avenue of Constantinople (the *Mese*), between the forum of Constantine and the hippodrome.

10. I.e., to the Asian side of the Bosporus.

11. These buildings (and others not mentioned by Prokopios) were not all set afire on the same day; his narrative compresses events. The church of Hagia Sophia was the predecessor of the one built by Justinian after the riots. The baths of Zeuxippos, the most popular and magnificent in the city, were adjacent to the palace grounds to the northeast of the hippodrome. In addition to other works of art, they housed an impressive collection of ancient statues. The Senate house burned along with the courtyard known as the Augousteion and the main gate of the palace (called the Propylaia here).

12. *Nika* ("win" or "victory") was what the fan-clubs chanted at the races.

while for the rest of the day he would devote himself to drinking and lustful bodily gratification. (15) As he could not in any way control himself, he ate until he threw up and was always ready to steal money—though he was even more ready to bring it out and spend it.[13] Such a person, then, was Ioannes. (16) Tribonianos, on the other hand, was also quite talented and was, moreover, second to none of his contemporaries when it came to the extent of his learning. But he was also abnormally addicted to making money and was always ready to sell justice to make a profit. Just about every day he would repeal some laws and propose others, selling each service according to the needs of his customers.[14]

(17) Now, so long as the populace was divided against itself and fighting on behalf of the names of these colors, no attention was paid to the crimes that those men were committing against the public interest. But when the fan-clubs came to an understanding, as was said, and began the uprising, they openly insulted these two men throughout the entire city and went about searching for them to kill. Hence the emperor, who wanted to win the populace back to his side, instantly dismissed both of them from their offices.[15] (18) And he appointed Phokas, a patrician, to be prefect of the court; he was a prudent man endowed by nature with a fine sense of justice.[16] He also ordered Basileides to take up the office of *quaestor*; he was known among the patricians for fairness and was in other respects esteemed.[17] (19) But even on these terms the uprising still raged no

13. The praetorian prefect Ioannes the Kappadokian is mentioned often in *The Secret History*. For his downfall (in 541), see Prokopios' account (*Wars* 1.25) translated in related text 7.

14. Tribonianos appears also at *Secret History* 13.12 and 20.16–17 (see note 114 in Part II for his career) and in *Wars* 1.25.1 (translated in related text 7). Prokopios' judgment regarding Ioannes the Kappadokian was shared by other contemporary intellectuals, for example Ioannes Lydos.

15. The rioters called for their dismissal as well as for the dismissal of the urban prefect Eudaimon on Wednesday 14 January, when Justinian tried to restart the games to pacify the crowds. These three men were the highest officials in the capital at that moment. For their careers after the riots, see related text 7.

16. For Phokas, a suspected pagan whom Prokopios admired, see *Secret History* 21.6 and note 28.

17. Basileides (or Basilides) had served as praetorian prefect of the East (before 528), praetorian prefect of Illyricum (529), on the first commission to codify the laws (528–529), and was deputy *magister officiorum* for Hermogenes (who was off in the East). He served as *quaestor* until 534/535. He, Konstantiolos, and Moundos had been sent out to hear the rioters' demands and returned to report that they were demanding the dismissal of Ioannes, Eudaimon, and Tribonianos.

less than before.[18] On the fifth day of the uprising, late in the afternoon, the emperor Justinian commanded Hypatios and Pompeïos, the nephews of the late emperor Anastasios, to go home immediately, either because he suspected that they were plotting some harm against his person or else because destiny led them to this. (20) But they were afraid that the populace might force them to claim the imperial position, which is in fact what happened, and so they said that it would not be right for them to abandon their emperor when he found himself in such a perilous position. (21) Hearing this, the emperor Justinian grew all the more suspicious and commanded them to leave right then and there. So these two men went to their homes and, for as long as it was night, remained there quietly.[19]

(22) But at dawn on the next day the people found out that the two men were no longer residing in the palace. So the entire populace rushed to them, proclaimed Hypatios emperor, and made as if to convey him to the forum where he would take charge of events.[20] (23) But Hypatios' wife, Maria, a discreet woman with the greatest reputation for prudence, took hold of her husband and would not let go, crying out in despair and pleading with all her friends and kinsmen that the fan-clubs were leading him away on the path to his death. (24) Overpowered by the press of people, however, she let go of her husband against her will and so the people led him, against his wishes too, to the forum of Constantine where they called him to the throne. Not having a diadem at hand, nor any of the things with which it is customary to invest an emperor, they placed a gold torque upon his head and acclaimed him

18. When the dismissal of his top three officials had no immediate effect, Justinian, probably still on Wednesday 13 January, sent out Belisarios with some Gothic soldiers to attack the militants. In response, they burned down more of the city and, on Thursday 14 January, rushed to the house of Probos (consul in 502), a nephew of the emperor Anastasios (r. 491–518), to acclaim him emperor. He was—wisely—not at home, and his older cousins were in the palace (see 19–21 below). They set fire to his house, but it didn't catch. On Saturday 17 January there was widespread fighting in the city between the rioters and army units that were brought in from Thrace, each side setting additional parts of the city on fire to smoke out the other.

19. This was probably the evening and night of Saturday 17 January. Hypatios and Pompeïos held high military commands under Anastasios, Justin (r. 518–527), and Justinian, though the former was singularly unsuccessful at almost everything he did.

20. On the morning of Sunday 18 January, Justinian appeared in the hippodrome in an attempt to negotiate with the rioters. When this failed the latter went off to find Hypatios.

as the emperor of the Romans. (25) The members of the Senate had already assembled—however many, that is, who were not still in the emperor's court—and many opinions were expressed about how they should go to the palace and fight. (26) But Origenes, a senator, stepped forward and said the following.[21] "Our present state of affairs, O Romans, cannot be settled except by war. Now it is understood that war and imperial power are the greatest of all things in human life. (27) But great actions are accomplished not by the shortness of the time in which they are executed but through sound judgment and hard work, which things people exercise over lengths of time. (28) If, then, we should march out against the enemy, our cause will be balanced on a razor's edge and we will risk everything in but a moment; for the sake of forcing an outcome, we will either have to adore Fortune afterward or blame her for everything. (29) For the most hazardous matters tend to fall in most cases under Fortune's dominion. But if, on the other hand, we handle the present circumstance with more caution and planning, we will be unable to seize Justinian in the palace even though we wish to do so, but he also will gladly seize the opportunity to flee the moment someone presents it to him. (30) And power that is scorned tends to collapse as its foundations weaken day by day. And we have other palaces besides, the Plakillianai and the other one named after Helene,[22] which this emperor can use as his base to conduct the war and govern other matters in the most advantageous way." (31) That was what Origenes said. But the others, as crowds tend to do, were all for hazarding the issue and believed that instant action was in their interest, not least among them Hypatios (for it was necessary that he would end up badly). He commanded them to head for the hippodrome. And some even said that he went there on purpose, because he was really on the emperor's side.[23]

21. Origenes is almost certainly a figure invented by Prokopios to deliver this speech. At the time that Prokopios was finishing the *Wars*, Justinian was trying to have the third-century theologian Origenes declared a heretic.

22. Or Flaccillianae, after Aelia Flacilla, the first wife of Theodosios I (r. 378–395); this palace was under rebel control, as insignia were brought from there for Hypatios' use. The Helenianai were possibly named after Constantine the Great's mother Helene.

23. Some historians suspect that Hypatios was acting secretly for Justinian—at least at first. Some sources report that when he was taken to the hippodrome he sent a message to Justinian telling him that he had assembled all of his enemies for him to do with as he pleased (cf. 56 below). But he then received the false information that Justinian had fled, at which point he "began to sit more confidently in the imperial box."

(32) Those with the emperor were holding a meeting to decide whether it would be better for them to stay or to take to the ships in flight. Many speeches were made on either side. (33) And Theodora the empress also spoke as follows. "The impropriety of a woman speaking boldly among the men or stirring up those who are cringing in fear is hardly, I believe, a matter that the present moment affords us the luxury of examining one way or another. (34) For when you reach the point of supreme danger nothing else seems best other than to settle the matter at hand in the best possible way. (35) I believe that flight, now more than ever, is not in our interest even if it should bring us to safety. For it is not possible for a man who is born not also to die, but for one who has reigned it is intolerable to become a fugitive. (36) May I *never* be parted from the purple! May I *never* live to see the day when I will not be addressed as Mistress by all in my presence! Emperor, if you wish to save yourself, that is easily arranged. (37) We have much money; there is the sea; and here are our ships. But consider whether, after you have saved yourself, you would then gladly exchange safety for death. For my part, I like that old saying, that kingship is a good burial shroud."[24] (38) When the empress spoke these words, all the others were emboldened and turned to thoughts of prowess, considering how they might defend themselves if the enemy moved against them. (39) All the soldiers, both those stationed at the imperial court and all the rest, were not favorably disposed toward the emperor nor willing to take a side openly; rather, they were waiting to see how events would turn out. (40) The emperor placed all of his hopes on Belisarios and Moundos, the first of whom had just returned from the war against the Medes leading a strong and formidable force,[25] in particular a large number of his personal guards and marshals who were trained in the actual struggles and dangers of war. (41) As for Moundos, he had been appointed general of the Illyrians and, just by some chance,[26] happened to have been summoned

24. The "old saying" actually has *tyranny* instead of *kingship*, and was said by the notorious tyrant Dionysios of Syracuse when a popular uprising had besieged him in his palace. Prokopios has made a subtle substitution that would have been recognized only by those who, like himself, had a good classical education; it covertly signals his own view of the regime.

25. For the campaigns in the East in 531, see *Wars* 1.17–18.

26. Here is where the fortune (*tyche*) feared by Origenes (28–29 above) worked against the revolt.

to Byzantion for some purpose, and had with him Eroulian barbarians.[27]

(42) When Hypatios reached the hippodrome, he immediately went up to the place where the emperor is accustomed to sit and there he sat on the imperial throne, from where the emperor watches the horse races and gymnastic contests. (43) Moundos, meanwhile, left the palace from the gate which is called the Spiral after the way in which it winds around as you go down.[28] (44) As for Belisarios, at first he went straight up for Hypatios and the imperial throne,[29] but when he reached the nearest structure, where a military guard has been posted since ancient times, he called out to the soldiers and ordered them to open the door immediately so that he could attack the tyrant. (45) But the soldiers had decided to assist neither side until one had unequivocally prevailed, so they evaded him by pretending not to hear. (46) Belisarios turned back and informed the emperor that all was lost, (47) for the soldiers in the palace guard were now in revolt against him. The emperor commanded him to go to the Bronze Gate and the Propylaia there. (48) Belisarios, with difficulty and not without great danger and exertion, traversed the smoldering ruins and went up to the hippodrome. (49) And when he reached the portico of the Blues, which is to the right of the imperial throne,[30] he decided to go against Hypatios himself first but, since the gateway there was small and also closed and guarded on the inside by Hypatios' soldiers, he was terrified lest the entire populace fall upon him and his company while they were fighting in that narrow place and destroy them all; and then it would be easy for them to move against the emperor, in fact no trouble at all. (50) Realizing now that he needed to move against the populace that had occupied the hippodrome—a multitude beyond number, being pushed this way and that in great disorder—he drew his sword from

27. Moundos (Mundo) was the son of a Gepid king. He served Theodoric the Great in Italy until the latter's death in 526 and then switched over to Justinian, who first appointed him general of Illyricum (529–530), then of the East (531), then again of Illyricum (532–536). The Erouls, like the Gepids, were a Germanic people.

28. Moundos' route took him to the south (curved) end of the hippodrome; he and Belisarios would eventually attack the crowd from opposite ends of the hippodrome (see 49–53 below).

29. Belisarios' first attempt was through the passage that connected the palace to the imperial box in the hippodrome.

30. Belisarios' second attempt took him around the north side of the hippodrome, through the ruins of the Bronze Gate.

its scabbard, ordered the others to follow his lead, and rushed at them with a cry. (51) The populace was in a press standing around in no particular order. When the people saw the armored soldiers, men who had earned great fame for their courage and knowledge of war, striking with their swords and giving no quarter, they rushed headlong into flight. (52) There was a great outcry, as can only be expected. Moundos, meanwhile, had been standing somewhere nearby, eager for a fight (for he was a daring and energetic man), but he did not know what to do in the present circumstances. When he ascertained that Belisarios was already hard at work, he immediately charged into the hippodrome through the entrance that they call the Dead Gate. (53) And then Hypatios' militants began to die as they were being attacked violently from both sides. Finally, when the rout was undeniable and a great slaughter of the people had already been done, Boraïdes and Ioustos, the cousins of the emperor Justinian,[31] pulled Hypatios down from the throne without anyone daring to lift a hand against them, and they marched him off to the emperor, delivering him along with Pompeïos. (54) More than thirty thousand of the populace died that day. But the emperor commanded that the two men be imprisoned in harsh conditions. (55) By then Pompeïos was crying and speaking pitiful words. For the man had little experience of such trials and misfortunes. Hypatios rebuked him severely and said that it was unbecoming for those who were about to be killed unjustly to lament their fate. (56) For at first they were compelled against their will by the populace and later, when they went to the hippodrome, it was not to harm the emperor. The soldiers executed both of them on the following day and their bodies were flung into the sea. (57) The emperor confiscated their properties to the treasury along with the properties of all the other senators who sided with them. (58) But later he restored to the children of Hypatios, Pompeïos, and all the rest the titles that they had held along with as much of their property as he had not already given away to his own associates. And that was the end of the uprising in Byzantion.

31. No offices are attested for Boraïdes. Ioustos was made general in 542.

3. Theodora Helps Monophysite Saints

Yuhannan of Amida [John of Ephesos], *Lives of the Saints*[32]

At Secret History *10.14–15 (cf. 13.9, 14.8), Prokopios claims that Justinian and Theodora deliberately took opposite sides in the main religious controversy of the age, regarding the refusal by many Christian communities in the East to recognize the Council of Chalcedon (451). He promised to elaborate on this in a separate work of ecclesiastical history that, unfortunately, he never wrote. Later he relates an episode in which Theodora took the side of those opposing Chalcedon while Justinian was working to enforce it (27.13). As we might expect, Theodora is presented positively in works written by opponents of Chalcedon (Monophysites), because she supported their leaders and even granted them refuge and hospitality in Constantinople. These sources corroborate Prokopios' claim and reflect exactly the gratitude that we would expect from Monophysites who gained her patronage during a persecution. They also reveal that Theodora was known for personally honoring ascetic holy men, though Chalcedonian monastic sources were not so favorable toward her and, as* Life *36 reveals, nor were her advances immediately welcomed by all Monophysite holy men.*

Yuhannan of Amida (507–589; called John of Ephesos by scholars) was one of the leading Monophysite missionaries and writers of this period. He wrote (in Syriac) an Ecclesiastical History *and a collection of fifty-eight* Saints' Lives. *Theodora makes occasional appearances there as a patron of Monophysite bishops and holy men. In* Life *13 (below), Yuhannan casually reveals that Theodora "came from the brothel." He does not say what he thought of this, but his statement, more than any other single piece of evidence, has prevented skepticism about* The Secret History *from going too far (see the Introduction).*

[*Lives of the Saints* 13*: Toma and Stephanos*] This saint [Mare of Amida], therefore, with Sargis[33] and Stephanos and Toma his notaries and *synkelloi* were sent to a hard and distant place of exile at Petra; and they accepted it and departed and went; and they were there in great distress exceeding their power of endurance, until

32. Translations are from E. W. Brooks, *John of Ephesus: Lives of the Eastern Saints*, in *Patrologia Orientalis* 17 (1923) 1–307 (here 157 and 188–189); 18 (1924) 511–698 (here 630–634 and 676–680); and 19 (1925) 151–284, slightly adapted.

33. I.e., Sergios.

their lives were near disappearing. By reason of this distress, therefore, the holy Mare was constrained to send the virtuous Stephanos his deacon and notary to the royal city in the hope that he might perhaps by the intercession of anyone whom God might put in his way be able to have that place altered for them. But, when he went up, the good God, who, as the divine apostle also says, "is faithful and just, who will not permit you to be tried more than you are able to be tried,"[34] directed the virtuous Stephanos to Theodora who came from the brothel, who was at that time a patrician but eventually became queen also with King Justinian.[35] She, therefore, when she learned of that distress, as if by divine instigation, because she saw that saint's distress, made her mercy manifest and made entreaty to Justinian her husband, who was master of the soldiers and also a patrician and the king's nephew, that he would inform his uncle and he might order relief to be given to these distressed men, making this entreaty even with tears. And through the grace which cares for every man's life, it was done and an order went out to them to come to Alexandria.

[*Lives of the Saints* 47*: Concerning the holy communities which Theodora the queen gathered together in Constantinople, communities from every place in the royal city which were gathered together in the royal mansion called that of Hormisdas by the believing queen Theodora whose soul is at rest.*] On the subject, therefore, of the community of blessed men which was gathered together in the royal city by the believing queen at the time of the persecution out of many people and various local tongues, we wish to leave a record at short length; and the history of it is sufficient to cause discerning men to marvel at it, since it was indeed composed of many blessed men who did not fall short of the number of five hundred, and including great and venerable old men. And the congregation of persecuted saints was so widely extended that it shone with many who had under the constraint of the persecution come down from columns and been ejected from places of seclusion and been expelled from districts, and their congregation was rendered illustrious by great and distinguished heads of convents from all quarters of the east and of the west, and Syria and Armenia, Kappadokia and Kilikia, Isauria and Lykaonia, and Asia and Alexan-

34. 1 Corinthians 10.13.

35. This refers to the period in the 520s between Theodora's marriage to Justinian and his accession to the throne in 527. For this period in *The Secret History*, see 9.30–54.

dria and Byzantion, countries which beyond others burned with zeal for the faith. One might consequently go into the palace itself, called that of Hormisdas, as into a great and marvelous desert of solitaries, and marvel at their numbers and wonder at their venerable appearance and at the same men's honored old age, and be affected by the crucifixion of their bodies and their practices of standing and the same men's spiritual songs which were heard from all sides, and at their marvelous canticles and their melancholy voices which were performed and uttered in all the chambers and courts and cells and halls of that palace. And they were ranged in order and full in every place, and they were crowded and packed and their cells were full, as well as every chamber and room in that place. One might see in each of the great halls that they were filled by rows of planks, for by the care of the queen cells had been made and provided for the old and great and honored men among them. . . . Severe labors and protracted fasts and constant vigils and perpetual prayers as well as celebrations and descents of the Spirit in every place were being carried on, while altars were fixed up everywhere, so that in consequence not only did the believing people[36] run to the amazing sight, and see and marvel and be astonished and wonder at these spiritual congregations, and run to each one of these saints to be blessed and to be assisted by their prayers, but even some of those who did not belong to their communion would run to that amazing community about which they had heard, and see and marvel and be astonished and dumbfounded and edified, and would give thanks to God, and in consequence a great number of people of the city like a full river turned aside to these holy communities, and flowed on and overflowed at all times; insomuch that many of the participators with the Synod of Chalcedon,[37] which was a cause of scandal and of the persecution of the blessed men, when they saw this marvelous community, and learned the causes of the persecution of it, had their mind filled with affliction and contrition, and renounced the Chalcedonian communion, and asked for communion with them, and thus many were added to the believers. And the believing queen also would regularly once in every two or three days come down to them to be blessed by them, being amazed at their community and their practices, and admiring their honored old age, and going round among them and making obeisance to them, and being regularly

36. I.e., those who rejected the Council of Chalcedon.

37. I.e., those who took communion from priests who recognized the Council of Chalcedon.

blessed by each one of them, while she provided the expenses required for them liberally in every thing. And the king also, who was ranged against them on account of the Synod of Chalcedon, marveled at their congregation and himself also was attached to many of them and trusted them, and was constantly received and blessed by them. And this great community became illustrious by a variety of practices all the days of the blessed queen's life, while even after her death she laid an injunction on the king about it, and it was preserved, and all the lifetime of Justinian the king he looked after them and honored them, and supported the remnant of them, even to the present time which is the year 877.[38]

[*Lives of the Saints* 10: *Simeon the Bishop, the Persian Debater*] It became known to all men living in the country of the Persians that the evil doctrine of Nestorios flourished there only, while all peoples and tongues abhorred it;[39] and this glorious old man was yet more emboldened against them. In this same zeal, then, some occasion called him up to the queen of the Romans, to ask her for a letter to the chief queen of the Persians about the affairs of the believers, and, if it were possible, to go up in the same zeal to the territories of Rome. And she gladly consented, because she had in fact been well acquainted with his earnestness and his zeal for some time; and she detained him there for the space of one year, holding him in great honor.[40] And God saw the saint's labor, and that he had grown old and very feeble, and his signal gave command and he fell asleep there, in our presence.

[*Lives of the Saints* 36: *Mare the Solitary*] A great disturbance arose in the city of Alexandria on account of the faith, insomuch that many were expelled and driven from their places, men who would not consent to conform to the Chalcedonian communion. And they [Chalcedonians] came even to the blessed Mare himself; and, when they had pressed him greatly and he did not acquiesce in their communion, they drove him also out and expelled him from his cell. And from such a reason as this he was seized by a vehement desire to go up to Constantinople, so that he applied himself to dealing a severe reproof to the king and queen; and he went up and

38. I.e., 565/566 according to the Seleucid calendar.

39. Nestorios was the patriarch of Constantinople who was condemned at the Council of Ephesos in 431.

40. Probably in 539–540.

reached the royal city. But with regard to the blessed man's entry into the presence of the king and queen, and the rough character of his meeting with them, and the insulting words which he addressed to them, and his audacity and his contemptuous conduct moreover to them, of this we have not thought it well to make a written record in the history of his life not only on account of their violence, and the insults and the contemptuous conduct which he used toward the rulers of the world, but further also because perhaps, even if they had been written, the difficulty of believing among the hearers would be very great. . . . But when he had sternly rebuked the royal pair as we have said with such freedom and sternness which he had indeed possessed from his boyhood, they, as by the grace of God, accepted it from him humbly and with fear and without violent action, as from a great man and a perfect solitary, especially because they saw the freedom of his speech, that he spoke and rebuked and reproved them courageously and without fear, not being frightened by the crown or alarmed by the purple, and they said, "This man is in truth a spiritual philosopher," his dress being as we described it above, hideous through the patching together of unsightly and ill-matched rags differing from one another, and fastenings whereby they were joined by unsightly cords of hair and wool. . . . But when the victorious king observed these things, he greatly wondered at him and gave him a promise that he would do for him whatever he commanded; and yet more the believing queen held him as a great and righteous man and continued entreating him to remain with her in her palace, that he might speak to her words of profit. And while she on her side was making this request of him, he on the other hand answered her with stern reproofs. And when she saw that he would not comply with her wishes, she quietly ordered her own treasurer to bring her a *kentenarion* of gold,[41] thinking that by this she would soften the blessed Mare and make him yield. And when it came and she offered it to him bound up and began entreating him to accept it and divide it between the poor and his needs, then, after gazing sternly at it he grasped the bag containing the *kentenarion* in one hand and hurled it and threw it no small distance, so that all the chamberlains and everyone who saw it were seized with great astonishment, to think that he was so powerful and of such well-knit frame, as we stated at the beginning, and since he had flung it to a distance just as if it were something full of light apples, saying to her,

41. I.e., 7,200 gold coins.

"*Thy money go to perdition with thee*,[42] because through this you wish to tempt me and mock me." And after answering her with many other stern words that we will refrain from recording, he left her and went out. And she remained in distress and fear, and she and all her chamberlains as well were wondering at the blessed man's bodily strength, how he thought nothing of throwing a weight of a hundred pounds of gold to such a distance, insomuch that the story was heard over the whole palace and over the whole of the city, and was spoke of with astonishment by many persons. . . . But the queen, because she was a believer and knew that she had distressed him in the matter of the *kentenarion* of gold, made careful search for him; and on learning that he had left the city and was dwelling on the other side among the mountains sent some of her most distinguished chamberlains to entreat him to forgive her, and as a favor to herself to receive from her something that his needs required, whatever he wished. And, having taken much trouble and with difficulty discovered him, because he used to move from place to place, they delivered an earnest request to him as they had been ordered, and, absolutely refusing to grant their request, he sent her a message through them, "Think not that you possess anything which God's bondmen need, except religion if it exists in you."

4. The Convent of Repentance: A Different View by Prokopios

Buildings 1.9.1–10

At Secret History *(17.5–6), Prokopios gives a hostile account of Theodora's foundation of a monastery for repentant prostitutes, claiming that she forced them to give up their profession against their will. In the* Buildings, *which he wrote at least four years after* The Secret History *(and possibly more), he would give a positive account of this foundation that probably matched the imperial couple's own view of it. This provides us with one of the rare glimpses that we have of*

42. Acts 8.20.

*Theodora's own self-image, however insincerely it may be reported here by Prokopios. Justinian in fact issued edicts striking against the power of the pimps discussed here (*Novellae *14 of 535; 51 of 537), and many historians have seen the hand of the former prostitute Theodora behind these measures. It is probably to those years that the following events should be assigned.*

(1) On this shore there happened to be, since ancient times, a most impressive palace.[43] The emperor Justinian dedicated it to God in its entirety, exchanging the immediate gratification that it could bring for the fruits of piety procured by this act, and he did so in the following way. (2) There was a large number of women in Byzantion who were forced to have sex in brothels against their will, subject to the violent lust of others. (3) Living in extreme poverty, they were fed by their pimps and were required, every day, to perform lewd acts. These poor wretches had to couple at a moment's notice with unknown men, even those who just popped in. (4) There had long been a large gang of pimps in that place, profiting from this lecherous traffic in their "workshops," selling the beauty of others in the public marketplace, and leading innocent people into lives of slavery. (5) So the emperor Justinian and the empress Theodora, whose piety was mutual in all that they did,[44] devised the following plan. (6) They cleansed society from the stain of the brothels, banished the very name "pimp," and freed the women who were pressed by great poverty into this servile lechery. By providing them with a means by which to live, they set virtue itself free. They brought this about in the following way. (7) By the shore of the straits that is on the right as one sails to the Black Sea, there used to be a palace which they converted into a magnificent monastery to serve as a refuge for women who repented of their former lives. (8) The aim was to enable them there, by promoting a pious lifestyle and worship of God, to cleanse themselves of the sins of their occupation in the brothel. (9) That is why they named this house of female discipline Repentance, so that the name matched its purpose. (10) And the emperors have endowed this monastery with many grants of money and built many dwellings that are exceptional in beauty and luxuriousness to serve as a consolation for these

43. See below for the exact location.

44. This statement is ironic in light of the claim made repeatedly in *The Secret History* that Justinian and Theodora pretended to oppose each other, especially in their religious policies (10.15, 13.9, 14.8, 27.13).

women, so that under no circumstances might they be compelled to abandon the practice of virtue. So much, then, for this matter.

5. An Attempt to Curb Corruption in the Provinces

Justinian, *Novella* 8, Preface[45]

Date: 15 April 535. When provincial governors had to purchase their offices they could recoup their investment only by squeezing their subjects or selling their verdicts to the highest bidder; worse, they felt entitled to do so. But the corruption of justice and administration led to unrest and instability in provincial life. In The Secret History, *Prokopios accuses Justinian of selling offices, then passing a law which banned that practice, then tacitly reinstating it (21.9–25). That law was* Novella *8, whose preface is presented here. After seven years on the throne (and more of ruling the empire behind his uncle's throne), Justinian pretends that he is unsure whether the sale of offices is going on—but best to ban it just in case ("if this is not the case at present, it has been so at other times"). But when he goes on to explain the horrible consequences of this practice, his account of the provincials' woes results, ironically and paradoxically, in an indictment of his own administration that would not be out of place in* The Secret History *itself ("we are unable to enumerate the evils resulting from thefts committed by the governors of provinces"). Prokopios was certainly aware of this text. (See below for the oath that Justinian required his governors to swear on taking office.)*

[The emperor Justinian] to Ioannes, praetorian prefect for the second time, former consul and patrician:[46]

Preface: We pass entire days and nights in reflecting on what may be agreeable to God and beneficial to Our subjects, and it is not in

45. The translation is by S. P. Scott, *The Civil Law* (Cincinnati: Central Trust Co., 1932), 16:51–53 and 63–65 for the oath (see below), slightly modified.

46. These were the titles of Ioannes the Kappadokian. The "second time" alludes to his temporary dismissal in 532 during the Nika riots (see related text 2). For his downfall two years later, see related text 7.

vain that We maintain these vigils but We employ them in attempting to deliver those who are subject to Our government from care and anxiety; and, undertaking this Ourselves, We attempt in every way to do what may render Our people happy and relieve them of all onerous charges and impositions, with the exception of duties and taxes. We have found that great injustice has been committed in many instances, and that this injustice is not ancient but recent, an oppression that has impoverished Our subjects to such an extent that they have been reduced to indigence, taxes cannot be collected, and the lawful and customary tribute cannot be obtained without the greatest difficulty; for, when the Emperors try to obtain money from magistrates by selling them their offices and the latter, in their turn, indemnify themselves by extortion, how can those subject to taxation endure these unjust impositions as well as the lawful contributions for which they are liable?

Hence We have thought that any changes which We make in Our provinces should be liberal and for the general welfare. We believe that this can be accomplished if the Governors invested with the civil administration of the provinces keep their hands clean and abstain from accepting anything, remaining content with the remuneration given them by the Treasury. This, however, cannot take place unless they obtain their offices without purchasing them and give nothing either to officials or to other persons in order to obtain their influence. Although the suppression of unlawful gains of this kind may cause the empire some financial loss, We nevertheless think that Our subjects will ultimately be benefited by it if they are not imposed on by magistrates, and that the government and the Treasury will obtain a great advantage in having wealthy subjects and that, under such circumstances, there will be a great increase of riches and extraordinary prosperity. For is it not clear to all that anyone who gives money to obtain an office does not merely disburse it for that purpose, but pays out still more to the persons who procure it for him, or promises to do so? Where money is thus corruptly used in the first place, many hands are required to aid him who made the donation and, if he does not make the payment out of his own property, he must borrow and in order to do so will appropriate that of the public, as he must obtain enough from his province to pay his debts, both principal and interest, and indemnify himself for what he has borrowed; and he will also, in the meantime, incur greater expense and the judges and subordinates attached to his office will do the same thing; and he will make secret acquisitions with a view to providing for the future when he will no longer be in authority.

For which reason he collects three times the amount of what he has paid out, and sometimes more, or even ten times as much, if the truth be told, and the revenues of the Treasury are diminished to this extent, for what should have been paid into it if they had been entrusted to honest hands is collected for the private use of the official, which renders Our taxpayers poor, and their indigence which is caused by his conduct becomes a source of reproach to Us. How impious is such conduct and of how many thefts is it the immediate cause? Those who administer the affairs of the provinces, thinking incessantly of what their offices will cost them, discharge many criminals by selling them freedom from prosecution and convict many who are innocent, in order that they may profit thereby; and this not only occurs in pecuniary cases but also in prosecutions for crimes in which the death penalty is inflicted; and many persons in the provinces, including priests, city councilors, various officials, owners of property, citizens, and farmers, flock to this city with good cause, complaining of injustice, and accusing the magistrates of theft. Not only do these things occur, but also the seditions in cities and public disturbances which take place everywhere go unpunished in consideration of money paid. Corruption is undoubtedly the cause of these evils, it being the beginning and the end of all wickedness, confirming the truth of the sacred precept that avarice is the mother of all crime; especially when it is not confined to private persons, but even takes possession of the minds of magistrates. For who cannot steal without danger? Cannot anyone commit robbery with the certainty of appearing innocent in the eyes of the magistrate when he knows that he has purchased everything with gold and that no matter what illegal act he may commit, he can escape by the payment of the penalty? The result of this condition of affairs is homicide, adultery, violence, wounds, the rape of virgins, commercial difficulties, contempt of the laws and judges, all of which are attributable to venality, and the immunity sold to criminals in the same manner as a vile slave. We are unable to consider or enumerate the evils resulting from thefts committed by the governors of provinces, and still no one is courageous enough to accuse them of having corruptly purchased their offices.

At the end of the Novella *(which contains fourteen articles) is appended, among other documents, a schedule of salaries to be paid to the provincial governors. After that follows the text of the oath that governors were required to swear, prefaced by instructions to the praetorian prefect of Illyricum as to the manner in which they were to swear it. Prokopios refers to this oath at* Secret History *21.16–19.*

Magistrates shall be sworn in accordance with the form of the oath communicated to Your Highness. Those whom you appoint to office shall be installed by virtue of commissions issued by Us, which commissions you will give them; and they shall take the abovementioned oath before the bishop of the city in which they are and the inhabitants assembled in your palace, as well as in the presence of members of your court, and those who exercise curial or other public employments, to whom We desire that Your Highness shall show all proper consideration. You must be careful not to obtain any profit by the appointment of magistrates. . . .

The Oath to be Taken by Magistrates Appointed to Office

I swear by omnipotent God, by his only Son Our Lord Jesus Christ, and by the Holy Spirit, by the glorious, perpetually Virgin Maria, by the four Gospels which I hold in my hand, by the holy archangels Michael and Gabriel, to be faithful to Our Imperial Masters Justinian and Theodora his wife; to discharge with the greatest fidelity the duties of the administration of that part of their empire and government that their kindness has entrusted to me; and that I will devote all my efforts to that end, without any fraud or deceit whatsoever. I also swear that I am a communicant of the Most Holy Catholic and Apostolic Church, and that at no time I will oppose it, or permit anyone else to do so, as far as lies in my power. I also swear that I have neither given nor will give anything to anyone for the sake of obtaining my office, or in consideration of his influence, and that I have promised to send nothing out of the province, and shall, by way of contribution, send nothing either to the Emperor, to the Illustrious Prefects, or their subordinates, or to anyone else whomsoever. As I have received my appointment without having paid anything for it, I swear to act honorably with the subjects of Our Most Pious Majesties, and to be content with the allotment of subsistence made to me by the Treasury. I also swear to devote especial attention to the levying of taxes; to collect them inexorably from persons who are not prompt in payment; to show no leniency to them; and not to have in mind any profit which I might be able to obtain in case I were more indulgent. I promise not to extort anything from anyone whomsoever; or grant anything to anyone either through favor or dislike, beyond what he legally may be entitled to; to treat with paternal kindness taxpayers who are prompt in discharging their duties, and to protect as much as I can the rights of all the subjects of Our Most Pious Majesties. I also swear to be impartial in deciding the cases of private individuals, as well as those which concern the maintenance of public order, and only to compel my subordinates to do what is equitable; to prosecute crimes; and in all my actions to practice the justice which may seem to me proper; and to preserve the innocence of virtuous men, as well as inflict punishment on the guilty, in conformity to the provisions of the laws. I also swear (as I have already done) to observe the rules of equity in all public and private transactions; and if I should ascertain that depredations have been committed against the Treasury, that I will not only see that they are punished, but will also supervise the officials under my control, and induce them to exert the same honest efforts in the performance of their duties that I do; and if any of them should be found to be dishonest, I promise that his delinquency shall be made good, and that he shall be immediately dismissed. If I should not observe all these things which I have sworn to, may I, in the future as well as at present, undergo the terrible punishment of Our God and Savior Jesus Christ, share the fate of Judas, the leper Gehazi,[47] and the anxiety of Cain, as well as undergo the penalties imposed by the law of Our Pious Majesties.

6. A Contemporary Philosopher's View of Justinian's Tyranny

Simplikios, *Commentary on Epiktetos* 14.19–32

*Date: after 529 (possibly as late as the 550s). Simplikios was one of the leading Platonist (non-Christian) thinkers of his age and among the seven philosophers who left Athens for Persia when Justinian moved against their schools in 529. According to Agathias, who tells the story (*Histories *2.30–31), they did not find Persia to their liking but secured the support of King Chosroes, who insisted that a clause guaranteeing their safety be added to the treaty that he was negotiating with Justinian (the Eternal Peace of 532). They returned to the empire and*

47. 2 Kings 5.

continued to teach and write, though we do not know where each settled. The following passage is from Simplikios' Commentary *on the* Encheiridion (Manual) *of the Stoic teacher Epiktetos (first century AD). Its indictment of the evils that a person may face resonates with Prokopios' attack on Justinian in* The Secret History. *It is possible that the two authors knew each other's work.*

But the following injunction may seem harsh and even impossible, namely that you should want things to happen exactly as they happen. For what person in his right mind *wants* the common misfortunes that come from the nature of the universe, such as earthquakes and floods and conflagrations, plagues and famines and the destruction of every kind of animal and produce, or those things that are done in an unholy manner by human beings to one another, such as the capture of cities and kidnapping and unjust murders and robberies and plunder and licentiousness and tyrannical violence that forces one to commit even impieties, not to mention the destruction of education and philosophy, of all virtue and friendship and trust in one another; and as for the arts and sciences, discovered and established over the course of many years, some have gone completely extinct, so that only their names are known, whereas of the majority of them, given by God for the improvement of our lives, such as medicine and architecture and carpentry and others of that kind, only shadows and images remain.

7. The Downfall of Ioannes the Kappadokian

Wars 1.25 and 2.30.49–54

Date: May–August 541. Ioannes the Kappadokian was the most hated of Justinian's officials, at least by Prokopios and Ioannes Lydos. He was also the only one to stand up to Theodora, though it was a contest in which he could never win but only hope to survive. His downfall is mentioned often in The Secret History *(1.14, 2.15–17, 4.18, 17.38–45, 21.5, 22.1), but the full narrative is given in the* Wars. *It has been supposed that the following narrative was part of the dossier that became* The Secret History, *but the death of Theodora in 548 enabled Prokopios to place it in his more public work (finished in 550). The historian was careful to avoid open denunciations of Theodora and Antonina here, but they still emerge as the characters we know from* The Secret History. *The narrative picks up immediately following the account of the Nika riots (see related text 2).*

(1) Tribonianos and Ioannes, having been dismissed from office in this way, were at a later time both restored to those same positions. (2) Tribonianos survived in office for many years and died of illness, suffering no further harm from anyone. For he was a smooth talker and pleasant in every other way as well as capable of casting the shadow of his prodigious learning over his addiction to profit.[48] (3) But Ioannes was as overbearing to all people as he was severe, harming everyone he met and plundering their entire property for no good reason. He remained in office for another ten years,[49] at which point he paid a just and fitting penalty for the illegality of his conduct. It happened in the following way.

(4) The empress Theodora hated him more than any other person. And while he came into conflict with her because of his criminal acts,[50] he made no effort whatever to endear himself to her or win her favor; rather, he openly set himself up as her enemy and slandered her to the emperor, neither respecting her station nor feeling any shame before the amazing affection that the emperor bore her.[51] (5) When the empress perceived what was being done, she pondered how she might kill the man, yet she could find no plan that would work because Justinian valued him so greatly. (6) But when Ioannes discovered what the empress had in mind for him, he was thoroughly terrified. (7) Whenever he entered his bedroom to sleep, he imagined every night that one of the barbarians would attack and kill him. He was always peeping out of his room and keeping watch over the entrances, so that he rarely slept at all, even though he kept many thousands of personal guards and field marshals in his employ, something that no prefect before him had

48. Tribonianos appears also at *Secret History* 13.12, 20.16–17 (see the notes there for his career). He may have died when the plague hit Constantinople in 542.

49. Ioannes was dismissed during the Nika riots of 532 (*Wars* 1.24, translated in related text 2) but was reappointed praetorian prefect a few months later. He held that position until 541, making many enemies along the way.

50. Prokopios gives the lie to this flattering assertion at *Secret History* 17.38: Theodora did not care one bit about his crimes.

51. For Justinian's erotic infatuation with Theodora, see *Secret History* 9.30–32.

done.[52] (8) But when morning came, all his fears of God and man would flee from him and he would again become the ruin of the Romans, both in public and in private. He consorted all the time with poisoners and magicians and was constantly soliciting sacrilegious oracles that portended for him the imperial office; it was manifest that he was "walking on the air and suspended up there" by the hope that he would gain the throne.[53] (9) Never did he give his wickedness a rest nor did he desist from his lawless way of life. (10) He had no regard at all for the word of God; in fact, if he ever entered a temple in order to pray and stay the night, he did not in any way behave in accordance with the customs of the Christians but donned a worn cloak of the kind appropriate for a priest of the old faith, which now they tend to call Hellenic, and for the duration of the night he would murmur some unholy words that he had memorized, in this way hoping to bend the emperor's mind even more to his own will and to protect himself against all harm that might come to him from other people.

(11) At this time Belisarios, having subjugated Italy, was recalled along with his wife Antonina to Byzantion by the emperor in order to march against the Persians.[54] (12) And while everyone else held him in honor and high regard, as was reasonable, Ioannes alone bore him ill will and positively plotted against him for no other reason than that *he* drew the odium of all people upon himself whereas Belisarios was esteemed more than anyone else. With the hopes of the Romans upon his shoulders, he immediately marched off against the Persians, leaving his wife behind in Byzantion.[55] (13) Now Antonina, the wife of Belisarios, was the most crafty of all people when it came to devising means by which to accomplish the impossible. In order to ingratiate herself with the empress, she contrived the following scheme. Ioannes had a daughter, Euphemia, who had a noted

52. Belisarios employed a large corps of personal guards and field marshals (the *bucellarii*), which numbered seven thousand in 540 (*Wars* 7.1.20). Other generals and magistrates like Ioannes had similar retinues, though not as large.

53. A mocking allusion to the caricature of Sokrates in Aristophanes, *Clouds* 225–228. One of Prokopios' favorite lines, it appears also at *Secret History* 13.11, 18.29, and 20.22.

54. Belisarios returned to Constantinople in 540 after securing the surrender of Ravenna and the Gothic king of Italy Vitigis, whom he brought with him along with much treasure. He was now so popular that crowds followed him as he went around the capital (*Wars* 7.1.3–7).

55. Belisarios set out against the Persians early in 541. The explanation for his wife staying behind this time is given by Prokopios at *Secret History* 2.1–2.

reputation for discretion but was still very young and, because of this, was quite vulnerable. Her father simply adored her, for she was his only child. (14) Antonina now cultivated a relationship with this girl over a period of many days and managed to win her absolute trust, in part because she did not even hesitate to reveal some of her own secrets to her. (15) Then one day, when she was alone with her in the room, she pretended to lament her present misfortunes, alleging that even though Belisarios had made the Roman Empire so much larger that it had been previously and had delivered two captive kings and such enormous amounts of treasure to Byzantion, he had found Justinian to be ungrateful. And in other respects she maligned the current administration for its lack of justice. (16) Euphemia was overjoyed at these words for she too hated the current rulers because of her terror of the empress. "But for all this, dearest friend," she said, "you yourselves are responsible, given that you are not willing to use the power that you currently have at your disposal." (17) Antonina quickly took up that thought: "But we are not able, my daughter, to attempt a rebellion in the camps unless someone on the inside joins with us in the attempt. Now if your father were willing, then we could easily put it into motion and accomplish all that God wants."

(18) When Euphemia heard this, she eagerly promised that it would be done. Departing from there, she immediately brought the matter to her father's attention. (19) He was pleased by the news for he fantasized that this would be the way by which the oracles about his ascent to the throne would be fulfilled. He heedlessly agreed and told his daughter to arrange a meeting with Antonina the next day so that they could discuss the matter and give pledges. (20) When Antonina learned Ioannes' intentions, she wanted to lure him as far away from the truth of the matter as was possible. So she said that it was not advantageous for her to meet with him now, lest some suspicion arise that could hinder their enterprise. She was about to depart for the East, to join Belisarios. (21) So when she had put Byzantion behind her and came to the suburb named Rouphinianai (which happened to be the property of Belisarios),[56] there Ioannes could come to her on the pretext that he was bidding her farewell and seeing her on her way; and then they could talk about the totality of things and give and receive their pledges of trust. This plan

56. This was a suburb on the Asiatic coast of the Sea of Marmara, named after the fourth-century praetorian prefect Rufinus. Antonina departed, and the plot was hatched, in May 541.

seemed good to Ioannes, and a day was appointed to carry it out. (22) Meanwhile, the empress heard it all from Antonina and had nothing but praise for the plot and urged her on, making her even more eager to see it through.

(23) When the appointed day came, Antonina bade the empress farewell and left the city. She stopped at Rouphinianai as if intending to depart on her eastward journey the following day. That night Ioannes arrived in accordance with their agreement. (24) But the empress, having denounced to her husband the things that Ioannes was doing to usurp the throne, sent the eunuch Narses and Markellos, the commander of the palace guard, to Rouphinianai with a large company of soldiers and instructions to investigate what was going on.[57] If they should find that Ioannes was plotting a rebellion, they were to kill the man on the spot and come back. (25) So these men departed to carry out these orders. But they say that the emperor found out what was happening and dispatched one of Ioannes' friends to him with orders to absolutely forbid him from meeting with Antonina in secret. (26) Yet Ioannes—seeing as it was necessary for him to end badly—disregarded the emperor's warning. He met Antonina around midnight next to a wall behind which she happened to have stationed the men with Narses and Markellos, so that they could hear what was said. (27) In that place Ioannes let his mouth run, confessing to the plot and swearing the most dread oaths to it.[58] Narses and Markellos suddenly rushed him. (28) In the confusion that ensued—as was only to be expected—Ioannes' guards, who were standing near him, rushed to his aid. (29) One of them struck Markellos with a sword, not knowing who he was, and so Ioannes managed to escape with his men, reaching the city in all haste. (30) And if he had been bold enough to go straight to the emperor, I believe that he would have suffered no harm from him. As it was, however, he sought refuge in the sanctuary, thereby giving the empress the opening that she needed to dispose of him according to her wishes.

(31) Thus from being a prefect he became a private citizen; and rising up from that sanctuary he was conveyed to another one in a

57. Narses was a general and steward of the palace who would, in 552, finally defeat the Goths in Italy. Markellos was *comes* of the *excubitores*, the only battleworthy unit of palatine guards. Eight years later he would undo another plot against Justinian: see related text 10.

58. According to *Secret History* 2.16, Antonina had already sworn dire oaths to both Ioannes and Euphemia.

suburb of the city of Kyzikos; the people of Kyzikos call this suburb Artake. There, against his wishes, he was invested with the garb of a priest, not of course that of a bishop but of that rank which they call a presbyter. (32) Now the last thing that he wanted to do was conduct holy services lest it prove to be an obstacle to his return to office one day; for he was in no way willing to set aside his lofty aspirations. His property was immediately confiscated to the public treasury. (33) The emperor, however, granted him the use of a substantial portion of it, for he was still in an indulgent mood toward him. (34) Now it was there possible for Ioannes to live heedless of all dangers in the possession of great wealth, both that which he had secreted away and that which the emperor had granted him, and to enjoy all the luxury that he desired and even, by putting things into perspective, to consider his current lot a happy one. (35) Hence all the Romans were simply disgusted at the man, for after having been more wicked than any demon he was now living a happier life than he deserved. (36) But God, I think, found it intolerable that the retribution of Ioannes should end in this way and so he raised his punishment to a higher level. It came about in the following way.

(37) There was in Kyzikos a certain bishop named Eusebios, a man who oppressed everyone whom he met, Ioannes not least among them. The people of Kyzikos denounced him to the emperor asking that he be brought to justice. (38) But they accomplished nothing, for Eusebios used his considerable influence to counter them. Therefore, some of the young men came to an agreement among themselves and killed him in the city's marketplace.[59] (39) Now it just so happened that Ioannes was especially hostile to Eusebios and, because of this, suspicion for the murder fell on him. (40) Men were accordingly sent by the Senate to investigate this polluted act. The first thing that they did was confine Ioannes to prison, and then this man, who had been a prefect so powerful, had been enrolled among the patricians, and mounted the curule seat of the consuls, a position that seems loftier than any other in the Roman state—this man, then, they made to stand naked as a brigand or a common thief and lashed his back repeatedly, forcing him to confess his past deeds. (41) And even though it was not proven beyond a doubt that Ioannes was responsible for the murder of Eusebios, it nevertheless seemed as though divine justice was exacting from him punishments on behalf of the entire world. (42) Stripping him of all

59. Possibly in 544. Theodora later tortured two of the young men implicated in this murder to obtain information against Ioannes; *Secret History* 17.38–45.

his property,[60] they placed him nude as he was upon a ship, wrapped in a single cloak, a coarse one at that, purchased for but a few obols. Those in whose charge he was placed ordered him, wherever the ship put in, to beg for bread or obols from passers-by. (43) He begged like this all the way until he was delivered to the city of Antinoos in Egypt. This is now the third year that they have kept him there in confinement and under guard.[61] Yet despite his wretched condition, he has not set aside his hopes for the throne and has even contrived to denounce some of the Alexandrians on the grounds that they owe money to the state. This, then, was the punishment for his political career that caught up to Ioannes the Kappadokian ten years after the fact.

Date: 548. The story of Ioannes continues at the end of Book 2 of the Wars.

[*Wars* 2.30] (49) In the year before that, Ioannes the Kappadokian was summoned back to Byzantion by the emperor, for it was when the empress Theodora had reached the end of her life. (50) Ioannes was utterly unable to salvage any of his former ranks and positions but retained, quite against his will, the dignity of the priesthood. And yet the vision had appeared often before the man's eyes that he would gain the imperial throne. (51) For some unearthly power likes to dangle visions of that which people find most seductive from the highest reaches of their loftiest hopes, especially if their minds are not solidly grounded in reality. (52) It was to Ioannes that the charlatans of portents were always peddling imaginary prophesies, and especially that which foretold that he would don the vestments of Augustus. (53) Now there was a certain priest in Byzantion named Augustus who guarded the treasury of the temple of Sophia. (54) So when Ioannes was tonsured and forced to take on the dignity of the priesthood, he had no clothes appropriate for a priest, and so those who were in charge of this matter required him to put on the cloak and tunic of this man Augustus, who was nearby. This, I think, was how the prophecy was fulfilled for him.[62]

60. His mansion in Constantinople was given to Belisarios (an indirect way of rewarding Antonina).

61. Prokopios seems to have written this account in 546 and left the date in it unrevised. He continued the story of Ioannes at the end of Book 2 of the *Wars* (see below).

62. This refers back to the events of 541. Yet at *Wars* 1.25.31 (see above), Prokopios stated that Ioannes was consecrated at Kyzikos and not Constantinople.

8. The Justinianic Plague

Wars 2.22–23

Date: 541–542. The plague that modern historians have labeled "Justinianic" (Prokopios would have approved) was by far the most destructive and deadly event of the century, and it ravaged Europe, North Africa, and the Near East for two hundred years. In some areas up to a third of the population may have died. Yet its historical existence is known only from literary sources. From archaeology alone we would not know, or could not be sure, that it had ever happened. And among those literary accounts, by far the most sober, detailed, reliable, firsthand, and skeptically scientific is that by Prokopios in two chapters of the Wars, *the first of which details the medical symptoms while the second describes the social disruption that it caused in the capital in 542. It has long been recognized that Prokopios' account is modeled on Thucydides' account of the plague that ravaged Athens at the beginning of the Peloponnesian War (*History *2.47–254, in 430 BC). Yet it has also been demonstrated that Prokopios was not an uncritical imitator and that he managed to preserve the distinctive features of the event of his time. Scientists and historians have recently joined forces to study this event; the reader may consult the books and articles cited in A Guide to Scholarship in English.*

[*Wars* 2.22] (1) During those times there was a plague that came close to wiping out the whole of mankind. Now for all the calamities that fall upon us from the heavens it might be possible for some bold man to venture a theory regarding their causes, like the many marvelous theories about causes that the experts in these fields tend to dream up which are, in reality, utterly incomprehensible to mankind. Still, they make up outlandish theories of natural science, knowing well that they are saying nothing sound and they are content with themselves if only they manage to deceive a few people whom they meet into accepting their argument. (2) But about this calamity there is no way to find any justification, to give a rational account, or even to cope with it mentally, except by referring it to God.[63] (3) For it did not afflict a specific part of the earth only, or

63. In many passages, Prokopios implied that "God" was close to what people normally thought of as "chance," that is, what remains left over when all rational factors are excluded. His account of the plague strongly indicates that, if the event must be ascribed to God, that God has no moral standards.

one group of people, nor did it strike during one season of the year, based on which it might have been possible to contrive some subtle explanation regarding its cause; instead, it embraced the entire earth and wrecked the lives of all people, even when those lives were as different from each other in quality as can be imagined, nor did it respect either sex or age. (4) For people differ from each other in the place that they live, the customs that shape their lifestyle, the manner of their personality, their profession, and many other ways, but none of these differences made the slightest difference when it came to this disease—and to this disease alone. (5) It struck some during the summer, others during the winter, and the rest during the other seasons. So each person should state his own opinion about how he understands all this, and so too should our subtle theorists and astrologers, but I, for my part, will now state where this disease originated and the manner in which it destroyed people.

(6) It originated among the Egyptians who live in Pelousion.[64] From there it branched out in two directions, the first moving against Alexandria and then to the rest of Egypt, the second coming to the Palestinians who live by the border of Egypt. From here it spread to the entirety of the world, always moving along and advancing at set intervals. (7) For it seemed to move as if by prearranged plan: it would linger for a set time in each place, just enough to make sure that no person could brush it off as a slight matter, and from there it would disperse in different directions as far as the ends of the inhabited world, almost as if it feared lest any hidden corner of the earth might escape it. (8) It overlooked no island or cave or mountain peak where people happened to live, and if it passed through a region on whose inhabitants it did not lay its hands or whom it did not affect in some way, it would return to that place at a later time: those whom it had previously ravaged it now left alone, but it did not let up from that place before it had exacted the proper and just toll in dead people, the very death toll that the inhabitants of the surrounding areas had also paid earlier. (9) This disease always spread out from the coasts and worked its way up into the interior. It arrived at Byzantion in the middle of the spring of its second year, where I happened to be at the time. And it struck as follows.

64. Most historians believe it originated in central Africa, but a minority supports a south Asian origin.

(10) Visions of demons taking every imaginable human form were seen by many people, and those who encountered them believed that they were being struck on some part of their body by that man whom they had met; the disease set in at the very moment that they saw this vision. (11) At first, those who met these creatures would try to turn them away by invoking the most holy names and otherwise exorcising them in whatever way each knew how, but it was all perfectly futile, for even in the churches where most people sought refuge they were perishing constantly. (12) Later they would not bother to notice even when their friends were calling out to them but shut themselves up in their rooms and pretended not to hear, even while the others were pounding on their doors; this was, of course, because they feared that the caller was one of those demons. (13) But others were not affected in this way by the plague; instead, they saw a dream-vision in which they suffered the same thing at the hands of the entity standing over them, or else they heard a voice predicting to them that their names would be placed on the lists of those who were about to die. (14) Most people, however, were taken ill without the advance warning of a waking vision or a dream. (15) They fell ill in the following way. Suddenly they became feverish, some of them when they rose from sleep, others while they were walking about, and yet others while they were doing any odd thing. (16) The body did not change its color or become warm as during a regular fever, nor, certainly, did it burn up; rather, the fever was so feeble from its beginning all the way to the evening that it gave no cause for worry either to the victims themselves or to their doctors who touched them. (17) In fact, no one who fell ill in this way believed that he would die from it. But then on the same day for some people, or on the next for others, at any rate no more than a few days later, a bubonic swelling appeared. This happened not only in that part of the body, below the abdomen, which is called the *boubon*, but also inside the armpit, in some cases by the ears, while in others at various points on the thigh.

(18) Up to this point the symptoms of the disease were more or less the same for everyone who contracted it. But as for what followed, I am not able to say whether the variation in its progression was due to the differences in bodies or because it followed the will of him who introduced the disease into the world. (19) While some fell into a deep coma, others developed acute dementia, but both felt the fundamental effects of the disease. Those who became comatose forgot all about their loved ones and seemed to be always asleep. (20) If someone cared for them, they ate in the meantime, but those who were abandoned died directly of starvation. (21) Those gripped by

the madness of dementia, on the other hand, could not sleep and became quite delusional. Imagining that people were attacking them in order to kill them, they became hysterical and fled at a run, shouting loudly. (22) So those who were caring for their needs were driven to exhaustion and constantly faced unheard-of difficulties. (23) For this reason everyone pitied the latter no less than their patients, not because they were at all affected by the disease through proximity—for no doctor or layman contracted this misfortune by touching any of the sick or the dead, given that many who were constantly burying the dead or caring for the sick, even those unrelated to them, continued to perform this service against all expectation, whereas many who contracted the disease from an unknown source died directly—rather, they pitied them because they had to endure a great hardship. (24) For their patients kept falling out of bed and rolling around on the floor, and they would have to put them back; and then they would long to rush out of their houses, and they would have to force them back by pushing and pulling them. (25) If any came near to water, they wanted to throw themselves in, but not because of a need to drink (for most rushed into the sea); rather, the cause was mostly the mental illness. (26) Food also caused them much pain, as it was not easy for them to eat it. And many died because they had no one to look after them, were done in by hunger, or threw themselves from a height. (27) Those who did not became delirious or comatose died unable to endure the pain brought on by the mortification of the buboes. (28) Now one might deduce that the same thing happened to the others too but, as they were utterly beside themselves, they were incapable of sensing the pain; the illness of their minds took all sensation away from them. (29) Some doctors, who were at a loss because the symptoms were unfamiliar to them and believing that the focus of the disease was to be found in the buboes, decided to investigate the bodies of the dead. Cutting into some of the buboes, they found that a kind of malignant carbuncle had developed inside.

(30) Some died immediately, others after many days. In some cases, the body blossomed with dark pustules about the size of a lentil. These people did not survive a single day; they all died immediately. (31) Many others suddenly began to vomit blood and perished straightaway. (32) I have this to state too, that the most eminent doctors predicted that many would die who shortly afterward were unexpectedly freed of all their maladies, and they also claimed that many would survive who were destined to perish almost immediately. (33) Thus there was no *cause* behind this disease that

human reason could grasp, for in all cases the outcome made little sense. Some were saved by taking baths, others were no less harmed by it. (34) Many who were neglected died but many others paradoxically survived. Likewise, the same treatment produced different results in different patients. In sum, no method of survival could be discovered by man, whether to guard himself that he not be exposed to the disease at all or to survive that misfortune once he had contracted it; for its onset was inexplicable while survival from it was not under anyone's control. (35) As for women who were pregnant, death could be foreseen if they were taken ill with the disease. Some had miscarriages and died while others perished in labor directly along with the infants they bore. (36) It is said, however, that *three* new mothers survived while their infants did not, and that *one* died in childbirth though her child was born and survived. (37) In cases where the buboes grew very large and discharged pus, the patients overcame the disease and survived, as it was clear that for them the eruption of the carbuncle found relief in this way; for the most part, this was a sign of health. But in cases where the buboes remained in the same condition, these patients had to endure all the misfortunes that I just mentioned. (38) It happened for some of them that the thigh would become withered and because of this the bubo would grow large but not discharge pus. (39) In the case of others who happened to survive, their speech was not unaffected, and they lived afterward with a lisp or barely able to articulate some indistinct words.

[*Wars* 2.23] (1) The disease ran through four months while it lasted in Byzantion but it was at its peak for three. (2) At first only a few people died above the usual death rate but then the mortality rose even higher until the toll in deaths reached five thousand a day, and after that it reached ten thousand, and then even more. (3) In the beginning each would arrange in person for the burial of the dead from his own household, whom they would even throw into the graves of others either by stealth or using violence. But then confusion began to reign everywhere and in all ways. (4) Slaves were deprived of their masters, men who were previously very prosperous now suffered the loss of their servants who were either sick or dead, and many households were emptied of people altogether. (5) Thus it happened that some notable people were left unburied for many days because there was no help to be had.

And so the responsibility of handling this situation fell, as was natural, on the emperor. (6) He posted soldiers from the palace and gave out funds, appointing Theodoros to supervise this task; this was the man in charge of imperial responses, that is, his job was to convey to the emperor all the petitions of suppliants and then always inform them of his decisions. In the Latin tongue, the Romans call this office a *referendarius*. (7) So those whose households had not fallen so low as to be entirely deserted attended in person to the burial of their own relatives. (8) Meanwhile, Theodoros was burying the dead that had been abandoned both by giving the emperor's money and spending his own as well. (9) And when the already existing graves were full of dead bodies, at first they dug up all the open sites in the city, one after another, placed the dead in there, each person as he could, and departed. But later those who were digging these ditches could no longer keep up with the number of those dying, so they climbed up the towers of the fortified enclosure, the one in Sykai, (10) tore off the roofs, and tossed the bodies there in a tangled heap. Piling them up in this way, that is just as each happened to fall, they filled up virtually all the towers; and then they covered them again with their roofs. (11) A foul stench would come from there to the city and bring even more grief to its inhabitants, especially if the wind was blowing from that direction.

(12) All the customs of burial were overlooked at that time. For the dead were neither escorted by a procession in the way that was customary nor were they accompanied by chanting, as was usual; rather, it was enough if a person carried one of the dead on his shoulders to a place where the city met the sea and throw him down; and there they were thrown into barges in a pile and taken to who knows where. (13) At that time also those elements of the populace who had formerly been militants in the circus fan-clubs set aside their mutual hatred and together attended to the funeral rites of the dead, carrying in person and burying the bodies of those who did not belong to their color.[65] (14) Even more, those who previously used to delight in the shameful and wicked practices in which they indulged, well, these very people renounced the immorality of their lifestyles and became religious to an extreme degree. However, this was not because they finally grasped what it means to be wise nor because they had suddenly become lovers of virtue. (15) For it is impossible for a person to so quickly change what nature has implanted in him or the habits he has acquired over a long period of

65. Prokopios introduces the fan-clubs at *Secret History* 7.1, and they appear repeatedly after that. See note 17 in Part II at 7.1.

time—unless, of course, some divine goodness touches him.[66] For the moment, however, almost everyone was so astounded by what was happening, and believed that they were likely to die immediately, that they temporarily came to their senses out of pure necessity, as could only be expected. (16) In fact, as soon as they overcame the disease and were saved, thinking that they were now in the clear given that the evil had moved on to some other people, they completely reversed course again in their character and became even worse than they had been before, making a spectacle of the inconsistency in their behavior; their malice and immorality now quite overpowered their better selves. One would not, therefore, utter a falsehood if he were to assert that this disease, whether by some chance or providence, carefully picked out the worst people and let them live.[67] But these things were understood only afterward.

(17) It was not easy in those times to see anyone out and about in Byzantion, for all were holed up in their homes. Those who happened to be healthy of body were either tending to the sick or mourning for the dead. (18) If you happened to chance upon someone going out, he was carrying one of the dead. All work came to a standstill and the craftsmen set aside all their trades as did anyone who had some project at hand. (19) And a true famine was careering about in a city that abounded in all goods. It seemed difficult to find sufficient bread or an adequate quantity of anything else; such a thing was, in fact, worthy of mention. Therefore it seemed that some of the sick too lost their lives before their time because they lacked the necessary sustenance. (20) The whole experience may be summed up by saying that it was altogether impossible to see anyone in Byzantion wearing the chlamys,[68] especially when the emperor himself fell sick (he too developed a bubo).[69] In a city holding dominion over the entire Roman Empire, everyone was wearing civilian clothes and privately minding his own business. (21) That was how the plague affected Byzantion and the rest of the Roman lands. It spread also to the Persian lands as well as to all the other barbarians.

66. I.e., the plague was not sent by God for the moral reform of mankind, or it was not sent by a God interested in the moral reform of mankind.

67. See below for Justinian specifically.

68. Public officials in the later Roman Empire wore colorful garments embroidered with the insignia and standards of their office.

69. See also *Secret History* 4.1 for the emperor's illness.

9. Porphyrios the Whale and Other Natural Disasters

Wars 7.29.4–20

Date: 547–548. As Chapter 18 of The Secret History *reaches a crescendo of death and doom, Prokopios lists the natural disasters of Justinian's reign such as earthquakes and the Nile flood failing to subside. He refers to a passage in the* Wars *where this event is described, and this is translated below. This account is less pessimistic than the one in* The Secret History. *It also features the whale Porphyrios, who is mentioned elsewhere in* The Secret History *(15.37). The name, referring to the imperial purple, has connotations of royalty, a sign of the respect in which the whale was held—until it washed ashore.*

(4) At that time extraordinarily powerful and destructive earthquakes occurred frequently during the winter months both in Byzantion and in other regions, all of them at night. (5) The inhabitants of those places were terrified at the thought that they might be buried alive, but, as it turned out, nothing bad happened to them after all. (6) At this time also the Nile River rose over eighteen cubits[70] and flooded Egypt, irrigating the entire country. In the Thebaid, which lies upstream, the waters subsided and withdrew on time, allowing the inhabitants of that place to sow the land and perform all the other labors to which they are accustomed. (7) But in the lower regions, once the water had flowed over them, it did not then withdraw but rather stayed there impeding the entire sowing season, something that had not happened before in the whole of time. And there were places where the waters flowed back in again even after they had withdrawn just a short while earlier. (8) In those places all the seed rotted that was sown in the earth during the interval. The people had no means by which to withstand this unprecedented disaster, and most of their livestock died because they had no feed.

(9) It was then too that the whale, which the residents of Byzantion called Porphyrios, was caught. This whale had harassed Byzantion and its surrounding regions for more than fifty years, but not continuously, for sometimes it would disappear for long periods of

70. A cubit was about eighteen inches (or forty-five centimeters). The rising of the Nile was carefully monitored and measured (on the Nilometers). Between twelve and fourteen cubits was considered optimal; Strabon, *Geography* 17.1.3.

time between appearances. (10) It sank many ships and terrified the passengers of many others, forcing them to make great detours from their course. The emperor Justinian made it a priority to capture the beast, but he could find no way by which to accomplish his purpose. I will now explain how it recently came to be captured. (11) It happened one day that the sea was utterly still and a large number of dolphins were swimming by the mouth of the Black Sea. (12) Seeing the whale suddenly, they fled, each in whatever direction it could, but most of them came to the mouth of the Sangarios River. Overcoming some of them, the whale immediately gulped them down. (13) Then it continued to pursue the rest no less excitedly than before, driven by hunger or some kind of rivalry, until it had unintentionally come too close to the land. (14) There it ran aground on a patch of deep mud and it began to struggle and convulse all over in an effort to escape from its predicament as quickly as possible. It was, however, utterly unable to get out of the shallows; rather, it sank still deeper into the mud. (15) When news of this was brought to all the people who lived around that area, they attacked it immediately. Yet even though they slashed at it vigorously on all sides with axes, they did not manage to kill it. Instead, they dragged it up with strong ropes. (16) Placing it on wagons, they found its length to be more than thirty cubits and its width ten cubits.[71] Breaking into groups, some of them ate from it on the spot whereas others decided to cure the portion allotted to them.

(17) Now the residents of Byzantion, feeling the earthquakes and hearing about the Nile and this whale, immediately began to prophesy about the future, each according to his liking. (18) For when people do not understand the present they like to find portents regarding the future, and, when they worry themselves to death about things that confuse them, they make groundless predictions about what will happen. (19) As for me, I leave these oracles and the science of portents to others. What I know well is this, that the Nile's swamping of the land became the cause of great misfortunes in the *present* time, while the demise of the whale had already proven to be a relief from many evils. (20) Some, however, say that this was not the same whale as the one I mentioned at first, but a different one that happened to be captured. But I will now return to the point in my narrative from which I made this digression.

71. A cubit was about eighteen inches (or forty-five centimeters).

10. A Plot to Kill Justinian

Wars 7.31–32

Date: 548–549. In addition to mass protests (such as the Nika riots of 532), Justinian faced a number of plots to kill or replace him during his long reign. The plot of Artabanes, Arsakes, and Chanaranges recounted in the Wars *by Prokopios is the one whose details we know best. Prokopios presents almost all plots from the viewpoint of the conspirators. Some have suspected that he himself may have come under suspicion at some point based on the pointed way that he twice praises Justinian in the preface to the* Buildings *(1.1.10, 1.1.16) for the mercy that he showed to conspirators (a topic totally unrelated to the main theme of the work). His narrative of the following plot links the conspirators' motives to the oppressive administration of the provinces as well as to Theodora's resented interference with the marital politics of the ruling class.*

[*Wars* 7.31] (1) At this time some men plotted to attack the emperor Justinian. I will now explain how they came to this decision and how their plot was foiled and came to nothing. (2) Artabanes, the man who felled the rebel Gontharis, as I related in an earlier book, conceived a vehement desire to marry Preïekta, the emperor's niece, to whom he was engaged.[72] (3) She too was very willing to do this, not that she was driven to this by any erotic passion for the man but she did recognize a great debt of gratitude to him for avenging the murder of her husband Areobindos and for coming to her rescue and snatching her away when she was a prisoner and about to be forced against her will to share the bed of the rebel Gontharis.[73] (4) As they both liked the idea, Artabanes sent Preïekta to the emperor while he, even though he was appointed general of the whole of

72. Artabanes was an Armenian of the (deposed) royal line of the Arsakids who had fought in the 530s against the Romans in his native land, killing a governor and defeating a general (*Wars* 2.3, 4.27.17). He then served under King Chosroes of Persia against the Romans, but by 545 (at the latest) he had defected to the Romans and accompanied Areobindos to North Africa (*Wars* 4.24.1–2), who was sent to fix the mess made by Sergios (see *Secret History* 5.31 and note). Areobindos took with him his wife, Preïekta, the daughter of Justinian's sister Vigilantia, but he was betrayed and killed by the commander Gontharis, who rebelled and took Carthage as his base (*Wars* 4.25–28). Artabanes pretended to side with Gontharis in order to kill him, which he did at a banquet. Preïekta gave him a large reward and Justinian made him general of Africa (*Wars* 4.28.40–43).

73. See *Wars* 4.27.22.

North Africa, continued to invent various specious pretexts to induce the emperor to recall him to Byzantion. (5) He was led to it by the hopes stirred in him by this marriage, both the many advantages that would issue from it and the fact that he would then not be far from the throne. (6) For human beings, when they come into good fortune accidentally, are not able to leave it at that in their minds but eagerly look forward to the next thing, and they are always moving forward in their expectations until, finally, they are deprived even of the happiness that has undeservedly come to them.

At any rate, the emperor granted the request (7) and recalled Artabanes to Byzantion, replacing him with another general for North Africa, as I narrated above.[74] (8) When Artabanes reached Byzantion, the populace admired him for his noble deeds and generally loved him. (9) For he was tall and beautiful of body, liberal in his character, and spoke little. The emperor, moreover, granted him the highest honors. (10) He appointed him general of the soldiers in Byzantion and commander of the federate units,[75] promoting him also to the honor of the consuls. (11) But as for Preïekta, he was unable to marry her, for it turned out that he already had a wife, a relation of his who had married him in childhood. (12) Long before this, however, he had separated from her, probably for one of those reasons that set husbands and wives at loggerheads. (13) This woman, so long as Artabanes' station was humble, had stayed at home and not meddled in his affairs, enduring her circumstances in silence. But now that his deeds were glorious and his fortunes magnificent, she could no longer bear her disgrace and came to Byzantion. Falling upon the mercy of the empress, she asked that her husband be restored to her. (14) The empress, then—for it was her nature to side with women in distress[76]—decided that Artabanes had to live with her whether he liked it or not, and that Preïekta would become the wife of Ioannes, the son of Pompeïos, the son of Hypatios.[77] (15) Artabanes did not endure this misfortune calmly but grew angry and said that one who had done so many noble deeds

74. *Wars* 4.28.44–45 (in 546): Artabanes was replaced with Ioannes Troglita, whose campaigns against the Moors were celebrated in epic verse by the Latin poet Corippus.

75. I.e., *magister militum praesentalis* and *comes foederatorum*. The so-called federate units no longer consisted exclusively of barbarian recruits; *Wars* 3.11.3–4.

76. See *Secret History* 17.24–26 for a less favorable view.

77. Hypatios was set up as a rival emperor during the Nika riots; see related text 2.

for the Romans [. . .][78] no one allowed him to marry the woman to whom he was engaged, when both of them were entering that union willingly, and that he was instead being forced to spend the rest of his life in the company of the one person who was more repulsive to him than anyone else. For this is indeed the kind of thing that can exasperate one's soul. (16) And so when the empress died not long after that,[79] he gladly and immediately sent this woman away, in fact as swiftly as possible. (17) Now it happened that the emperor's nephew Germanos had a brother named Boraïdes.[80] This Boraïdes, then, the brother of Germanos, had recently died, leaving most of his property to his brother and to his brother's children. (18) Even though he had a wife and daughter, he instructed that his daughter inherit only so much as the law required. Because of this, the emperor insisted on siding with the daughter, which greatly annoyed Germanos.[81]

[*Wars* 7.32] (1) This, then, was how matters stood between the emperor on the one hand and Artabanes and Germanos on the other. Now there happened to be a certain Arsakes in Byzantion, an Armenian by origin, one of the Arsakids, who was related to Artabanes. (2) This man had been caught not long before in an attempt to harm state interests and had, beyond any doubt, been convicted of treason as he had been working for Chosroes, the king of the Persians, against the Romans. (3) But the emperor did him no harm other than to have him lashed on his back a few times and paraded in disgrace through the city on a camel. He removed nothing from his body or even his property; he did not even send him into exile. (4) Yet Arsakes was furious at what had happened and began to plot treason against Justinian and the state. (5) When he saw that Artabanes was also disgruntled, being his relative, he provoked him even further, ambushing the man with abuse during their conversations. Without letting up day or night, he insulted him by saying that he had picked the wrong times to be, first, manly and, then, some sort of androgynous thing. (6) When facing the hardships of *others* he had

78. There is a problem in the text here.

79. On 28 June 548.

80. Boraïdes played a role in the suppression of the Nika riots; see related text 2. Germanos had held a series of distinguished military commands under Justin and Justinian, but Theodora was his enemy; see *Secret History* 5.7–15.

81. Justinian had sought to limit testators' right to dispose of their property however they wished in their wills and stipulated minimum shares to which different kinds of heirs were entitled; see *Novella* 18 (of 536).

risen bravely to the occasion and undone the usurpation: even though Gontharis was his ally and his host, he had seized him with own hands and slain him without any provocation whatever. (7) But present circumstances had unmanned him, so here he sat like a coward while his own country was under a harsh occupation and being bled by unheard-of taxes;[82] his father had been killed for the sake of the terms of some treaty;[83] and his entire family had been enslaved and scattered to every corner of the Roman Empire.[84] (8) And yet, with all these things being so, Artabanes was satisfied with himself just to be appointed general of the Romans and bear but the *name* of consul. "Moreover," he said, "you hardly commiserate with me even though I am your kinsman and have been horribly treated, while I, friend, sympathize with what you suffered over these two women, how you lost the one unjustly and were forced to live with the other. (9) And yet it is hardly likely that anyone who had even a trace of spirit left in him would shrink back from murdering Justinian, nor need there be any hesitation or dread about it—for that man is always sitting unguarded in some lobby at untimely hours of the night explicating the Christian scriptures in the company of some superannuated priests.[85] (10) Nor," he added, "will any of Justinian's relatives oppose you. The one who is indeed the most powerful of them all, Germanos, will, I believe, be most eager to join you with his own sons, who are young men and boiling with rage against him on account of their age and spirit. In fact, I am hopeful that they will even do the deed on their own initiative. (11) For they happen to have been treated unjustly by him, more so than have we or any other Armenian." With such words was Arsakes constantly working a spell on Artabanes, and, when he saw that the man was opening to the idea, he brought the matter before another Persarmenian,[86] Chanaranges by name. (12) This Chanaranges was

82. In the *Wars*, Prokopios is consistently critical of Justinian's administration of Armenia, as being oppressive and corrupt.

83. Artabanes' father, Ioannes, was murdered by the Roman general Bouzes in 539 while negotiating on behalf of the Armenian rebels; *Wars* 2.3.28–31. See *Secret History* 4.4–12 for Bouzes' sufferings at the hands of Theodora at a later time.

84. Presumably referring to the Arsakids.

85. For Justinian's nocturnal habits, see also *Secret History* 12.20 and note 104 in Part II.

86. This was the part of Armenia under Persian rule; the other part was under Roman rule.

a young man, but well built; he was not, however, altogether serious, inclining rather to a childish personality.

(13) When Arsakes had ensured that he and Artabanes shared the same intentions and had expressed their agreement to each other, he took his leave of them, stating that he was going to secure the assent of Germanos and his sons to their enterprise. (14) Now the eldest of Germanos' sons, Ioustinos, was a young man who still had his first beard, but he was energetic and quick to action. (15) Hence a short time earlier he had even mounted the curule seat of the consuls.[87] Accosting him, Arsakes said that he wished to meet with him secretly in a sanctuary. (16) When the two met in the church, Arsakes first demanded that Ioustinos declare an oath that he would not reveal what was about to be said to any person in the world except for his father. (17) And when he had sworn to that effect, he began to upbraid him for being a very close relative to the emperor and yet watching as these common and vulgar people held the offices of the state to which they had no right. He was already of an age to manage his own affairs but had to suffer the fact that not only he but his father also, who had reached the peak of virtue, as well as his brother Ioustinianos were forever confined to a private station. (18) He had not even been allowed to inherit the property of his uncle despite the fact that he was the rightful heir, at least according to Boraïdes' intentions; almost all of it had unjustly been taken away from him. (19) And it was, in fact, very likely that they would be all the more snubbed in the near future, given that Belisarios was swiftly returning from Italy. For he was reported as being halfway through the land of the Illyrians by then.[88] (20) With this as his premise, Arsakes incited the young man to join in the plot against the emperor and revealed to him what had been agreed among himself, Artabanes, and Chanaranges concerning this action. (21) Ioustinos was shocked when he heard all this and grew dizzy at the prospect of it but told Arsakes that neither he nor Germanos, his father, could ever do these things.

(22) Arsakes now told Artabanes what had happened, while Ioustinos reported the entire matter to his father. The latter then confided in Markellos, who was the commander of the palace guards, and they deliberated whether it was advisable for them to bring the issue to

87. Flavius Mar. Petrus Theodorus Valentinus Rusticus Boraïdes Germanus Iustinus was consul in 540.

88. Belisarios was returning from Italy for the last time in 549; for his circumstances, see *Secret History* 5.1–27.

the emperor's attention.[89] (23) Now this Markellos was a most serious man who kept his silence in most matters, did nothing for the sake of money, and did not tolerate jokes or frivolous behavior. He took no pleasure in relaxation but lived an austere life, always maintaining a personal lifestyle in which pleasure played no role. He handled everything with a carefully honed sense of justice and burned with a passion to know the truth. (24) At that juncture, he would not allow any report of this to reach the emperor. "It is inadvisable," he said, "for *you* to become an informant in this matter. For if you should wish to speak to the emperor secretly, those around Artabanes will immediately suspect that you have reported on this very thing, and if Arsakes should manage somehow to get away, the accusation will remain unproven. (25) For my part, I am not in the habit of believing anything myself or reporting it to the emperor that I have not first thoroughly examined. (26) I would prefer either to hear these words with my own ears or for one of my close associates to hear the man saying something unambiguous about the matter, if you can arrange it." (27) When he heard this, Germanos bade his son Ioustinos to bring about what Markellos had requested. (28) But he had nothing more to say to Arsakes about the matter given that he had, as I stated, flatly refused to participate. (29) So he inquired of Chanaranges whether Arsakes had recently come to him on behalf of Artabanes. "For I, at any rate," he said, "would never dare to entrust any of my secrets to him, seeing the kind of person that he is. (30) But if you yourself should be willing to tell me something helpful, perhaps we could deliberate together and even perform some noble deed." (31) Conferring with Artabanes about this, Charananges explained to Ioustinos all that Arsakes had told him earlier.

(32) When Ioustinos agreed to carry everything into execution himself and to secure his father's assent, it was decided that Charananges should discuss the matter personally with Germanos, and a day was appointed for the meeting. (33) Germanos reported this to Markellos and requested that he detail one of his close associates to witness what Charananges would say. (34) Markellos chose Leontios for the task, the son-in-law of Athanasios, who professed a strict

89. Markellos was *comes* of the *excubitores*, the only battle-worthy unit of palatine guards. In 541, he had been used by Theodora in the plot to bring down Ioannes the Kappadokian; see related text 7.

regard for justice and always spoke the truth.[90] (35) Germanos brought this man into his house and placed him in a room across which a heavy curtain had been hung as a screen for the couch on which he was accustomed to dine. (36) He hid Leontios inside this curtain while he and his son Ioustinos remained outside. (37) When Charananges arrived, Leontios clearly heard him divulge all that he, Artabanes, and Arsakes were plotting. (38) Among it all this too was said, namely that if they killed the emperor while Belisarios was still on his way to Byzantion, none of their plans would advance; even if it was their intention to place Germanos on the throne, Belisarios would muster a large host in the towns of Thrace and, once he moved against them, they would not by any means be able to turn him back. (39) It would therefore be necessary to postpone the deed until such a time as Belisarios was present, but as soon as the man arrived at Byzantion and went to the emperor in the palace, then, sometime late in the evening, they should go there with daggers but without warning and kill Markellos and Belisarios along with the emperor. (40) It would then be much easier for them to arrange matters to their liking.

Markellos learned all this from Leontios but decided not to bring it to the emperor's attention because he was still apprehensive lest, out of excessive zeal, he bring about the condemnation of Artabanes on insufficient grounds.[91] (41) But Germanos did reveal everything to Bouzes and Konstantianos,[92] fearing, which is indeed what happened, that some suspicion might fall on him because of the delay. (42) Many days later, when it was announced that Belisarios would soon arrive, Markellos reported the entire matter to the emperor, who immediately ordered that those with Artabanes should be taken to prison, and he appointed some officers to torture them for information. (43) When the whole conspiracy had come to light and

90. Athanasios was praetorian prefect of Italy in 539–542 and then North Africa in 545–548/549. He had been sent to Africa with Areobindos and, according to some sources, had orchestrated the murder of the rebel Gontharis that Artabanes had carried out; see note 72 above.

91. The involvement of Artabanes in the plot was, at this point, known only through the unreliable assertions of Arsakes (and at third-hand via Ioustinos at that) and the frivolous Chanaranges.

92. Bouzes seems not to have held any office since his imprisonment by Theodora (on which see *Secret History* 4.4–12). In the 550s he would be appointed general in Lazike. Konstantianos had served as general in Italy for many years.

everything had been explicitly written down, the emperor convened all the members of the Senate to the palace, where they meet in order to resolve cases in which there is doubt. (44) When they had read everything that those under investigation had recounted, they went so far as to involve Germanos and his son Ioustinos in the indictment, until Germanos brought forth the testimony of Markellos and Leontios, at which point the suspicion was lifted. (45) For they, along with Konstantianos and Bouzes, declared under oath that Germanos had concealed nothing whatever from them regarding this matter but that everything had happened exactly in the way in which I have just described it. (46) So the senators immediately and unanimously cleared both him and his son, finding that they had committed no offense against the state.

(47) But when they all went inside to the emperor's court, the emperor himself, who had become furious, was openly displeased and spoke with great anger against Germanos, blaming him for the delay in the disclosure. And two of his officials, seeking to ingratiate themselves with him, agreed with his opinion and made as if they too were distressed. In doing so they incited the emperor to become even angrier, as their purpose was to indulge him when it concerned the misfortunes of others. (48) The rest cowered in fear and yielded to him by not resisting his wishes. Markellos alone managed to save the man by speaking in candor. (49) He took the responsibility on himself and stated, as emphatically as was in his power, that Germanos had revealed to him what was going on at the earliest opportunity but that he himself had reported the matter in a more deliberate fashion in order to conduct an exacting investigation. (50) In this way he placated the emperor's anger. For this Markellos earned great fame among all men as one who gave proof of his virtue at a most dangerous moment. (51) The emperor Justinian dismissed Artabanes from his office and harmed him in no other way, nor did he harm any of the others beyond keeping them all under guard, though with no dishonor attached, indeed in the palace and not in a public prison.[93]

93. Justinian reappointed Artabanes to a military command the following year, in 550, and he subsequently served in Italy under Narses.

11. Silkworms Are Smuggled into the Roman Empire

Wars 8.17.1–8

Date: 552–553. The establishment of an imperial monopoly over the internal Roman silk trade (probably in the late 540s) is one of the grounds for Prokopios' indictment of Justinian in The Secret History *(25.13–26). At that time silk was obtained from Persian middlemen; the material itself originated mostly in China (which Prokopios calls Serinde). Justinian had sought to circumvent the Persian intermediaries in the north and south, but he had failed and the Persians were raising their prices. It was in this context that the following events took place. Prokopios has tripped up most modern historians by saying that the monks came to Justinian from India "at this time" (552–553). In fact they must have come long before, then traveled to China to obtain the eggs, and returned to Byzantion. It was this second return that happened "at this time," for their journey must have lasted at least two years.*

China and Rome were distantly aware of each other, more and more so toward the end of late antiquity, as many literary sources demonstrate. Silk became one of the most profitable and prestigious imperial businesses in the Byzantine Empire.

(1) At this time some monks arrived from India, and when they learned that the emperor Justinian was keen to find a way so that the Romans no longer had to buy silk from the Persians, they came before the emperor and declared that they could arrange it so that the Romans would no longer have to purchase this item from their enemy the Persians, or indeed from any other people. (2) For they had spent much time in a land situated far to the north of the nations of India which is called Serinde, and there they had learned exactly by what process silk could be produced in Roman lands too. (3) The emperor questioned them in detail and sought to discover whether this was true, whereupon the monks explained that the makers of silk were certain worms that knew how to do this by their nature, which compelled them to work it continually. (4) It was, however, impossible to convey these worms here alive, but it could be done altogether easily with their offspring. The offspring of each of these worms consisted of countless eggs. (5) Men cover these eggs with dung long after they are laid and, by heating them in this way for a sufficient time, they thus produce the animal itself. (6)

When they said this, the emperor promised to give the men great gifts and persuaded them to prove their words through action. (7) So they went back to Serinde and brought the eggs to Byzantion, where they transformed them into worms in the manner just described, feeding them on mulberry leaves. From that time onward silk has been produced in the lands of the Romans. (8) So that was how affairs stood between the Romans and the Persians regarding both the war and silk.

Many readers will wonder, where is the famous hollow cane in which the monks were said to have secretly smuggled the eggs out of China? That part of the story comes from Theophanes of Byzantion, a historian writing toward the end of the sixth century. His work is lost, but a brief summary was written by the future patriarch of Constantinople Photios in the mid ninth century. Even though Theophanes' work covered the years after 567, he had looked back to the importation of the silkworm.

[He talks about] the breeding of the silkworms, which was not formerly known in the Roman Empire and which was revealed by a Persian man at the time that Justinian was ruling in Byzantion. He set out from the land of the Seres [China] having preserved the eggs of the worm all the way to Byzantion by placing them in a receptacle.[94] When spring came, he laid the eggs down on mulberry leaves to feed and, by feeding on the leaves, they grew their wings and did all the rest that follows.

94. Translating *narthex*. A *narthex* can be a cane though it can also be a jar of some kind.

Index

Citations are to chapter and section number or to related text number.